IS AUTHORITARIANISM
STAGING A COMEBACK?

Is Authoritarianism Staging a Comeback?

Mathew Burrows, *Co-Editor*

Maria J. Stephan, *Co-Editor*

An Atlantic Council Publication

IS AUTHORITARIANISM STAGING A COMEBACK?

Copyright © 2015 by The Atlantic Council.

Co-Editor: Mathew Burrows
Co-Editor: Maria J. Stephan

Project Editor: Karl Grindal

ISBN-10: 0986382213
ISBN-13: 978-0-9863822-1-5

LCCN: 2013909024

Table of Contents

Contributor Bios

Peter Ackerman is the Founding Chair of ICNC, and one of the world's leading authorities on nonviolent conflict. He holds a Ph.D. from The Fletcher School, Tufts University, where he presently is the Chairman of the Board, and he is co-author of two seminal books on nonviolent resistance, A Force More Powerful: A Century of Nonviolent Conflict (Palgrave/St. Martin's Press, 2001) and Strategic Nonviolent Conflict: The Dynamics of People Power in the Twentieth Century (Praeger, 1994).

Nada Alwadi was a reporter for Alwasat, the most popular newspaper in Bahrain, a monarchy on a small island in the Persian Gulf. Alwadi covered the pro-democracy protests this spring against the Al Khalifi monarchy prior to government authorities closing the newspaper. She earned a BA from Kuwait University and an MA in Mass Communications from the Universiti Sains, Malaysia. She has served as a freelance journalist, writer and researcher for several media outlets, including Women Gateway in Arabic and English and USA Today. Ms. Alwadi is founder of the Bahrain

Press Association, which seeks to defend journalists from government repression. In 2011, she received one of the first James Lawson Awards for Nonviolent Achievement from the International Center on Nonviolent Conflict.

Howard Barrell worked in the underground and exile organizations of the African National Congress (ANC) during the struggle against apartheid in South Africa. His doctorate at Oxford University examined the narrative of ANC operational strategy between 1976 and 1986. He is a former editor of the *Mail & Guardian*, the award-winning South African political weekly. He currently teaches aspects of journalism and insurgency at Cardiff University in the United Kingdom, and serves on the academic advisory board of the Washington-based International Centre on Nonviolent Conflict.

Maciej Bartkowski is the Senior Director for Education and Research at the International Center on Nonviolent Conflict and an adjunct professor at Johns Hopkins

University's Krieger School of Arts and Sciences where he teaches about strategic nonviolent conflict. He is the editor of *Recovering Nonviolent History: Civil Resistance in Liberation Struggles*, published by Lynne Rienner in 2013 that highlights the role of nonviolent resistance in numerous cases of national struggles for self-rule and independence. He holds a PhD in Political Science and MA in International Relations and European Studies from Central European University in Budapest.

Shaazka Beyerle is a Senior Advisor with the International Center on Nonviolent Conflict, and a visiting scholar at the Center for Transatlantic Relations, School of Advanced International Studies, The Johns Hopkins University. She is the author of *Curtailing Corruption: People Power for Accountability and Justice* (Lynne Rienner 2014). Ms. Beyerle is on the editorial board of *State Crime*. She is a Friend of the International State Crime Initiative (Queen Mary University-London, Harvard University, University of Hull), an elected coordinating committee member of the United Nations Convention Against Corruption (UNCAC) Civil Society Coalition, and part of the ASK (Anti-Corruption Solutions and Knowledge Programme) Network of Experts.

Dennis Blair leads the Sasakawa Peace Foundation, USA. He serves on the Energy Security Leadership Council, the boards of Freedom House, the National Bureau of Asian Research and the National Committee

on US-China Relations. From 2009 to 2010, as Director of National Intelligence, Admiral Blair led sixteen national intelligence agencies. Prior to retiring from the Navy in 2002, Admiral Blair was the Commander of the US Pacific Command. A graduate of the US Naval Academy, Admiral Blair earned a master's degree in history and languages from Oxford University. He has recently written *Military Engagement: Influencing Armed Forces Worldwide to Support Democratic Transitions*.

Mathew Burrows serves as Director of the Atlantic Council's Strategic Foresight Initiative in the Brent Scowcroft Center on International Security. His recent book is entitled *The Future Declassified: Megatrends that Will Undo the World Unless We Take Action* (Palgrave/Macmillan). In August 2013 he retired from a twenty-eight year career in the CIA and US Department of State. His last appointment was Counselor in the United States National Intelligence Council (NIC) where he managed a staff of senior analysts and production technicians who guide NIC products from inception to dissemination. He was the principal drafter of the last three editions of the NIC's Global Trends series, which has received praise in the international media.

Erica Chenoweth is an Associate Professor at the Josef Korbel School of International Studies at the University of Denver and Associate Senior Researcher at the Peace Research Institute of Oslo (PRIO). Her book (with Maria J. Stephan)

Why Civil Resistance Works: The Strategic Logic of Nonviolent Conflict won the 2013 Grawemeyer Award for Ideas Improving World Order and the 2012 Woodrow Wilson Foundation Award. She holds a MA and PhD in political science from the University of Colorado and a BA in political science and German from the University of Dayton. *Foreign Policy* magazine ranked her among the Top 100 Global Thinkers of 2013.

Larry Diamond is a Senior Fellow at the Hoover Institution and at the Freeman Spogli Institute for International Studies at Stanford University, where he directs the Center for Democracy, Development, and the Rule of Law. He is also the Peter E. Haas Faculty Co-Director of the Haas Center for Public Service at Stanford. Diamond is the founding co-editor of the *Journal of Democracy* and the author or editor of numerous books on democracy, including, *The Spirit of Democracy: The Struggle to Build Free Societies throughout the World*.

Jeremy Kinsman directs and co-authors the international project *A Diplomat's Handbook on Democracy Development Support* now in its third edition. Postings over forty-years in the Canadian Foreign Service included Deputy Permanent Representative to the United Nations in New York, Minister for Political Affairs in Washington, Ambassador in Moscow (1992-1996) and Rome (1996-2000), High Commissioner in London (2000-2002), and Ambassador to the European Union in Brussels (2002-2006). Kinsman was 2007-2008 Diplomat-in-Residence at Princeton University. In 2009 he was named Regents' Lecturer at the University of California, Berkeley (Institute of Governmental Studies) and is also attached to Ryerson University, Toronto.

George Lopez is the Vice President of the Academy for International Conflict Management and Peacebuilding at the United States Institute of Peace in Washington, D.C. He assumed this position in September 2013 after 27 years at the University of Notre Dame's Kroc Institute, where he is the Rev. Theodore M. Hesburgh, C.S.C., Chair Emeritus in Peace Studies. He has edited or written 6 books and over 40 articles on economic sanctions.

Hardy Merriman is President of the International Center on Nonviolent Conflict. His work focuses on how grassroots civil resistance movements around the world can successfully fight for rights, freedom, and justice. He has contributed to the books: *Waging Nonviolent Struggle: 20th Century Practice and 21st Century Potential* (2005) by Gene Sharp and *Civilian Jihad: Nonviolent Struggle, Democratization, and Governance in the Middle East* (2010) by Maria Stephan (ed.). He has also written about the role of civil resistance in countering terrorism and co-authored *A Guide to Effective Nonviolent Struggle,* a training curriculum for activists.

Regine A. Spector is an Assistant Professor in the Department of Political Science at the University of

Massachusetts, Amherst. She holds a Ph.D. in political science from the University of California, Berkeley and a B.A. and M.A. in International Relations and International Policy Studies from Stanford University. Her research interests and teaching fall at the intersection of political economy, development, and politics in Eurasia. Regine has published in Problems of Post-Communism, Post-Soviet Affairs, Central Asian Survey, and numerous edited volumes. She has been employed previously at Smith College, the Woodrow Wilson Center's Kennan Institute, and the Brookings Institution.

Maria J. Stephan is a Senior Policy Fellow at the United States Institute of Peace and a Nonresident Senior Fellow at the Atlantic Council, where she focuses on the dynamics of civil resistance and democratic development. Previously, she served in the US Department of State's Bureau of Conflict and Stabilization Operations. She is the editor of *Civilian Jihad: Nonviolent Struggle, Democratization, and Governance in the Middle East* (2009) and the co-author of *Why Civil Resistance Works: The Strategic Logic of Nonviolent Conflict* (2011); the latter was named the best book published in political science by the American Political Science Association. She holds a MA and PhD from the Fletcher School of Law and Diplomacy and a BA from Boston College.

Julia Taleb has worked in the field of journalism and international relations for several years, with a focus on Middle Eastern politics and cultural affairs. A Syrian, fluent in both Arabic and English, Ms. Taleb focuses on the Syrian conflict and the issue of resistance movements within an authoritarian context. She earned her MA degree in conflict resolution and BA in journalism from Carleton University in Canada. Her work was featured in places like the Middle East Institute, Voice of America, Atlantic Council, and the International Center on Nonviolent Resistance.

Zeynep Tufekci is an Assistant Professor at the University of North Carolina. She was formerly a fellow at the Princeton Center for Information Technology Policy as well as at the Harvard Berkman Center for Internet and Society where she remains a faculty associate. Her research interests revolve around the interaction between technology and society with special focus on social movements, civic and public sphere(s), privacy and surveillance. Besides her academic publications, she is a frequent contributor to national and international publications as well as her own blog, www.technosociology.org.

Elizabeth Wilson is Assistant Professor at the School of Diplomacy and International Relations at Seton Hall University where she teaches human rights and international law. She earned her J.D. from Harvard University and holds a PhD in Comparative Literature and Literary Theory from the University of Pennsylvania.

Foreword

Dear Reader:

Determining an appropriate strategy for outsiders to follow in assisting locally-led democratic movements across the world is one of the most challenging policy dilemmas for the United States and other democracies. In the wake of US military interventions in Iraq and Afghanistan, and four years into a tumultuous Arab Spring, a popular backlash is growing against promoting democratic development in other countries. The result is that most democratic governments and democracy promotion organizations today view assistance to groups that engage in nonviolent struggles for rights and freedoms as a step too far despite the world being in the throes of a nearly decade-long democratic recession—and despite the demonstrated efficacy of civil resistance in advancing democratic development.

Democratic breakdowns in strategically important countries like Russia, Nigeria, Pakistan, Egypt, and Venezuela are cause for serious concern, as are reversals in Turkey and Hungary. Vladimir Putin's revanchist policies in the heart of Europe highlight how domestic democratic setbacks can have serious negative regional reverberations. At the same time, protests in Tehran, Tahrir, Gezi Park, Euromaidan, and Hong Kong have ushered in what some have called a "fourth wave" of democratization, with people's power sometimes fueled by social media upending state-society relations.

This volume completes the first phase of the "Future of Authoritarianism" project in which the Atlantic Council's Strategic Foresight Initiative—with the generous help of the International Center for Nonviolent Conflict—aims to assess why and how authoritarian regimes have become smarter. Why have aggregate Freedom House numbers declined in each of the last eight years? To what extent are trends like the rise of a global middle class, migration to cities, and the Internet and social media making it harder or not for authoritarians to rule? Is the resource curse linked with authoritarians' ability to fend off democratic pressures? Are increasing corruption levels bolstering or undermining authoritarian regimes?

The second half will focus on the roles and responsibilities of outside actors for furthering democratic development. How will the principal of sovereign immunity develop in the next 10-15 years? Is there an evolving international norm that recognizes the responsibility of outside actors to assist pro-democratic nonviolent movements? How can diplomats and development practitioners, militaries, NGOs/ IOs, private foundations and businesses provide timely and sustained support to those seeking to organize nonviolently under repression?

Failure to reverse the troubling global trends of democratic decline could have serious negative repercussions for US, regional, and international security. There is a policy imperative for external actors, governmental and nongovernmental, to find creative and effective ways to engage nontraditional civil society actors, helping to create space for nonviolent political transitions and providing pathways to meaningful political participation in the new democracies. This second part will focus on the roles, responsibilities, and tools available to outside actors to improve the chances of democratic consolidation.

We want to thank the co-editors of this volume, Mathew Burrows, the Atlantic Council's Director of the Strategic Foresight Initiative and Maria J. Stephan, Atlantic Council nonresident senior fellow, for spearheading the effort and putting together—with the help of a number of outside experts—this first volume focused on the future of authoritarianism. We invite readers' comments and also help in forging a strategy for countering authoritarianism and helping local civil societies and activists advance nonviolent democratic change – even in those places where conventional wisdom might suggest that such change is impossible.

Frederick Kempe
President and CEO
Atlantic Council

Peter Ackerman
Founding Chair
International Center on
Nonviolent Conflict

Is Authoritarianism Staging a Comeback?

THE LATE SAMUEL HUNTINGTON, the Harvard political scientist, famously talked about democratization as a series of wave motions forward and backward. Scholars label the burst of democratization in Latin America, Asia, and Eastern Europe in the 1980s and 1990s as the Third Wave. The recent uprisings in Tunisia and Egypt in 2011 and regime changes in Myanmar and Ukraine in 2014 have been seen by some as a possible Fourth Wave. At the same time, for the eighth year in a row, Freedom House announced in its 2014 *Freedom in the World* report that more countries registered declines in political rights and civil liberties than gains. Even as the number of electoral democracies in the world increased, there were "serious setbacks to democratic rights in other large, politically influential countries, including Russia, Azerbaijan, Turkey, Venezuela, and Indonesia."[i] In fact, "thirty-five percent of the world's population, living in 25 percent of the polities on the planet, found themselves in countries that aren't free. As we enter a year in which more people will vote in elections than ever before, democracy appears to be in a holding pattern around the world—if not outright retreat."[ii]

There is controversy over how far the recent backsliding repeats earlier patterns of "two steps forward, one step back." Jay Ulfelder, a political scientist, believes what we are seeing is a normal part of that wave motion. "The slippage we've seen in the past several years is happening where and when we would have expected it to happen, given that so many of those democracies were "born" in a wave of transitions that occurred in the early 1990s. If those reversals were to continue until they had reversed most or all of the post–Cold War gains, then we should be both surprised and alarmed."[iii]

This collection of essays is organized around this central question: what is the future for authoritarianism? Are we at an inflection point where authoritarianism will regain more territory than is usual during these periods of democratic backsliding, undermining what has been a long-term trend toward democratization over the past several decades? Are there deeper, structural trends like the growth of the global middle class and hyper-connectivity that should give us confidence about the long term health of the democratization? Finally, in reversing the current backsliding and re-accelerating toward democratization, what kind of civil resistance efforts have proven effective against authoritarianism, which will work in the future, and why?

Our bias is to believe that the stalling of democratization is temporary, but as many of the authors underline in this volume, authoritarians are also increasingly adept in countering opposition. Outside actors have to be more aggressive in supporting nonviolent civil resistance groups, but civil resistance groups have to learn the lessons of others' attempts that failed because they opted for violence.

Part I provides a long term prognosis of democratic prospects from different angles. First, **Mathew Burrows**, Director of the Atlantic Council's Strategic Foresight Initiative, draws on the Council's work with the National Intelligence Council's global trends project and looks at various political, social and economic factors that help explain current patterns of democratic backsliding and smarter authoritarians. **Regine A. Spector**, political science professor at the University of Massachusetts at Amherst, provides a case study of the relative resilience of Central Asian authoritarian regimes where many of the leaders have shown themselves to be "adaptable autocrats." **Larry Diamond**, longtime democracy expert at Stanford University, explains why "democracy is a tough system to institutionalize and sustain." **Zeynep Tufekci** of the University of North Carolina at Raleigh shows how authoritarians have used social media to be more adaptable and agile in countering the opposition.

Part II examines trends in civil resistance. **Erica Chenoweth**, University of Denver professor and co-author of an award-winning book on civil resistance, discusses why nonviolent resistance campaigns are becoming more frequent in recent years, but not necessarily more effective. **Peter Ackerman**, founding chair of the International Center for Nonviolent Conflict (ICNC), and **Hardy Merriman**, ICNC's President and Director , believe the skills of civil resistance groups are on balance more important than conditions in determining outcomes. **Shaazka Beyerle**, visiting scholar at John Hopkins' School of Advanced International Studies , examines how corruption, often the glue holding the regime together, is also its Achilles' heel, engendering widespread public outrage and dissent.

Part III offers several case studies of civil resistance, providing concrete examples of what tactics have worked in building up opposition and overcoming pressures from authoritarians. **Nada Alwadi**, a Bahraini independent journalist, details how the 2011 civil resistance in Bahrain lacked a unified strategy, thus leading the movement to take premature actions—such as calls for widespread civil disobedience—that its supporters in the broader public were not prepared for. **Howard Barrell**, a former journalist and African National Congress activist, examines how political mobilization can help achieve the encirclement of a regime not merely from without but also from within. **Maciej Bartkowski,** ICNC's Senior Director for Education and Research and adjunct professor at Johns Hopkins University, and **Julia Taleb**, independent journalist with a focus on the Middle East, examine the fatal and short-sighted decision by the Syrian opposition to turn to violence despite the success of the nonviolent civil resistance movement in gaining public support, government concessions, and growing numbers of defections.

Part IV looks at the role of outside actors in helping civil resistance to topple authoritarian leaders. **Dennis Blair**, former Commander of US Pacific Command (PACOM) and Director of National Intelligence, believes there are many opportunities for the armed forces of the established democracies to affect the thinking of their counterparts in authoritarian regimes. **Elizabeth A. Wilson,** human rights law professor at Seton Hall University, examines the international legal basis for outside support to nonviolent movements. **George A. Lopez**, Vice-President of US Institute for Peace, makes the argument that "smart sanctions" provide an array of coercive measures to the international community that have proven somewhat effective in particular cases of massive rights abuses and ongoing atrocities. **Jeremy Kinsman**, former Canadian diplomat, illustrates critical ways that foreign diplomats have played to create space for civil resistance. **Maria J. Stephan**, Senior Policy Fellow at US Institute of Peace, concludes by providing a checklist for external assistance to nonviolent movements.

Notes

i.   *Freedom in the World 2014*, annual publication of Freedom House, available at *http://www.freedomhouse.org/report/freedom-world/freedom-world-2014#.U1-4x6PD-Uk*.

ii.   Uri Friedman, "Report: Global Freedom Has Been Declining for Nearly a Decade," *The Atlantic*, January 23, 2014, available at *http://www.theatlantic.com/international/archive/2014/01/report-global-freedom-has-been-declining-for-nearly-a-decade/283279/*.

iii. Ibid.

PART ONE

DEMOCRACY'S PROSPECTS

CHAPTER 1

The Long View on Authoritarianism's Second Wind

Mathew Burrows

Director, Strategic Foresight Initiative, Brent Scowcroft Center on International Security
Atlantic Council

TAKING THE LONG VIEW, democracy has done pretty well over the past couple decades. According to Freedom House's 2014 report, "the state of freedom reached its nadir in 1975, when 40 countries, just 25 percent of the world's independent states were ranked as Free, compared with 65 countries, or 41 percent, ranked as Not Free."[iv] In 1975 democracy was largely limited to Western Europe and North America, and with communism seemingly entrenched, there was little cause for optimism.

However, the next couple decades were to see democratization in South Korea, Taiwan, and other Asian states; the fall of military dictatorships in Africa and Latin America; and the end of communism in Eastern Europe and the breakup of the Soviet Union itself. By 2000, "the number of countries designated as Free had surged to 86, or 45 percent of the total, while the number of Not Free states had declined to 48, or 25 percent."[v] Few of the countries that moved toward democracy between 1980 and 2000 sank back into authoritarian rule. Europe's post-communist countries have maintained a high standard of rights and liberties, in part due to the EU's imposition of democratic criterion for new member states. There have been problems in Latin America—most prominently in Venezuela—but on balance the region has experienced the longest period of stable democracy in its history. In the early part of the twenty-first century, the Middle East remained the only major part of the world that had been relatively untouched by democracy.

Since then, the outlook has been more challenging. The color revolutions in Ukraine, Georgia, and parts of Central Asia gave hope that authoritarian regimes there were seeing their last days. Instead, with the possible exception of Kyrgyzstan, most authoritarians survived and grew smarter. The 2011 Arab Spring raised hopes for establishment of a number of budding democracies in the Middle East. Egypt—which could have been the most important trendsetter—is reverting back; Syria looks set to be pulled apart by civil war; this leaves Tunisia as the only possible new member of the democracy club in the region.

The past eight years have been the longest stretch of reported deterioration since Freedom House began tracking 1972. The march of democracy has met with a wall of resistance in three major settings: China, Eurasia, and most of the Middle East. Are the past eight years a blip or a new trendsetter?

My work on global trends at the National Intelligence Council would suggest both good and bad news on this score. On the good news side, today there is an increasingly broad global consensus about the legitimacy, at least in principle, of liberal democracy.[i] We live in the most democratic and least authoritarian world in the history of the modern state system. Even in China, party intellectuals talk about democracy being China's ultimate destiny.

At the same time, advances towards democracy may zigzag as democratization takes time to root itself. A key difference now from past decades is that with the emerging multipolar world, non-Western countries are moving into global leadership roles; some like China remain authoritarian while other emerging powers are trying to consolidate their democracy. In an age which puts so much stress on economic development, historic examples suggest democracy is not that vital. Developing states that had sustained rapid growth in the post-war period were most often either authoritarian or one party.[ii] The path forward is not as clear cut as it may have seemed in 1989 with the fall of the Berlin Wall and democracy enjoying one of its biggest surges.

TRENDS FAVORING DEMOCRACY...

Democracy has always had a close link with growing middle classes. Over the past couple of decades, the global middle class has been growing spectacularly—more than at any other time in history. Middle classes almost everywhere in the developing world are exploding both in absolute numbers and as a percentage of the population that can claim middle-class status. Even the more conservative models project a rise in the global total of those living in the middle class from the current 1 billion to over 2 billion over the next 15 years. Other estimates are even more optimistic, forecasting that over half of the world's population will be middle class by 2030. The bulk of this new middle class is appearing in developing states where democracy is not necessarily well-rooted.

Education is increasingly critical for human and material development and, like the growth of the global middle class, is largely a good news story. We have seen the developing world catch up with advanced nations and the gender gap begin to close with young girls getting the same education opportunities as young boys.

Insecurity and conflict have often retarded democratic development; one has only to think of Thomas Hobbes' famous treatise on *Leviathan* in which citizens trade disorder for a strong state that can protect them against violence. Civil conflicts are also debilitating because they tend to last a long time. The average intrastate conflict that began between 1970 and 1999 continued without a one-year break in fatalities for about six years.

Conflict has been decreasing over the past several decades and there are reasons that over the long term this trend could continue. There is a high correlation between civil conflict and countries with youth bulges. With global aging, there will be fewer countries with large proportions of their populations below the age of 25. Today more than 80 countries have populations with a median age of 25 years or less. Roughly 80 percent of all armed civil and ethnic conflicts have originated in countries with youthful populations. Due to fertility decline, the tally of countries with youthful populations is projected to fall to about 50 by 2030. We have to be careful in our projections because there has been a gradual increase in intrastate conflict with more mature country-level populations that contain a politically dissonant, youthful ethnic minority. Moreover, for the next two decades regions such as the Middle East, sub-Saharan Africa, and Central Asia where democracy is not well-rooted are also those with continuing large youth bulges.

...BUT THE FUTURE ISN'T ALWAYS STRAIGHTFORWARD

High levels of educational attainment and the presence of a large middle class don't necessarily translate into democracy—at least not right away. A democratic deficit exists when a country's developmental level—as measured by the growth of an educated and prosperous middle class, for example—is more advanced than its levels of governance. Many of the Gulf, Middle East, Central Asian, and Asian countries—Qatar, the UAE, Bahrain, Saudi Arabia, Oman, Kuwait, Iran, Kazakhstan, Azerbaijan, China, and Vietnam—fall into that category.

We would expect many of these democratic deficit countries to begin to democratize over the next couple decades. China is slated to pass the threshold of US $15,000 per capita (PPP) in the next five years or so. This level is often a trigger for democratization, especially when coupled with high levels of education and a mature age structure.

However, resource-rich countries have been able to delay democratization even when per capita incomes rise. These rentier states, dependent on large-scale resource exploitation, such as those industries involving oil, gas, and minerals, are able to provide economic well-being for their citizens. In most cases, large energy assets have been a "dictator's friend," although in some cases—that of Nigeria, for example—large-scale energy industry has spurred a sizable number of coups d'etat because of the rewards it offers rivals. In practically all cases, large amounts of oil or gas have been a detriment to democratization.

Take the example of Qatar,[iii] whose fundamentals otherwise make it look like a prime candidate for democratization. One of the biggest natural gas exporters in the world, Qatar has high education and literacy rates and a median age near 30 which means it no longer has a youth bulge. Transparency International gives it a low rating on corruption. Moreover, its GDP per capita is at $56,000 (PPP[1]) which puts it well beyond the level at which democratization is triggered. However, the high standard of living—achieved through its extensive gas exports—is probably the reason for the lack of strong democratization pressures.

In 2010, energy exports constituted 10 percent or more of the GDP of 27 countries; for 15 countries, including some with the greatest governance problems, the value exceeded 20 percent. The top five dependent countries, in descending order, were Angola, Trinidad, Libya, Azerbaijan, and Kazakhstan. Resources revenues are typically used to buy off opposition. Because of the lack of economic diversity, middle classes in these countries are tied more closely to the state's fortunes and are therefore less apt to rock the boat.

High levels of corruption are a typical byproduct of large energy industries, particularly in many resource rich states with big inflows of resource rents. There has been a large and persistent gap on corruption between developing states and rich Western countries. Corruption is insidious, particularly when institutions like the judiciary fall prey, which makes it all the harder to root out. Unfortunately, we know that, historically, rapid economic development often fuels corruption and organized crime. For people in the developing world, in survey after survey, people cite corruption as one of the top issues which needs to be solved.

For budding democracies, high levels of corruption can have an eviscerating effect, turning public opinion against democracy. For authoritarian regimes, corruption can function as an essential glue keeping together elite support for the regime; at the same time opposition groups can use corruption as a flashpoint for gaining support for moving against dictators. Egyptians listed "lack of democracy" and "corruption" as top concerns, for example, before the Mubarak regime fell, according to Pew surveys.[iv] According to recent surveys by Transparency International, many countries "believed to be

---

[1] Purchasing Power Parity

on a trajectory toward greater transparency have largely stalled and only a few countries marginally managed to improve their standing" in recent years.[v]

In *Global Trends 2030*, we used the International Futures (IFs) modeling and Polity's 20-point scale measuring a state's level of democracy based on political participation, openness, and limits on executive power to track where countries would be in 15 to 20 years in the trajectory between autocracy and democracy.[vi] Currently about 50 countries are in the awkward stage between autocracy at one end and democracy at the other in Policy's 20 point scale. Over time, we would expect that as global growth continues, educational levels—already at historically high levels in the developing world—will increase further, and the pressures for democratization will increase. Using IFs modeling, roughly four out of the current 50 in the awkward mid-stage, graduate to democracy and 17 move from autocracy (below 5 on the Polity scale) into the awkward middle. Based on rapidly rising levels of income and education, the greatest number of these are likely to be in sub-Saharan Africa, followed by Asia, and then the Middle East and North Africa. This is the base case.

A more pessimistic forecast of even fewer graduations out of autocracy to the mid-range and decreased numbers of new full democracies could easily occur if we see sharp reductions in economic growth, undermining progress toward better governance and increasing the chances of greater populism and authoritarianism in even currently strong democratizing countries. Middle East, Gulf, and Eurasian countries are increasingly economically vulnerable as energy production surges in the US, Canada, and potentially elsewhere due to shale and deep water exploitation of oil and gas deposits. The International Monetary Fund (IMF) has recently identified a large number of Middle East and Gulf countries who depend on high energy prices to balance their state budgets and fund domestic programs.[vii] A sharp downward turn in economic fortunes could be the needed trigger to begin the transition to more democratic rule in many of these countries, but with such economic instability that transition is likely to be tortuous.

Increased conflict in the short term—either internal conflict or spillover from broader regional wars—would undermine democracy's chances. The last couple of decades have comprised a period of historically low rates of intrastate and interstate conflict. However, as noted in *Global Trends 2030*, there has been an uptick in intrastate conflict in the past few years, and the risks of interstate conflict are growing. The civil war in Syria is particularly disconcerting because of its potential to spread to Iraq, Jordan, Lebanon, and other Middle Eastern countries, undermining prospects in those countries for democratization.

Increasing the risk of instability are the likely increased pressures on critical resources. Based on current trajectories, the OECD estimates that by 2030 nearly half the world's population will live in areas with severe water stress. Africa, the Middle East, and South Asia are the regions where the perfect storm of climate change impacts, rapid population growth, and food and water scarcities are going to be felt the most. They are also areas containing many of the countries lacking strong governance capacity and struggling to consolidate democracy.

MORE OPPORTUNITIES TO AFFECT CHANGE

Historically, democratization has gone through three basic stages. As described by Professor Barry Hughes in his latest volume *Strengthening Global Governance*, the first stage began with "overcoming anarchy through consolidation of territorial governing authority to establish sovereignty."[2, viii] For Western democracies, this happened in the sixteenth through early nineteenth centuries with the rise of the nation-state. The second stage involved improving state competencies, such as the development of civil service and increased taxes. For Western democracies, this happened beginning in the nineteenth century. The final stage was the process of widening inclusion. Britain's

---

[2] Barry Hughes of the University of Denver kindly shared with me his latest volume on governance in manuscript which uses his international futures model to "forecast the next 50 years." He examines a number of factors, such as the levels of economic development and governance, to determine likely movement towards democratization.

1832 Reform Act, for example, widened the franchise significantly and reduced the number of "rotten" parliamentary boroughs.

For Western democracies, this process was mostly sequential: "government effectiveness has usually preceded and been a precondition for expanding political inclusion." However, since decolonization, "an increasing global trend has been to encourage greater social participation in government in earlier stages of state capacity-building."[ix] Our better understanding of the mechanics of democratization combined with looser, less sequential, and less structured processes, which are now typical, means that we can modulate our efforts to give democratization the biggest push possible. For countries like Afghanistan, the Democratic Republic of Congo, and Somalia, achieving security is a priority and, according to the IFs modeling, could give the biggest push toward greater human development which is essential for democratization. In other countries which have achieved security, building governmental capacity or greater inclusiveness would have bigger impacts.

Finally, democracy has been attractive because it is equated with ensuring the greatest possible good for the greatest number. If advanced Western democracies are no longer seen as "for the people" and "by the people" and instead become increasingly associated with inequality and lack of opportunity for the majority, the democratic model itself will become tarnished and won't be the ideal that others strive to emulate.

Notes

i.   Freedom House, Freedom in the World 2014: The Democratic Leadership Gap, Freedom House, 2014. Accessible at: *www.freedomhouse.org/report/freedom-world/freedom-world-2014, p. 15.*

ii.   Ibid., p 15.

iii. Francis Fukuyama, *Foreign Affairs*, "The Future of History: Can Liberal Democracy Survive the Decline of the Middle Class?" January/February 2012, available at *http://www.foreignaffairs.com/articles/136782/francis-fukuyama/the-future-of-history.*

iv.   Pew Research Center, Global Attitudes Project: Egyptians Embrace Revolt Leaders, Religious Parties and Military, As Well, Pew Research Center, April 2011. Accessible at: *http://www.pewglobal.org/files/2011/04/Pew-Global-Attitudes-Egypt-Report-FINAL-April-25-2011.pdf.*

v.　　Christoph Wilcke, "CPI 2013: Crackdown on Middle Eastern Civil Society Must Stop," Transparency International, December 3, 2013. Accessible at: *http://blog. transparency.org/2013/12/03/cpi-2013-crackdown-on-middle-eastern-civil-society-must-stop/.*

vi.　　National Intelligence Council, *Global Trends 2030: Alternative Worlds*, National Intelligence Council, December 2012. Accessible at: *http://www.dni.gov/files/ documents/GlobalTrends_2030.pdf.*

vii.　　International Monetary Fund, Middle East and North Africa Regional Economic Outlook, International Monetary Fund, November 12, 2013. Accessible at: *https:// www.imf.org/external/pubs/ft/reo/2013/mcd/eng/pdf/mreo1113p.pdf.*

viii.　　Barry B. Hughes et al. Strenthening Governance Globally: Patterns of Potential Human Progress, Vol. 5, Colorado: Paradigm Publishers, 2014.

ix.　　Ibid.

CHAPTER 2

The Pillars of Authoritarian Resilience in Central Asia

Regine A. Spector
Assistant Professor, Department of Political Science
University of Massachusetts, Amherst

INTRODUCTION

Almost a quarter of a century after the Soviet Union's collapse in 1991, most of the Central Asian successor states remain distinctly authoritarian. In light of significant sums of foreign aid dedicated to democracy promotion in the region since the 1990s, and numerous waves of political change in Eurasia[1] and the Middle East[2] in the 2000s, some have suggested that Central Asian countries are ripe for revolution.[i] Others counter that the region's current authoritarian equilibrium was shaped by Soviet-era institutions and interventions.[ii]

Neither perspective captures the dynamics of authoritarian stability in Central Asia today. The relative resilience of Central Asian regimes can be best understood by conceptualizing the leaders of these countries as "adaptable autocrats."[iii,3] While leaders in the region draw upon past Soviet institutions and other structural resources at

---

[1] Serbia in 1999, Georgia in 2002, Ukraine in 2003.

[2] Tunisia and Egypt in 2011.

[3] In his book *Adaptable Autocrats* Stacher compares relative stability after regime change in Egypt to the civil war and violence that has ensued in Syria. He asks, "Which autocrats are most successful at adapting their political systems?" and conceptualizes autocratic change not as reform but adaptation, defined as "political change that adjusts a state to changes in its environment… without giving up power or sacrificing the cohesion of elites." (21-22). This chapter conceptualizes autocratic adaptation more broadly focusing also on the management of society and political culture.

their disposal, they continually respond to domestic and international pressures to ensure their survival. For the Central Asian leaders, one of the gravest threats over the past decade has been the perceived threat of popular revolutions. This chapter first briefly explains why Kyrgyzstan has been the only country in Central Asia in which the leader has been unwillingly ousted. The remainder of the chapter investigates the ways in which the leaders of Uzbekistan, Kazakhstan, and Tajikistan responded to the perceived threat of regime change after 2005.[4] In particular, it focuses on the five pillars of authoritarian resilience: the regimes' selective use of violence, appropriation of economic resources, control of political institutions, creation of compliance and persuasion, and management of foreign influence. Two main findings from this analysis emerge. First, adaptations and changes the leaders have made in recent years must be viewed as extensions or adaptations of ongoing processes of authoritarian consolidation that well predate any of the more recent revolutionary waves; and second, the ways in which the leaders adapt differ due to varying ideational and structural constraints. Thus, while these pillars form the backbone of a general "toolkit" leaders use to respond to regime challenges, the precise combination and nature of adaptations vary country by country.

KYRGYZSTAN AS EXCEPTION

Nestled among the mountains bordering China, Kyrgyzstan surprised outsiders and citizens alike in 2005 when the country's first president fled amidst street protests. Unlike in other Eurasian countries (such as Georgia and Ukraine) that had experienced electoral revolutions in years prior, in Kyrgyzstan the role of youth movements and civil society proved limited. Instead, wealthy politicians and elites mobilized their local supporters to protest the Akaev regime in regional cities and later in a more coordinated fashion in the capital Bishkek.[iv] While the proximate cause of these protests rested in elite discontent with the rigging of parliamentary elections in February and March

---

[4] Turkmenistan is not considered in this chapter due to the closed nature of the regime and the limited scholarship on the country. See McFaul and Spector (2010) for details on the ways in which the Russian government responded to the electoral revolutions, and Robertson (2009) for the ways the Russian government managed civil society and protest in the 2000s.

of that year, combined with President Akaev's announcement that he was not running for president later that year resulting in a "lame duck" moment,[v] the underlying cause of Akaev's overthrow lies in the fragmented and decentralized political elite and the ways in which Akaev managed wealthy elites throughout the 1990s and early 2000s.

Specifically, the relative dispersion of economic resources in Kyrgyzstan (as well as in Georgia and Ukraine) to elites outside a narrow presidential circle allowed for economic and political power bases to emerge in those countries in the 1990s. Years later, those individuals had become the main challengers to incumbent autocrats, and were responsible for funding political movements and media outlets.[vi] Akaev's unwillingness to use state violence in this moment, combined with his history of ineffectively managing opponents, discourses, and political institutions, spelled the end of his rule in 2005.[vii] After the subsequent President Bakiev's ousting a mere five years later, in 2010 and 2011 liberal reformer Roza Otunbaeva led Kyrgyzstan to adopt a new constitution, becoming the region's first and only (semi) parliamentary democracy.

THE FIVE PILLARS OF AUTHORITARIAN RESILIENCE

Unlike in Kyrgyzstan, the leaders in Uzbekistan, Kazakhstan, and Tajikistan have resisted challenges to their regimes throughout the 2000s up to the present day. They developed unique strategies for remaining in power, all relying on some combination of the following five pillars.

Selective Use of Violence and Repression

Kyrgyzstan's more modest and ineffective use of violence and repression serves as a stark contrast to the other three Central Asian regimes under consideration. Uzbekistan's "hard authoritarian" regime has demonstrated the capacity and willingness to use violence. In May 2005, President Karimov responded to mass protests in the southern city of Andijon with a strong show of force resulting in hundreds of dead civilians. This event in Uzbekistan was triggered by protests in favor of the release of 23 locally influential Islamic businessmen who had been imprisoned in 2004 in an attempt by a new governor of Andijon province to break up increasingly entrenched small business networks.[viii] The particularly violent response in May 2005 must be viewed against the backdrop of events just months before in neighboring Kyrgyzstan, where that country's first president was deposed. Seeking to prevent the spread of this "revolutionary" fervor, the Uzbek government responded arguably more harshly than it would have in a context in which no such neighboring threat existed.[ix,5]

This massacre, combined with the regime's longstanding practices of silencing political opponents, Islamic groups, and mafia networks through repression, torture, intimidation, and other harsh tactics, has led to descriptions of the regime as "violent."[x] Yet even in what has been described as a "police state," the use of repression had been targeted and selective until the Andijon massacre in 2005. Throughout the 1990s and early 2000s, protests and social unrest erupted in Uzbekistan in response to perceived violations of economic rights and human suffering—for example, when the government closed borders or attempted to install cash registers in bazaars to formalize the economy. Yet few deaths occurred; central and local authorities forged compromises or backpedaled in response to social pressure. The electoral revolution in Kyrgyzstan that preceded Andijon by two months heightened the fear of "revolution" and likely led to a harsh response impacting a broader range of civilians than in the past.

Other regimes in Central Asia have used violence more selectively; the "rationing" of coercion is targeted for occasions when persuasion, co-optation, and other strategies fail. Soft authoritarian regimes such as Kazakhstan seek to avoid undermining the country's international legitimacy. As Schatz observes, "the mass killing spree gives way to the rare targeted assassination, the jailing of crucial regime opponents, and the erection of obstacles to upend regime critics."[xi] These tactics

---

[5] Hill and Jones 2006 write that "Karimov saw Andijon as a clear sign that Uzbekistan was now infected with the "contagion of revolt" from the Coloured Revolutions..." 114. In other words, the way in which he framed and interpreted the events impacted his particularly violent response. By all accounts, the circumstances that led to this event were wholly domestic and local, not internationally inspired or influenced.

targeted against particular individuals and political organizations long predate the electoral revolutions; for example the dismantling of a well-funded elite-led opposition movement, Democratic Choice Kazakhstan, took place in 2000 and 2001.[xii] The January 2011 incident in which protests by laborers in the oil sector in the western town of Zhanaezon, Kazakhstan which culminated in a show of force that left dozens dead is more of an exception than the rule. This governmental response was similar to that in Andijon, albeit on a smaller scale, and resulted from long-standing labor disputes between workers and oil companies that had not been addressed.[xiii]

Tajikistan resembles Kazakhstan in its use of violence and repression; the regime led by President Rahmon has been constrained in its ability to use violence due to the historical legacy of the brutal civil war between 1992 and 1997. Violence-wielding militias with strong allegiances to region, clan, and other ascriptive tendencies were incorporated into state bodies in a 1997 peace agreement, making it challenging for Rahmon to consolidate state security forces. Targeted repression is more common than mass violence; common tactics include imprisonment and disappearance of opposition leaders and activists.[xiv]

While all the regimes in the region use violence and repression, Uzbekistan resembles much more of a police state with sustained forms of torture and repression as well as mass execution. While the causes of discontent are homegrown, the regime has pointed to foreign Islamic extremists or foreign-funded revolutionary waves in its justification of violence and repression. Grievances in the other countries are similarly local and homegrown, often related to the provision of social services (or the lack thereof) and the ability of locals and laborers to survive economically. Violent repression is circumscribed in Kazakhstan and Tajikistan to particular individuals and groups of regime opponents.

Appropriating Economic Flows

In addition to control over the use of violence, the ways in which authoritarian regimes control and appropriate economic resources has shaped their prospects for resilience. In contrast to Kyrgyzstan where wealth was dispersed among a broader base of elites throughout the country, in countries such as Kazakhstan and Uzbekistan, wealth primarily originating from the development and sale of commodities on the international market (oil, gas, and minerals in the former, and cotton and gold in the latter), remains tightly controlled by the presidential families and close allies and friends.[xv] Importantly, the leadership in these countries does *not* permit economic elites to simultaneously build political power and social bases of support, which could be mobilized on behalf of the elites to challenge existing power.[6] Wealthy businesspeople in these two countries do not hold parliamentary seats, for example; those who do hold positions in government or at the regional level are constantly rotated to prevent the emergence of independent power bases.[7] In Tajikistan, while the country's economy does rely on a centralized cotton sector, this sector is considerably smaller than Uzbekistan's. The government faces greater challenges managing the country's significant foreign aid and drug trafficking flows, which Markowitz attributes to the legacy of the civil war and the institutionalized inability of the state to consolidate power.[xvi]

While the leadership of these countries controls and directs rents from commodities, the majority of the populations rely on other capital flows that bypass the state and more directly support the needs of everyday people in the countries. One crucial capital flow is the billions of dollars of remittances sent back annually by millions of labor migrants from Uzbekistan, Tajikistan, and Kyrgyzstan working in the oil-boom economies of Kazakhstan and Russia. Cross-border trade also allows for small-scale traders and middle-men to earn profits. When these options were foreclosed via border closures, bazaar restrictions, and labor disputes, significant bottom-up social protest emerged. Leaders understand that they must keep these flows open to allow for some economic opportunity, and thus social stability.[8]

---

[6] See Radnitz 2010 for a contrast between Uzbekistan and Kyrgyzstan, and see Junisbai and Junisbai 2006 for the case of Kazakhstan.

[7] For example in the 1990s in Uzbekistan, regional governors were rotated on average every 3 years by Karimov, and he also managed encouraged and managed intense competition and rivalries among Ministries and Security Agencies as part of broader patronage bargains. Ilkhamov 2007. Returning to the violent case of Andijon, the underlying cause of the conflict originated the exceptionally long duration of the akim of Andijon, which allowed relatively independent wealth and power bases to emerge. Radnitz 2010.

[8] State leaders and other elite capture the rents from the commerce by controlling land. See Spector 2008.

This contrast between the centralized sale of commodities and the decentralized flows of remittances and other commercial flows highlights the different ways in which these regimes are tightly integrated into the international economy. While commodity flows such as oil and gas, minerals, cotton, and gold bolster regimes because of the ways in which wealth is centralized and distributed to prevent alternative elite pillars of power backed by society, other flows such as remittances from migrant laborers and profits from cross-border trade serve as decentralized social safety valves for everyday citizens. They allow for investments in weddings, celebrations, and other community festivities that both bring meaning to local people as well as serve as a mechanism through which ongoing reciprocal relations can continue in the absence of local jobs.[xvii]

Finally, while government provision of public services was radically challenged in the 1990s in the aftermath of the Soviet Union's collapse, governments have increased the provision of social services in the region, especially after 2005. The cotton economy in Uzbekistan, for example, was reformed by the mid-late 2000s, allowing famers more crop choice. The government also co-opted local customary organizations such as neighborhood associations, or *mahallahs*, both to distribute social welfare and solve local conflicts, as well as to collect information and maintain control of local populations. Functioning now as "agents of state administration," *mahallahs* in Uzbekistan provide an example of the ways in which leaders adapt social and economic policy by co-opting informal institutions.[xviii] In mineral-rich Kazakhstan, the government has re-aligned patronage relations and built considerable bureaucratic strength as part of a broader state- and nation-building strategy involving the capital relocation from Almaty to Astana in 1998.[xix] President Nazarbaev has also reshaped business-state relations since the 2000s. After Nazarbaev dismantled opposition movements comprised of new Kazakh elites in 2001-2002, he shortly thereafter embarked upon a broader program to co-opt small and medium businesses. Through business reforms and the creation of state-led business associations, the leadership sought to avert political instability from the business sector. He articulated the reasons for the 2005 revolution in Kyrgyzstan as lying "not in some mythical plots by outside forces, but [rather] the result of the logic of internal developments. Poverty and unemployment….are fertile grounds for people's dissatisfaction with the authorities."[xx] Corporatization and formalization of business-state relations is an adaptation to strict patron-client relations that dominated the first decade of rule in Kazakhstan.

Controlling Political Institutions and Reshaping Politics

Upon independence from the Soviet Union, the Central Asian leaders have controlled political institutions and shaped formal politics. Uzbekistan has been the most restrictive from the onset; between 1991 and 1993 various laws were instituted that prevented mass gatherings and the organization of political parties. As a result, political and religious parties and movements have been suppressed or dislodged. [xxi] Political dynamics in Uzbekistan revolve around center-region tensions and intra-elite struggles, not electoral politics.[9]

Kazakhstan and Tajikistan are softer forms of electoral authoritarian regimes where elections are held and political parties exist, yet the principles and processes are manipulated so as to "render elections instruments of authoritarian rule rather than instruments of democracy."[xxii] The Kazakh government has shaped both the actors and the institutions involved in politics. Oligarchic parties and movements were sidelined in the late 1990s and early 2000s, well before the electoral revolutions became significant perceived threats to the regime. Legislation in 2002 required 50,000 signatures representing all regions and major cities of the country for the creation of a new party, up from 3,000 in the past. The events in the 2000s—especially neighboring Kyrgyzstan's electoral revolution in 2005—both sped up and intensified these institutional changes. Kazakhstan's electoral reforms that were adopted at this time banned street demonstrations and meetings organized by individuals, public organizations, or political parties until an election campaign has ended and vote tallies are officially

---

[9] Regional elites in the 1990s had representation in the national parliament although the nature and details of this bargain have shifted continually over the past 20 years: "stability is very much predicated on the continuing ability of central and regional leaders to reach mutually satisfactory agreements…." Ilkhamov 2004, 181.

announced. Legislators who supported the law openly admitted that it was designed to prevent the kind of protests that happened in Georgia, Ukraine, and Kyrgyzstan following their elections.[xxiii] Perhaps the most important trend has been the centralization of political control through the creation of pro-presidential parties;[10] this process has been ongoing in Kazakhstan since the 2000s, and has resulted in the incorporation of three smaller political parties into current-day state-led party, "Nur-Otan."[xxiv] Similarly, between 2003 and 2006, Tajikistan reversed electoral reforms by changing the constitution to allow President Rahmon to run for president for two more 7-year terms; other trends included rigging elections, stuffing ballots, and intimidating and arresting opposition figures, often by using the official electoral administration.[xxv]

In sum, Uzbekistan's restriction of political opposition and alternative movements dates to the inception of the independent state in 1991. In contrast, more liberal hybrid electoral regimes in Kazakhstan and Tajikistan have allowed for more openness, while consistently controlling elections and consolidating political power in a centralized party apparatus. The threat of electoral revolutions in the 2000s served to hasten and deepen this ongoing process.

Creating a Culture of Compliance and Persuasion

Crucial to authoritarian stability has been the ability of the region's leaders to create generally compliant populations, especially in the absence of political legitimacy. Creating compliance goes beyond the use of violence, economic resources, and political institutions. It entails mobilizing culture and discourses, setting the sociopolitical agenda, and controlling information in effective ways. In Uzbekistan one form of compliance is achieved through the elaborate planning and performing of regular Olympic-style mass spectacles and celebrations that elevate Uzbekistan's national identity and celebrate the country's national culture.[xxvi] These events dominate public TV airspace and channel the creative energy of the intelligentsia, serving to both project state power

---

[10] Brownlee (2007) finds that the strength and solidarity of ruling parties matters in explaining authoritarian durability.

and shape cultural discourse—even if people have become tired of the scripted and unchanging nature of these events.

Soft-authoritarian rulers have been particularly effective at political persuasion, which rests on the ability of the elite to define the political agenda and channel political outcomes.[xxvii] For example, in Kazakhstan the regime manages media flows and information, without completely dominating media so as not to discredit the press entirely. The leadership sets the political agenda by engineering political drama to undermine opponents while simultaneously employing rhetoric of democratization and human rights promotion. The consolidation of parties discussed above was framed as "democratization"; preventing political fragmentation and strengthening the presidential party served as a core democratizing goal for the country. Debate and discussion is not quashed and silenced, but rather countered and strategically managed.[xxviii] In the mid-2000s, the government skillfully juxtaposed televised flashbacks to chaos and riots in Kyrgyzstan with sunny pictures of the country's beautiful snow-capped mountains and the Kazakhstani national flag. The narratives of stability and development continue to predominate in a variety of media—TV, billboards, and print media.[xxix]

Tajikistan's President Rahmon has justified his rule rhetorically not using the contrast of color revolutions but rather by reminding the population of the instability, brutality and the chaos of the civil war in the 1990s. Popular memories of the death and destruction from this time bolster the effectiveness of this discursive strategy. He has also focused on creating narratives emphasizing nationalism and moderate Islamic identity.

Managing Foreign Influence

Finally, the leaders in Central Asia have addressed challenges they perceive from the international community. The region's independence in 1991 coincided with a broader movement in the West to support democratization-from-below by funding local civil society organizations and NGOs.[xxx] On one end of the spectrum, Kyrgyzstan's President Akaev embraced international influence, ranging from international economic integration to foreign-funded NGOs. On the other end of the spectrum, Uzbekistan's Karimov adhered to more autarkic ideas about economic integration and limited foreign aid presence, although some domestic NGOs and foreign-funded organizations were working in Uzbekistan by the early-2000s.[xxxi]

In the middle of the spectrum, in both Kazakhstan and Tajikistan, international relationships proliferated not out of an intentional or strategic calculation by the leadership to invite Western influence, but rather as a result of unintended consequences of other goals and events. For Kazakhstan, the relative openness to foreign aid and foreign NGOs resulted from the ways in which the leadership defined the legitimacy of the new state based on international recognition in the early 1990s: "the elite chose to base its legitimacy claim on external recognition broadcast inward to domestic audiences" which meant engagement with and integration in myriad international structures. [xxxii] Significant foreign aid and support for civil society in Kazakhstan proved an unintended consequence of the broader goal of attaining international legitimacy, and had the effect of moderating potentially more authoritarian and coercive practices. For Tajikistan, the influx of aid and assistance resulted from the post-civil war bargain and the interest in having the international community help address humanitarian and other challenges in the poorest of the Central Asian countries.

In the 2000s, against the backdrop of the Eurasian electoral revolutions and the perception that foreign NGOS and foreign-financed civil society groups were complicit in instigating political change, countries in the region began restricting and limiting this influence. A 2006 report by the National Endowment for Democracy (NED) finds that new legislation restricting NGO activities and weakening civil society adds up to more than isolated events.[xxxiii] Yet the degree and nature of these restrictions varied dramatically in Central Asia. To the extent that certain international organizations and NGOs were allowed in the 1990s, Uzbekistan squeezed out 200 domestic NGOs and expelled most international NGOs after 2005. Tajikistan's response has been more "selective and temporary" compared to neighboring Uzbekistan. While the regime has ordered the reregistration of NGOs as a form of pressure, and fewer were registered in 2007 than in 2006 after the law was instated, they still permitted over a thousand organizations in the country primarily working on economic development and institution building. The government has also closed down the country's main independent publishing house and independent press, and has limited the activities of other Internet sites and broadcasters. Yet, these have been short-term strategies, and not nearly as extensive as in other countries such as Uzbekistan and Russia.[xxxiv]

Kazakhstan's response has focused also on selectively preventing mass demonstrations and protests, while both rhetorically and practically reframing the role of NGOs and civil society in the country. In order to prevent a "Kyrgyz scenario," the government enacted legislation to ban demonstrations during and after elections and broke up peaceful protests on numerous occasions.[xxxv] Policy toward NGOs and civil society has been different. The Nazarbaev government (via the Constitutional Council) rejected restrictive legislation on NGOs and the media that the government itself had engineered so as to demonstrate the President's "moderate... and liberal values."[xxxvi] Nazarbaev invited Russian and other post-Soviet observers to monitor the 2005 presidential election, which they deemed to meet international election standards, in contrast to the OSCE's critique of the election process. Moreover, the money that foreign organizations such as the United States Agency for International Development (USAID) have channeled into strengthening civil society and elections often did not make any difference in the transparency and conduct of the elections. Instead, the tools and techniques imported via foreign aid by local parties—including pro-presidential parties—were used to "wage a battle that was quintessentially Kazakhstani—that between the informal patron-client networks of power in the country."[xxxvii]

Finally, governments such as Uzbekistan and Kazakhstan have increased their own budget allocations for supporting NGOs.[xxxviii] These two governments have also actively courted more direct relationships between civil society organizations and the government in the provision of public services and other forms of collaboration. While these activities are relatively new in Uzbekistan; in Kazakhstan, the government's 2006 through 2011 "Concept of Civil Society Development" is now being updated and the next 2014-to-2020 platform will soon be released. These plans, together with bi-annual civic forums and other state-sponsored initiatives, indicate the leadership's ability to manage and oversee civil society discourse and activities.

CONCLUSION

Central Asian autocrats have adapted over the last 25 years to a variety of pressures and challenges. This investigation into the discourses and practices of authoritarian resilience in Central Asia reveals two broad trends. First, Central Asian "varieties of authoritarianism" range from "hard" authoritarian regimes such as that of Uzbekistan, to "soft" authoritarian regimes including those of Kazakhstan and Tajikistan. This distinction suggests that despite a common Soviet background and history, the Central Asian regimes are increasingly following divergent trajectories. Hard authoritarian regimes have utilized more systematic repression and coercion, as well as restricted certain forms of international influence more heavily. Soft authoritarian regimes such as those of Kazakhstan and Tajikistan rely on more selective and targeted forms of repression and coercion, and have managed foreign influence instead of fully restricting it. All of these regimes—both hard and soft— appropriate and manage economic resources and business interests to prevent alternative economically-backed power centers, and all create cultures and discourses that attempt to engender a compliant public.

Second, while all the leaders continually adapt and respond to challenges, the Soviet period and early transitions in the 1990s bequeathed a set of particular constraints and opportunities for the new leaders, and leaders themselves held different ideas that guided and shaped their rule throughout the 1990s and 2000s. The particular perceived external "threat" of electoral revolutions—especially after Kyrgyzstan's changes in 2005—led to increased violence and restrictions in the political and public sphere, and also prompted proactive government initiatives related to social services and political consolidation. This suggests that we look closely at the interactions between adaptable autocratic leaders and their particular national contexts to understand reactions to broader regional and global processes and challenges.

Notes

i.   Examples of media headlines in 2012 capturing the search for the "Central Asian Spring" include Joanna Lillis, "Will there be a Central Asian Spring," *Foreign Policy Magazine*, January 26, 2012, *http://www.foreignpolicy.com/articles/2012/01/24/will_there_be_a_central_asian_spring* ; Scott Radnitz, "Waiting for Spring," *Foreign Policy Magazine*, February 17, 2012 *http://www.foreignpolicy.com/articles/2012/02/17/waiting_for_spring* . For an analysis that critiques the mainstream Western press for "emphasizing broad, sweeping similarities – religion, resources, repression" between the Arab world and Central Asia, see Sarah Kendzior, "The Reverse Orientalism of the Arab Spring," *Registan*, January 16, 2012 http://registan.net/2012/01/16/the-reverse-orientalism-of-the-arab-spring/.

ii.   Eric McGlinchey, "Exploring Regime Instability and Ethnic Violence in Kyrgyzstan." *Asia Policy*, no. 12 (July 2011): 79–98.; Radnitz, Scott. Weapons of the Wealthy: Predatory Regimes and Elite-Led Protests in Central Asia. Cornell University Press, 2010.

iii. Joshua Stacher, *Adaptable Autocrats: Regime Power in Egypt and Syria* (Stanford, CA: Stanford University Press, 2012), p. 21-22.

iv.   Scott Radnitz, *Weapons of the Wealthy: Predatory Regimes and Elite-Led Protests in Central Asia*. Cornell University Press, 2010.

v.   Ibid.

vi.   Scott Radnitz, *Weapons of the Wealthy: Predatory Regimes and Elite-Led Protests in Central Asia*. Cornell University Press, 2010.

vii. Edward Schatz, "The Soft Authoritarian Tool Kit: Agenda-Setting Power in Kazakhstan and Kyrgyzstan." *Comparative Politics* 41, no. 2 (January 2009).

viii. Fiona Hill and Kevin Jones, "Fear of Democracy or Revolution: The Reaction to Andijon." *The Washington Quarterly* 29, no. 3 (2006): 111–25., Radnitz 2012.

ix.   Ibid.

x.   McGlinchey 2011. For additional examples of state use of imprisonment and torture, see CIVICUS 2013. And US Department of State Human Rights reports, for example *http://m.state.gov/md369.htm*.

xi.   Edward Schatz, "The Soft Authoritarian Tool Kit: Agenda-Setting Power in Kazakhstan and Kyrgyzstan." *Comparative Politics* 41, no. 2 (January 2009) p. 206.

xii. Barbara Junisbai and Azamat Junisbai, "The Democratic Choice of Kazakhstan: A Case Study in Economic Liberalization, Intra-Elite Cleavage and Political Opposition." *Demokratizatsiya: The Journal of Post-Soviet Democratization* 13, no. 3 (2005): 373–92.

xiii. Aitolkyn Kourmanova, "Lessons from Zhanaozen. Bringing Business, Government and Society Together." *Voices from Central Asia* 6 (September 2012).

xiv. Lawrence Markowitz, "The Sub-National Roots of Authoritarianism: Neopatrimonialism and Territorial Administration in Uzbekistan." *Demokratizatsiya: The Journal of Post-Soviet Democratization* 20, no. 4 (Fall 2012).

xv. Scott Radnitz, *Weapons of the Wealthy: Predatory Regimes and Elite-Led Protests in Central Asia.* Cornell University Press, 2010.

xvi. Lawrence Markowitz, "The Sub-National Roots of Authoritarianism: Neopatrimonialism and Territorial Administration in Uzbekistan." *Demokratizatsiya: The Journal of Post-Soviet Democratization* 20, no. 4 (Fall 2012).

xvii. Ibid.

xviii. Jennifer Murtazashvili, "Coloured by Revolution: The Political Economy of Autocratic Stability in Uzbekistan." *Democratization* 19, no. 1 (February 2012): p. 89.

xix. Edward Schatz, "The Soft Authoritarian Tool Kit: Agenda-Setting Power in Kazakhstan and Kyrgyzstan." *Comparative Politics* 41, no. 2 (January 2009) p. 206.

xx. Wojciech Ostrowski, *Politics and Oil in Kazakhstan.* Routledge, Central Asian Studies, 2009, p. 350.

xxi. Alisher Ilkhamov, "The Thorny Path of Civil Society in Uzbekistan." *Central Asian Survey* 24, no. 3 (September 2005): 297–317.; McGlinchey, Eric. "Exploring Regime Instability and Ethnic Violence in Kyrgyzstan." *Asia Policy*, no. 12 (July 2011): 79–98.

xxii. Schedler 2006, 3. For more on the ways in which nominally democratic institutions such as legislatures can strengthen incumbent leadership, see Gandhi, Jennifer and Przeworski, Adam "Authoritarian Institutions and the Survival of Autocrats" *Comparative Politics* 40, no. 11 (November 2007).

xxiii. Antoine Blua, "Kazakhstan: Movement Elects to Transform Itself into a True Opposition Party." Eurasianet, December 5, 2003.; Yermukanov, Marat. "Kazakhstan Amends Electoral Law, but Reforms Still Lacking." Eurasia Daily Monitor 2, no. 52 (March 15, 2005). *http://www.jamestown.org/single/?no_cache=1&tx_ttnews%5Btt_news%5D=27691#.VSLyEfnF-SE.*

xxiv. See *http://carnegieendowment.org/2012/04/05/background-on-nur-otan-party/a6os*

xxv. Lawrence Markowitz, "The Sub-National Roots of Authoritarianism: Neopatrimonialism and Territorial Administration in Uzbekistan." *Demokratizatsiya: The Journal of Post-Soviet Democratization* 20, no. 4 (Fall 2012), p. 108–109.

xxvi. Laura L. Adams, *The Spectacular State: Culture and National Identity in Uzbekistan. Politics, History, and Culture.* Durham: Duke University Press, 2010.

xxvii. Edward Schatz, "The Soft Authoritarian Tool Kit: Agenda-Setting Power in Kazakhstan and Kyrgyzstan." *Comparative Politics* 41, no. 2 (January 2009) p. 206.

xxviii. Ibid.

xxix. TV segments and billboards witnessed by the author in Almaty in 2006.

xxx. For a review of this trend, see Schatz 2006, p. 266-67.

xxxi. Keith A. Darden, *Economic Liberalism and Its Rivals: The Formation of International Institutions Among the Post-Soviet States.* Cambridge ; New York: Cambridge University Press, 2009.

xxxii. Schatz 2009, p. 270. In contrast to Kazakhstan's legitimacy claim based on internationally recognized statehood, Uzbekistan's legitimacy claim was focused more inward on an anti-Islamist and Uzbek national identity.

xxxiii. Carl Gershman and Michael Allen, "The Assault on Democracy Assistance" *Journal of Democracy* 17, no. 2 (April 2006); See also The International Center for Not-for-Profit Law, "Recent Laws and Legislative Proposals to Restrict Civil Society and Civil Society Organizations," *International Journal for Non-for-Profit Law* 8, no. 4 (August 2006).

xxxiv. Markowitz 2012, 98. For additional details see the International Center for Non-Profit Law page on Tajikistan: *http://www.icnl.org/research/monitor/tajikistan.html*.

xxxv. Holly Cartner, "Kazakhstan: New Restrictions put Elections at Risk," Human Rights Watch Letter, October 12, 2005. *http://hrw.org/english/docs/2005/10/12/kazakh11853.htm*.

xxxvi. Edward Schatz, "The Soft Authoritarian Tool Kit: Agenda-Setting Power in Kazakhstan and Kyrgyzstan." *Comparative Politics* 41, no. 2 (January 2009) p. 211.

xxxvii. Sean Roberts, "Doing the Democracy Dance in Kazakhstan: Democracy Development as Cultural Encounter" *Slavic Review* 71, no. 2 (Summer 2012). While foreign aid organizations might view electoral assistance and other programming as technical problem, Roberts finds that it is a contested and negotiated process.

xxxviii. Vsevolod Ovcharenko, "Government Financing of NGOs in Kazakhstan: Overview of a Controversial Experience," *The International Journal of Not-for-Profit Law,* Volume 8, Issue 4, August 2006. Available at: *http://www.icnl.org/research/journal/vol8iss4/special_2.htm*. See also International Center for Non-Profit Law page on Uzbekistan: *http://www.icnl.org/research/monitor/uzbekistan.html*; and International Center for Non-Profit Law page on Kazakhstan: *http://www.icnl.org/research/monitor/kazakhstan.html*.

CHAPTER 3

From People Power to Democracy Building

Larry Diamond
Senior Fellow, Hoover Institution
Stanford University

O NE OF THE DISTINGUISHING features of world politics in the past quarter-century has been the surprising number of peaceful popular uprisings for democratic change. These have sometimes been called eruptions of "people power" because ordinary people have driven political change, the mobilizations have been at the grassroots and often quite spontaneous, and the consequences have certainly been quite powerful: in many instances, longstanding dictators have fallen suddenly and unceremoniously.

People power has been a prominent means of transition from authoritarian rule during the past four decades of what has been termed "the third wave" of global democratization. The paradigmatic early case was the Philippines in 1986. In the wake of efforts by the dictator, Ferdinand Marcos, to steal the February "snap" presidential election, hundreds of thousands—and then ultimately millions—of Filipinos came out in the streets, using tactics of nonviolent civil resistance to split the regime and bring down the dictatorship. Manila became ungovernable as people filled the streets in the "miracle at Edsa," significant portions of Marcos's own armed forces defected, and, with the United States joining in on the pressure at the end, Marcos was forced to depart the country, leaving the duly elected new president, Corazon Aquino, to assume the presidency. This was the first "color revolution," in which mass peaceful, popular protests after a stolen election tipped the balance toward democratic change. The pattern was repeated in Serbia in October 2000, in Georgia after the fraudulent November 2003 elections, and in Ukraine, following the blatant fraud in the December 2004 presidential election. In Ukraine, democrats adopted the color Orange, and that gave the iconic name to their struggle, "The Orange Revolution."

More recently, popular uprisings toppled dictators in four Arab countries during what has come to be called the "Arab Spring." None of these uprisings were immediately triggered by a stolen election. Rather, years of pent-up frustration with corruption and misrule finally ignited popular mobilization. Once the spark was lit in Tunisia in December 2010, it quickly spread to Egypt, Libya, Bahrain, Yemen, Syria, and elsewhere. But so far, Tunisia is the only Arab country where "people power" has given rise to a genuine democratic transition. Freedom House data show that of the sixteen Arab countries in the Middle East, seven had worse average freedom scores at the end of 2013 than they did at the end of 2010, and only two (Tunisia and Libya) were improved. The Arab Spring has become an Arab freeze. Libya has become a semi-failed state; Syria has been devoured by catastrophic civil war; Bahrain has seen the ruthless crushing of its movement for democracy; and many Arab countries have seen a constriction of political and civic space, even while the Gulf oil regimes have been pouring money into clientelistic payoffs and public services and subsidies as a way of buying off or tamping down dissent. A transition is still under way in Yemen, though it has been precarious and has required intensive international mediation.

There is a larger sobering set of facts. Democracy is a tough system to institutionalize and sustain. Looking back on the 40-year history of the "third wave," roughly one-third (56) of the 170 democratic regimes that have existed during this period have failed. If we remove the 26 rich, mainly Western, democracies that preceded the third wave (in Western Europe, the US, Canada, Australia, New Zealand, and Japan), the failure rate is even higher, nearly 40 percent. Then consider the countries where popular mobilization against authoritarian rule never gave rise to genuine democracy. That has been the sad fate to date not only of a number of Arab countries, but of China (with the suppression of the 1989 Tiananmen protests), Iran (with the crushing of the Green

Movement in 2009), and of Zimbabwe, where pro-democracy forces appear to have won and then been robbed of the 2008 elections, but managed to win a place in a power-sharing arrangement, only to squander the opportunity in the subsequent 2013 elections. Elections can be a way to topple dictators, but broadly supported democratic movements can also fall short in elections. This has repeatedly happened of late in Venezuela, where the opposition may well have had the most votes in the last two presidential elections, which were "won" by the dictator Hugo Chavez and then by his designated successor Nicholas Maduro. And it happened in 2013 in Malaysia, when the opposition Pakatan Rakyat coalition broke through to win 51 percent of the parliamentary vote but was only able to capture 40 percent of the seats due to gerrymandering.

All of this raises a profoundly important question. How does a country move beyond "people power" protest to democracy—real democracy, sustainable democracy? What is necessary for a non-violent uprising to become a transition to democracy? And what role can the international community play?

DOMESTIC INGREDIENTS FOR SUCCESSFUL TRANSITIONS TO DEMOCRACY

I consider here first the domestic factors that can affect the likelihood of a transition to democracy. Then in the concluding section I will ponder the implications for international actors. This is the right sequence, because international actors cannot help move countries toward democracy without a strong domestic base of action and support. International actors *may* be able to help empower local democratic actors and to tip the balance toward them over time. But the people in a country must initiate, drive and "own" their own transition. The most that international actors can do is to help, to facilitate, and to protect. But they cannot initiate and they cannot impose.

The single most conducive factor to a democratic transition is a ruling elite that, for whatever reason, wants to see it happen. This is not as far-fetched as it seems. Many military regimes get to the point where a combination of domestic and international pressures leads them to see the need for extrication. Sometimes this happens with civilian rulers or parties or coalitions; for example with Adolfo Suarez following the death of Francisco Franco in Spain, or with Lee Teng-hui and the KMT following the death of Chiang Ching-kuo in Taiwan in the late 1980s, or Ernesto Zedillo deciding in the late 1990s that Mexico needed to institutionalize truly free and fair elections. After many years of ruling as an authoritarian (and initially military) strongman, Jerry Rawlings made the same decision as Zedillo, and around the same time. And in the early 1990s, many African dictators felt they had no choice but to yield to international pressure for free and fair multi-party elections. But what if authoritarian ruling elites do not decide to lead or permit a democratic transition? Then what makes for a successful transition?

Getting to democracy requires effective political and civic organization, and sustaining democracies require effective institutions. That, in a nutshell, is the main message of this short essay. Democratic transitions typically fail because opposition forces lacked the organization, leadership, strategy, and resources to bring down a very clever, agile, determined, resourceful, and entrenched autocracy. And new democracies typically fail because of weak institutions of representation and governance, and poor leadership.

The first requirement is for democrats to have some kind of political organization that is capable of performing the following essential tasks:

- Mobilizing but also restraining, disciplining, and targeting mass protests and other means of non-violent resistance, such as strikes and boycotts.

- Waging an effective national election campaign (if competitive elections are in the mix, as they often are), and mobilizing voters.

- Mounting a broad and effective national election monitoring effort, with a parallel vote tabulation.

- Delineating and articulating at least a rudimentary policy program or agenda for a post-authoritarian era (which would presumably include significant governance reforms and possibly constitutional reforms as well).

- Mobilizing international public opinion and the governments of major democracies to lean in favor of a democratic transition in the country.

There is no way to ignore or neglect the obvious fact that these are essentially the tasks of a political party or coalition of parties. Democracy is much more than elections, but it cannot take root in the absence of elections, and he who says "democratic elections" must also say "democratic political parties." The weaker political parties are in the transition, the weaker are the prospects for transition, for several reasons. First, it is harder to sustain and discipline protest over an extended period of time without some kind of prominent role for one or more opposition parties. Second, parties play a crucial and indispensable role in all of the other functions above. Third, it is nearly impossible to govern a large-scale, modern democratic state without a political party or coalition to structure an agenda and mobilize legislative support for a prime minister or president. And fourth— and this point is less obvious—strong, institutionalized (and internally democratic) parties are necessary not only to produce effective democratic leadership, but also to restrain it. If, under authoritarian rule, opposition parties are weak, they tend to be dominated by strong individuals, and these individuals may then ride roughshod over democratic norms and restraints once they come to power. One thing that enables "people power" to be about democracy, and to produce democracy, is a political party (or party coalition) that advocates for and then works to advance a set of principles and interests, rather than just the glorification of a new strongman.

Second, implicit in the above is that successful democratic movements need the broadest possible support, and this often requires a wide-ranging, inclusive coalition of opposition parties and political forces, in which rival opposition leaders sometimes have to find a way to submerge their egos and ambitions in the service of a larger cause.[i] In 2004 and

2005, the pro-democracy forces in Ukraine ultimately succeeded in defeating both Kuchma's neo-communist successor regime and his chosen candidate, Viktor Yanukovich. This was possible because the two most compelling candidates, Viktor Yuschenko and Yulia Tymoshenko, joined forces in a common front. Similarly, in the Philippines in 1986, Aquino was only able to win against long odds because virtually all the opposition parties united behind her. In October 1988, Chile's democrats succeeded in defeating General Augusto Pinochet's bid to extend and re-legitimize his authoritarian regime in a referendum only because all the significant center and left parties united in the Concertacion alliance against Pinochet. And in 1990 the liberal publisher Violetta Chamorro led a 14-party alliance to unseat the incumbent authoritarian president of Nicaragua, Daniel Ortega. More recently, opposition forces assembled in very broad coalitions behind clear and unified leadership allowed upstarts in Zimbabwe in 2008, Venezuela in 2012 and 2013, and Malaysia in 2013 to come very close to victory.

And leadership matters. That is the third important point. People power movements need clear, shrewd, and courageous leadership. And, of course, they need democratically committed leadership if they are to get to democracy. One thing that undermined the Green Movement in Iran is that the "opposition" presidential candidate that it rallied behind, Mir-Hossein Mousavi, did not in turn unequivocally rally behind the movement. The electoral debacle suffered in 2013 by Morgan Tsvangirai's opposition party, the Movement for Democratic Change (MDC-T), was not merely the result of fraud and intimidation by Robert Mugabe's authoritarian regime; the MDC also lost a significant amount of public support as a result of having grown too comfortable—and corrupt— during the power-sharing arrangement of the previous four years, while the party's organization and campaign spirit atrophied.[ii] This was partly a failure of leadership on the part of Tsvangirai, who was criticized for organizing a lavish wedding for himself while his supporters were suffering. In the case of Ukraine, what enabled Viktor Yanukovich to win the presidency in 2010 and then decimate democracy was the infighting, ineffective governance, and corruption of those who had led the Orange Revolution just five years previously, beginning with Yuschenko and Tymoshenko. The situation became so embittered that

Yuschenko (who could not manage to win more than 5 percent of the vote in his bid for reelection) refused to endorse Tymoshenko (and tacitly supported their mutual nemesis, Yanukovich) in the February 2010 presidential run-off election.

The Venezuela situation is more complex. In the 2012 and 2013 presidential elections, which first returned Chavez to power and then promoted his successor Maduro, Henrique Capriles mounted a broader, more pragmatic and sophisticated opposition campaign than anything that the Bolivarian socialist regime constructed by Chavez had confronted previously. But some critical observers believe Capriles should have been more outspoken in challenging the clear evidence of electoral fraud and denouncing the results as illegitimate. The problem, of course, is that denunciation, confrontation, and then mobilization all entail risks. If Capriles had done that, it would have needed to have been part of a broader strategy to mobilize non-violent civil resistance to change the regime then and there. Capriles was not ready for that. The regime in Venezuela is still not fully authoritarian. He no doubt judged that he had too much to lose, and that Venezuela had too much to lose. On the other hand, the result is that the regime persists, is becoming more authoritarian, and order is disintegrating, as crime rises and Venezuela creeps toward a broader societal decay if not collapse. There should be no illusions that the struggle for democracy involves easy and obvious strategic choices.

But democratic forces do need a strategy, and that is the fourth requirement. They need to understand the pillars of support that sustain an authoritarian regime, and figure out specific means to knock them away. It is not only important to unify the opposition, it is also essential to divide the regime and then rip away a portion of its base. Almost everywhere, the military and the broader security apparatus are key pillars of regime support. But often autocrats don't trust their own militaries and instead build rival security forces or presidential guards that are more tightly under their personal control (or so they think). Corruption, factionalism, ethnic divisions and simple human paranoia may generate divisions in the authoritarian regime that can be exploited. Members of the business community may become disaffected by corruption and crony "capitalism" that is, as it was in the

Philippines under Marcos and in Tunisia under Ben Ali, increasingly concentrated within a narrow elite around the ruler and his family, or in the ruling party. A good strategy looks for weaknesses in the authoritarian armor and potential assets and opportunities among the opposition forces. It then develops a sequence of political moves and a plan for mobilizing and deploying resources (human, financial, organizational, and technical) in asymmetrical ways to overcome the apparent advantages of the authoritarian regime. There is considerable evidence to suggest that efforts to bring down dictators are much more likely to bring about democracy if they steadfastly avoid violence. People power is much more likely to produce popular sovereignty if it understands and utilizes in a well-strategized and disciplined fashion techniques of non-violent civil resistance. This requires a plan. But democrats must also remain flexible, able to adapt as a political struggle unfolds, and keenly aware that in politics as in war (to quote Clausewitz on war), "No campaign plan survives first contact with the enemy."

The fifth requirement is resources: people, money, organization, and technology. Effective, sustained, adroit mobilization against authoritarian rule requires some degree of financing to stage rallies, wage campaigns, move organizers around the country, construct alternative media, disseminate messages, monitor elections, expose human rights violations, and so on. Alternative media are especially critical; some means by which democrats may counter the relentless propaganda machinery of the authoritarian regime and put opposition coalitions on something slightly closer to a level playing field. During the Serbian revolution, the radio station B-92 served this purpose. In many of the recent popular uprisings, including during the 2009 Green Movement and the Arab Spring, social media such as Facebook and Twitter played a crucial role.

The sixth potent factor contributing to a democratic transition is a strong and democratically-minded civil society. This is often where romantic portraits of the formula for democratic breakthrough begin, but it is where I will end. A robust, pluralistic civil society, with strong, horizontal relations of trust and reciprocity,[iii] is not only immensely helpful in organizing the initial protests and in breaking the climate of fear and passivity. It can also help to build and entrench a culture of democracy and to tackle the hugely important task of mass civic education for democracy, rising from the moral ashes of a cynical, exploitative, and demoralizing authoritarian regime. A vigorous civil society gives voice to the previously disempowered, often advancing women and minorities into the front ranks of democratic action and representation. Down the road, it can help to simulate and train political participation, monitor and check state power, generate an alternative sphere of news and opinion outside state or dominant elite channels, improve the representation of interests, break down surviving patterns of authoritarianism and corruption at the local or regional level, and recruit and prepare political leaders.[iv]

WHAT INTERNATIONAL ACTORS CAN DO

International democratic actors cannot (and certainly should not try to) choose leaders for a country. They cannot give them a strategy or a moral rationale. But there are some important ways that international assistance can help to diminish the enormous inequality in power and resources between authoritarian regime and opposition, and help as well to tilt a political regime crisis toward a democratic outcome. Fortunately, international actors already do these things. The questions to be pondered and researched are how they can do them more effectively, with what kind of timing and coalitions, and for how long.

First, international actors can transfer resources and skills. Movements for democracy need money and equipment (including transportation, information, and communication tools) to build and sustain their organization and activities. So do independent media organizations. Often the soil for an eventual democratic transition is tilled years in advance through financial and technical support to a wide range of independent organizations and media in civil society. This has been true for almost all the cases mentioned above, and many others including Poland and South Africa. There are a host of other strategies and skills—the methods and diverse forms of non-violent civil resistance, the specific skills of conducting a parallel vote tabulation—that international actors can help expose local democratic forces to. Training is particularly effective when it brings democratic politicians and civil society leaders from previous transitioning countries to countries in the thick of a transition challenge. There is only so much that an American, Swedish, or German trainer can convey. Training becomes more vivid when people who have been through similar challenges share their concrete experiences.

A crucially important and often under-appreciated element of assistance is political party assistance. To repeat, civil society can mobilize against authoritarian depredations, but it cannot on its own deliver a country to the promised land of democracy. That requires effective political parties that are capable of performing the essential roles of political parties: recruiting and selecting candidates, canvassing and surveying public opinion, crafting effective messages and policy platforms, waging electoral campaigns, mobilizing voter turnout, forming governing coalitions, and then representing interests and passing legislation. While civil society organizations may help with some of these functions, all of them require the involvement of political parties and some can only be done by parties. Especially where democratic parties are emerging for the first time or after a long period of slumber due to authoritarian suppression, international assistance can make a tangible difference. Yet it often must walk a fine line between the need to engage on behalf of democratic aspirations and the need to not pick a specific "winner."

Second, international actors can help to train opposition forces in the tools of "liberation technology." Opposition forces need help on both "offense" and "defense." On the one hand, they can learn how to make more effective use of social media to build civic infrastructures and mobilize supporters. On the other hand, they need training in basic safety precautions—how to utilize these tools, and the Internet more broadly, through means that limit the potential for monitoring, intervention, sabotage and subversion by the authoritarian state. Some of these involve diffusing the basic protocols of Internet "hygiene." Some of it involves training in the use of encryption tools and software programs like Tor to circumvent Internet controls, widen access, and improve security. Some of what needs to be conveyed involves the *limits* of these information technologies and some sober lessons on when *not* to use them, or rely on them.

Third, ambassadors and their embassy staffs from established democracies can reach into what has been called "the diplomats toolbox" to find ways of supporting and protecting democrats on the ground in these countries. This can involve the use of diplomatic immunity to engage civil society, to bear witness at trials, to stand in solidarity with democratic protestors and to try to protect them from punishment or arrest; diplomatic or public reporting to expose and publicize authoritarian abuses; private diplomatic démarches against repressive policies or actions; economic or other bilateral or multilateral sanctions to raise the costs to autocrats of suppressing democratic mobilization; and public diplomacy to raise the democratic consciousness, hope, and self-confidence of anti-authoritarian actors in civil society as well as the public at large. Many of these diplomatic tools have their impact by imposing costs or risks on the authoritarian regime and limiting its freedom of action to defy or punish demands for democratic change. In a low-profile way, diplomats may also be able to provide a neutral and safe place for different elements in the opposition (or potential opposition) to meet and begin to forge the relations of trust and cooperation that could mature into a formal political coalition.[v] And when the confrontation between regime and opposition is peaking, a powerful democracy like the United States may use its leverage (if it has any) to persuade the dictator not to use bloody force, but rather to permit a transition to unfold, or even to leave the country. Such diplomatic pressure may have tipped the balance in ensuring peaceful transitions to democracy in the Philippines in 1986 and South Korea in 1987, and it at least helped in Chile in 1988.[vi]

An important distinction must be made between the assistance that international actors offer when a transition game is on—when the confrontation is underway and the transition is going to unfold or fail in a defined period of time—and the more prosaic forms of assistance that flow in the absence of any sign of a "transition moment." Perhaps the most important way that international actors help democratic transitions move beyond protest to actual democracy is through a protracted, patient flow of investments to political parties (if they are permitted) and to a civil society so that it is sufficiently robust, skillful, resourceful, broadly based, and democratically committed that it can keep propelling the transition moment forward to democracy. Partly because of this long period of democratic engagement, "In South Africa, Chile, Poland, and Serbia, frustration that might have been channeled into more violent antiestablishment forms took a more incremental, electoral, civic, peaceful approach. In Iran, the failure of the United States to do much to assist opposition forces [during the resistance to the Shah] left the field open for the Islamists to dominate organizational space."[vii] And the same could be said for the situation in Egypt after the fall of Mubarak.

The truth is, both social scientists and policy makers are poor prognosticators. We are not very good at predicting when and where a movement for democracy will erupt, or when the sands of political opportunity in the desert of authoritarianism will shift. Thus, "External actors must be prepared to support democratic actors in civil society for a long period of time, even in the absence of any clear prospect of democratic transition."[viii] The potential for people power to graduate to popular sovereignty will be greatly enhanced if both governmental and non-governmental organizations in the world's established democracies enter the arena of assistance early on, and for the long haul.

Notes

i.   For a seminal analysis identifying the elements of success behind the post-communist color revolutions, seek Michael McFaul, *Journal of Democracy* 16 (July 2005): 5-19. The relative weight of domestic and international factors affecting the success or failure of democratic transitions is assessed in Kathryn Stoner and Michael McFaul, *Transitions to Democracy: A Comparative Perspective* (Baltimore: Johns Hopkins University Press, 2013).

ii.   Adrienne LeBas, "A New Twilight in Zimbabwe? The Perils of Power Sharing," *Journal of Democracy* 25 (April 2014): p. 52-66.

iii. Robert Putnam, *Making Democracy Work: Civic Traditions in Modern Italy* (Princeton: Princeton University Press, 1993).

iv.   Larry Diamond, *Developing Democracy: Toward Consolidation* (Baltimore: Johns Hopkins University Press, 1999), chapter 6.

v.   Council for a Community of Democracies, *The Diplomats' Handbook,* chapter 3, *http://www.diplomatshandbook.org/pdf/Handbook_CH3.pdf.*

vi.   George Shultz, *Turmoil and Triumph: My Years as Secretary of State* (New York: Charles Scribner and Sons, 1993).

vii. Kathryn Stoner, Larry Diamond, Desha Girod, and Michael McFaul, "Transitional Successes and Failures: The International-Domestic Nexus," in Stoner and McFaul, *Transitions to Democracy,* p. 19.

viii. Ibid.

CHAPTER 4

Authoritarian Use of Social Media

Zeynep Tufekci
Assistant Professor, School of Information & Department of Sociology
University of North Carolina at Chapel Hill

THIS SHORT CHAPTER COVERS two intertwined dynamics: the evolution of both authoritarianism and authoritarian tendencies in the age of the Internet as well as social activism in countries that experience these phenomena. I especially examine countries where the Internet is neither fully free, nor fully restricted, and look at the range of options available to the actors in these countries for both retaining and challenging power under the new conditions.

THE CHANGING ENVIRONMENT

It's gotten harder to be an authoritarian regime. Resting on previous ways of maintaining power or assuming complete control of the public sphere, pillars of authoritarian rule in the past, are increasingly unjustified. While the story is complex, one clear underlying reason for much of that loss of control over the public sphere is the rapid explosion in digital connectivity, enabled by the spread of the Internet, as well as the lowly cell phone with its Internet-connected camera in everyone's pocket. It's no longer enough to control television and other mass media, and it's certainly not easy or straightforward to control information distribution on the new digital media. Hence, the dynamics of remaining in power in an authoritarian or authoritarian-leaning manner have changed drastically in just a decade or two.

To put the sudden nature of this upheaval into perspective, consider that it was not until 2009 that Facebook was first translated into Arabic. There were less than 30,000 Facebook users in Tunisia in 2009, a mere five years ago.[i] Afghanistan's cell phone penetration has recently reached a staggering 70 percent from nearly zero in 2001.[ii] Such connectivity creates new opportunities for dissidents to find and draw strength from each other, get the word out, and organize street protests and visible occupation of public spaces.[iii] From Russia to Taiwan, from Iran to Brazil, from Madrid to New York, and from Tahrir to Taksim--in other words, from more established democracies to more authoritarian states—the world has witnessed a surge in protest activity, which research suggests has more than doubled since 2006,[iv] and continues to accelerate.

However, with a few exceptions, social media-fueled challenges to authoritarian regimes in most cases have faltered. (This is also true in the case of protests in more democratic countries, such as the Occupy movement or the M15 anti-austerity protests in Europe, but those are outside the scope of this chapter). I'm referring to countries such as Egypt, Turkey, and Russia which, despite profound differences, share certain characteristics in terms of growing centralization of power and erosion of the (already weak) rule of law. In Egypt, multi-decade autocratic rule was brought down by street protests and replaced by a one-year experiment with an imperfect democracy in which the military and the state never fully let go of control. This ended with a full-scale military coup, followed by the election of the military leader to the presidency under coercive conditions. Turkey is an imperfect multi-party democracy with more than 70 years of experience with electoral politics, interrupted by military coups. Its current ruling party, the AKP, had just been elected for a third term when it was rocked by protests that erupted over the razing of the centrally-located Gezi Park. This was followed later in the year by a massive corruption scandal, the news of which was also carried online. And Russia, also an electoral regime—albeit a rocky one—has been run by Vladimir Putin, whether as a President or a Prime Minister, since 1999. Russia has undergone multiple crises, including one in neighboring Ukraine, and all seem to have yielded more power for Vladimir Putin.

In all three cases, a strong leader has been in charge for a long time, and is likely to remain in charge. Putin's reign in Russia is in its 15th year. Turkish Prime Minister Erdogan has left that post, held since 2002, to become the president of the country, potentially ruling it for another decade. Egyptian President Sisi, while newly established as ruler, is also showing signs of strengthening his control and settling in for a long term. All three regimes, with different degrees of democracy and rule of law, have undergone great changes in the public sphere during the past decade. Their trajectory is indicative of broader trends in governmental response to the Internet and social media's expansion, and of the options and range of actions that have been undertaken by activists using these tools.

THE REGIMES

In fact, we can roughly divide current Internet regimes around the world into three categories, keeping in mind that categorization may obscure variation within categories and continuity between them. It's important to note that neither Egypt, nor Russia, nor Turkey completely filter or block the Internet on the scale of Iran or China, both of which have expended a great deal of resources, energy, and effort into creating a "Great Firewall" or a "Filternet" in their respective countries.

On one end of the spectrum lie China and Iran with their large infrastructure of censorship and blocking, making practical use of the global Internet quite difficult, and where popular social media platforms such as Facebook and Twitter remain blocked. In both cases substantial circumvention of this censorship exists, but this remains limited to smaller portions of the population, especially in China. In Iran, according to the religious police, about 17 million people are on Facebook, despite the blocking, and their president and prime minister have just joined Twitter. Still, for ordinary Iranians, circumvention is cumbersome, and repressive countermeasures such as throttling, or slowing down key sites, are common.

At the other end of the spectrum are democratic countries, including the US and the EU where most of the large Internet companies reside to begin with, and where government regulation and suppression of content is based mostly on intellectual property considerations rather than policing political speech. We should note that many of these governments have recently been revealed to be conducting sizable surveillance programs, although there is little evidence that there has been government interference in what gets published online, or that political speech has been targeted; the surveillance capacity of the state remains worrisome, however.

Between these two poles—significant suppression of Internet based on concerns about political speech and organizing, and relative free-for-all, subject to commercial considerations—lie many countries that neither fully censor the Internet, nor can afford to let it become a free-for-all, especially if they are to maintain control over the public sphere.[v]

There are multiple reasons why these middle countries cannot afford or pull off what China has done. First, it's too late. It's not easy to create the kind of massive infrastructure required to effectively censor the Internet as an afterthought, and it's much harder when a population has already gotten used to a relatively free environment on the Internet. Second, it's not cheap: China reportedly spends hundreds of millions of dollars on Internet censorship infrastructure, and employs hundreds of thousands of human censors[vi]. Third, being China requires a home-grown tech industry: Chinese people are increasingly wired through domestic companies that are privately-owned but heavily controlled or overseen by the government. Fourth, censoring the Internet and suppressing circumvention tools such as Virtual Private Networks, which also provide security for businesses, makes a country an undesirable environment for many multinational companies to operate in. That may be less of a worry for China, which is still an appealing target for foreign investors given its low-wage workers and huge domestic market, but it's a bigger consideration for a country like Turkey, which carries a significant trade balance and hence depends on a continuing influx of foreign money and investment to keep its economy going.

What has happened is that many countries have taken a third route to Internet control: demonization and targeted suppression, along with increased pressure to keep even stronger control of traditional mass media. For example, while Turkey made headlines when it blocked YouTube, the block itself was lax and due to somewhat arcane laws about insulting the founder of the country, Mustafa Kemal Atatürk. Prime Minister Erdogan himself joked that he, too, circumvented the ban, and implied that so should everyone else. However, this relaxed attitude changed with the Gezi protests of 2013 when Twitter emerged as a strong organizing tool. "Twitter is a menace to society," Erdogan roared from televisions, which were so tightly censored during the height of the protests that CNN Turkey was showing a documentary on penguins at exactly the same time as the scale and scope of the events had CNN International—and other international news organizations—reporting live from Istanbul.

Censorship in mass media has also taken a new turn in many of these "middle-range" countries. Media-owning tycoons in countries like Russia and Turkey generally operate other businesses beholden to the government's patronage or good graces.[vii] Self-censorship is thus imposed by media bosses, who routinely fire journalists who try to do their job. Moreover, mass media outlets that dare cross the government may end up being hit with huge and spurious tax bills, ranging up to a billion dollars, which can then disappear with similar ease, as happened in Turkey.[viii]

Through 2013 and 2014, Erdogan repeatedly made similar statements against social media, blaming social media for a decline of family values, proliferation of pornography, lies, unrest, and conspiracies by foreign governments who he charged wanted to weaken Turkey— or him. Indeed, first Twitter, and then YouTube, were blocked in Turkey during the crucial election period, even though they were later unblocked by the Constitutional Court—after the elections.

Meanwhile, Russian President Putin has made similar moves, passing laws that require blogs to register with the government and threatening their owners with harsh punishments for defamation and disrupting public order, while also keeping close tabs on the mass media that most ordinary Russians depend on for news. The harshest and most "old-style" repression has been seen in Egypt, where the country's most prominent blogger, Alaa Abd-al Fattah, has been sentenced to 15 years in prison for opposing an "anti-protest law" which bans protests. The screws tighten on self-expression online just as mass media converges toward uniform pro-regime propaganda: Al Jazeera journalists in the country were charged with conspiracies and sentenced to seven years in prison.

Similar statements targeting social media as a source of evils are heard from politicians from Azerbaijan to Malaysia, even as Internet censorship in most of those countries remains far short of what China has undertaken. Unable to unplug the Internet (as Mubarak did to his detriment) or to keep their opponents from using circumvention and other tools to access it if selectively blocked, these regimes have taken to demonizing the medium, and also flooding it with their own propaganda, while increasing their surveillance of all media. It should be noted that the revelations of extensive spying by the government in the US, home to most Internet platforms, has increased tensions, and further promises to fuel both the rhetorical and practical case of countries who want to have tighter controls over their national Internet, to protect themselves from future spying, or, in some cases, both.

All this has created a schizophrenic public sphere in many countries. Government opponents and activists have relatively free access to social media, while government supporters and those either unwilling or unable to use social media or circumvent government blocks when present (even when circumvention is not that difficult or costly) continue to watch mass media that operates as a quasi-government arm. For example, in Turkey leaked audiotapes, which were later authenticated by Prime Minister Erdogan, show that during the Gezi protests he personally called heads of television stations, chiding them for minor infractions such as running an opposition leader's statements on the small ticker on the screen. The manager can be heard snapping to attention, saying "yes sir," to the Prime Minister's requests, obviously not an unusual situation. The ticker Erdogan expressed displeasure at, containing the words of a parliamentary opposition leader, promptly disappeared. Prime Minister Erdogan shrugged off the leak saying that he had a right to express his displeasure to TV executives.[ix]

THE ACTIVIST CHALLENGE

The activist experience on social media in these middle-range countries has been mixed. Increasingly, in Egypt, online spaces are a place of caution and quiet, given the repressive conditions. However, during the lead-up to the initial protests that overthrew Mubarak, the activists had used it as a public space where they could find and draw strength from each other, and share important news that was censored by their own government. That is likely one of the most important uses of social media for activists across many countries: finding common cause with other people, and helping alter the public dialogue on crucial issues. Activists of all stripes use the Internet to discover that they are not alone.

Social media has also been crucial to organizing logistics during protests. In Egypt, for example, during the height of another round of protests in November 2011, four activists in their early twenties emerged as an *ad hoc* volunteer group to organize and coordinate the ten field hospitals set up around the area of clashes. This was not a minor operation, as more than 40 people were killed and thousands injured.[x] Through a Twitter account, a website, and a Google spreadsheet with cell phones for volunteer doctors, nurses, and workers at the field hospitals (remarkably, none of the organizers were physically present at the hospitals), organizers were able to keep accurate count of supplies and personnel needs for many days, and organize transfers and rebalancing as necessary. In post-crisis interviews that I conducted, it became apparent that none of the young organizers were familiar with the history or trained in the methods of logistics, a problem that has brought down many armies. Armed with nothing but youthful energy, caffeine, and digital technology, these volunteers have altered the dynamics of protests themselves: it is no longer the police or the army—the official, trained forces—that have the unilateral advantage of communication and logistics.

Similarly, censorship has become much harder to make effective, at least when targeting populations who are willing to trust or access social media. In Turkey another group of four college students has organized a remarkable citizen network news organization called @140journos which uses Twitter as a platform to gather, verify, and publicize news. [xi]

Remarkably, in a very polarized country they follow a strategy of reporting news from a variety of communities, many of which are angry with one another, such that their platform has also become what traditional news media might have been: a neutral and objective source of information. At the same time, their existence has repeatedly pushed back mainstream media censorship; it is harder to ignore news when it will be covered by alternative platforms, if only on Twitter. As a result of such means of spreading news, censorship isn't effective by itself.

However, this should not be understood to mean that the regimes have no way to respond. Besides demonizing social media, most of these governments have supporters who also go online to challenge and sometimes harass opposition activists.[xii] In some cases, such as that of the so-called 50-cent army in China and that of the "trolls" in Bahrain who harass activists, there is increasing evidence that some opposition comes from people paid by those in power to challenge activists.

It is not correct to view online spaces as solely occupied by the opposition. In Turkey, for example, trending topics often alternate between pro- and anti-government causes, often the result of organized campaigns by both parties. However, this highlights another difference between governments and challengers: online government campaigns tend to have identifiable leaders and appear more hierarchical in nature. Online opposition is more diffuse and is not necessarily identified with the parliamentary opposition. In Russia, blogger Alexei Navalny has emerged as a politician who often challenges Putin's rule, but he also remains in the regime's crosshairs. Currently under house arrest and banned from blogging, he is facing new charges as well as defamation lawsuits.[xiii]

The leaderless and diffuse nature of opposition movements is both a strength and a weakness. In Egypt, the initial protests were without a single clear leader or spokesperson, though some activists garnered more attention than others. A telling story is that of Wael Ghonim, administrator of the "We are all Khaled Saed" website, which was the initial page that organized the January 25th protests—though the Tunisian revolution had greatly inspired Egyptians and January 25th was already a long-standing day of protests. Ghonim was arrested during the protests. At first, the regime did not know they had him, and after they found out, they brought him to the presidential palace to "negotiate"—in other words, buy him off so that he'd call off the protests going full strength in Tahrir.[xiv] As Ghonim explained to the bewildered leaders of the *ancien régime,* he had no such power to call off the protests as he was neither a leader, nor even a person with that kind of influence—nobody was. Being administrator of the original website gave him some clout and influence, but unlike traditional organizations, he had no ability to cut a deal.

This is in fact a double-edged sword for protest movements.

Consider the case of the Gezi movement in Turkey, which was quite leaderless, as most participants wanted it to remain. The hundreds of interviews I conducted during the protest confirmed this. This certainly made the protest harder to control, "decapitate," or otherwise target. But it was also a weakness when, toward the end of the protests, the government indicated a desire to negotiate. The protesters did not have a delegation they could send, or an approved mechanism through which they could negotiate with the government, and in the ensuing confusion the government seized the opportunity to go into the park and raze the protest site with overwhelming police force. Tellingly, in local elections in March 2014, the AKP government was able to retain control of key mayoral positions, including Istanbul as a whole, and the municipality of Beyoglu, in which Gezi Park is located.

CONCLUSION

It's a new information environment, and most of the struggle to define and control it is not happening in the few outliers, such as China and Iran, that have implemented the strictest censorship, built from the ground up, and from the first moments, into their Internet infrastructure. Rather, it is occurring in middle-ground countries, where governments try to manage a public sphere that cannot be ruled in the old ways. Challengers find themselves with new capabilities for organizing among themselves, for public dialogue, breaking censorship, protest logistics, and more, but are unable, yet, to fully counter government onslaughts on their digital capabilities, often coupled with even tighter controls on mass media. It is a difficult interregnum with new rules, new players, and much tension, and as yet no clear winners.

Notes

i.   Zeynep Tufekci, "New Media and the People-Powered Uprisings," MIT Technology Review (August 30, 2011), accessed November 18, 2014, *http://www.technologyreview.com/view/425280/new-media-and-the-people-powered-uprisings/*.

ii.   Michael Dean Krebs, "Afghanistan: mobile phones an 'affordable luxury'" Media Global News, (February 16, 2012), accessed November 18, 2014, *http://www.mediaglobal.org/2012/02/16/afghanistan-mobile-phones-an-%E2%80%9Caffordable-luxury%E2%80%9D/*.

iii. Zeynep Tufekci and Deen Freelon, "Introduction to the Special Issue on New Media and Social Unrest," *American Behavioral Scientist* 57 no.7 (July 2013), p. 843 – 847.

iv.   Ortiz, et al., "World Protests: 2006-2013," Initiative for Policy Dialogue and Friedrich-Ebert-Stiftung New York Working Paper, 2013, accessed November 18, 2014, http://cadtm.org/IMG/pdf/World_Protests_2006-2013-Final-2.pdf.

v.   Ronald Deibert, et al., *Access Controlled: The Shaping of Power, Rights, and Rule in Cyberspace,* (MIT Press: Cambridge, MA, 2010).

vi.   Katie Hunt and Cy Xu, "China employs 2 million to police internet," CNN, October 7, 2013, accessed November 18, 2014, *http://www.cnn.com/2013/10/07/world/asia/china-Internet-monitors/*.

vii. Marc Piernini and Markus Mayr, Press Freedom in Turkey, Carnegie Endowment for International Peace, 2013. *http://carnegieendowment.org/files/press_freedom_turkey.pdf.*

viii. Ayla Jean Yackley, "Turkey Gov't hits media group Dogan with tax fine," Reuters, September 8, 2013. *http://uk.reuters.com/article/2009/09/08/turkey-dogan-idUKL815352620090908.*

ix.   Ayla Albayrak and Joe Parkinson, "Turkey Leader Called to Lean on Media Boss." Wall Street Journal, Febarury 11, 2014. *http://online.wsj.com/news/articles/SB10001424052702304104504579377070864032320.*

x.   "Egypt: The legacy of Mohammed Mahmoud Street." BBC November 19, 2012 *http://www.bbc.com/news/world-middle-east-20395260.*

xi.   Engin Onder, "A Sense of Exhilaration and Possibility" Nieman Reports, Spring 2014 *http://www.nieman.harvard.edu/reports/article/103103/A-Sense-of-Exhilaration-and-Possibility.aspx.*

xii. Zeynep Tufekci, "'Not this one': Social Movements, the Attention Economy, and Microcelebrity Networked Activism," *American Behavioral Scientist,* 57, no .7, (2013a), p. 848-870.

xiii. BBC, "Profile: Russian opposition leader Alexei Navalny," BBC, December 30, 2014. Accessible at: *http://www.bbc.com/news/world-europe-16057045*

xiv. Wael Ghonim, *Revolution 2.0: The Power of the People Is Greater Than the People in Power: A Memoir,* (Houghton Mifflin Harcourt: New York, NY, 2012).

PART TWO

TRENDS IN CIVIL RESISTANCE

CHAPTER 5

Trends in Civil Resistance and Authoritarian Responses

Dr. Erica Chenoweth
Associate Professor
Josef Korbel School of International Studies, University of Denver

INTRODUCTION

Although nonviolent resistance campaigns are becoming more frequent in recent years, they are not necessarily becoming more effective. Part of this puzzling finding may be driven by learning among authoritarian regimes, which have established a set of generalized responses to domestic political challenges—what I call the authoritarian playbook. I identify 11 of these measures and conclude by calling for a new response to the authoritarian playbook that reinforces the potential for people power movements to emerge and thrive.

TRENDS IN CIVIL RESISTANCE

The Nonviolent and Violent Campaigns and Outcomes (NAVCO) Data identified 323 campaigns of nonviolent and violent resistance worldwide from 1900 to 2006. Campaigns were included if they featured at least 1,000 observed participants and possessed maximalist goals of removing the incumbent leader from power or establishing an independent territory. When the data were released in 2008, it was already clear that nonviolent campaigns were becoming more frequent and more effective over time.[i] With the onset of a new wave of uprisings in the late 2000s and the Arab Awakening, however, observers wonder about the record of nonviolent resistance since 2006. Figure 1 shows that through the end of 2013, nonviolent campaigns have continued to diffuse worldwide. Strikingly, the 2010-2013 period has already seen the onset of more campaigns than happened in the entire decade of the 1990s, suggesting that the world is indeed in the midst of a highly contentious era.

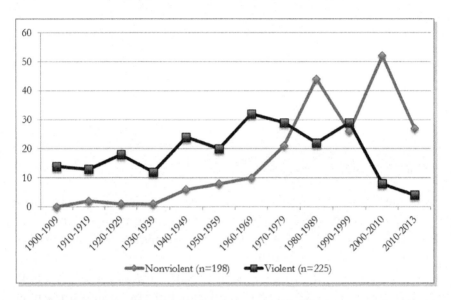

FIGURE 1: Onsets of Nonviolent Campaigns Worldwide, 1900-2013.
Source: Author calculations.

As Figure 2 illustrates, the success rates of nonviolent campaigns rose dramatically from 1940 to 2010. But just in the initial three years of the current decade, this trend has reversed to a rate of success comparable to that of the 1950s—a time when civil resistance was far less common than it is today.

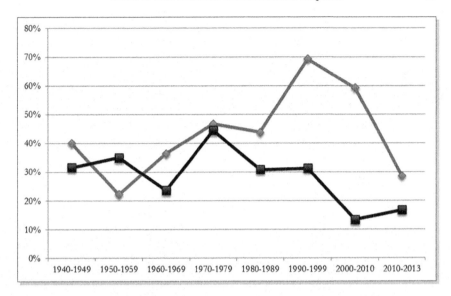

FIGURE 2: Rates of Campaign Success Worldwide from 1940-2013.
Source: Author calculations.

Of course, it may yet be too early to make the claim that civil resistance has become much less effective. It may be that the record will return to average levels by 2020. Moreover, the alternative to civil resistance—namely armed struggle—has become so ineffective that few would argue that it is a viable substitute.

Nevertheless, observers must take seriously the possibility that civil resistance campaigns are becoming less successful in recent years. If so, perhaps the best explanation is that learning is a two-way street—that as grassroots movements have learned from watching others wield this technique, authoritarian governments have also learned from one another how to effectively suppress these movements.

TRENDS IN AUTHORITARIAN RESPONSES: UNCOVERING THE AUTHORITARIAN PLAYBOOK

Regime opponents used lethal repression against over 80 percent of nonviolent campaigns occurring during the 1900-2006 period. Since

2007, however, this trend has increased to nearly 92 percent, indicating that brute force remains the most common tool that authoritarian leaders use to combat challenges from nonviolent campaigns.

Perhaps seeing the unreliability of violent coercion in disrupting civil resistance campaigns, however, in the past decade authoritarian leaders have also established a more sophisticated playbook by which to suppress domestic challengers—including nongovernmental organizations (NGOs), opposition leaders, and civilian-led movements alike. I identify 11 common methods below.

First, authoritarian leaders under pressure tend to pin the blame on foreigners and outsiders. Vladimir Putin has routinely accused Western governments of deliberately stoking domestic dissent to threaten his grip on power at home, as well as in his spheres of influence. When faced with the Gezi Park protests in summer 2013, Turkish Premier Reycip Erdogan quickly blamed outsiders for the unrest, citing an international conspiracy against Turkish interests. And Nicolas Maduro's government in Venezuela responded to protests in February by expelling American diplomats, citing evidence that the US government had conspired to support a coup against his government.

Related to this strategy are attempts to mischaracterize domestic oppositionists as terrorists, traitors, or coup plotters.[ii] Bashar al Assad routinely referred to peaceful demonstrators as "terrorists" to drum up fears of violence and sectarian divisions before the start of the Syrian Civil War. In Russia, a new website called "traitor.net" encourages users to "suggest a traitor" and lists names of people thought to oppose Putin's regime.[iii] And even Erdogan referred to Gezi Park demonstrators as left-wing "extremist" groups, trying several protestors under Turkey's harsh terrorism laws.

At times, authoritarian regimes have attempted to co-opt oppositionists by making legislative reforms, such as allowing them to compete in elections or appointing opposition leaders to administrative posts.[iv] Separating regime challengers into largely ineffective, disunited opposition parties allows the regime to effectively divide and rule while keeping a watchful eye on skillful challengers, as has occurred in Belarus, Azerbaijan, and Uzbekistan, among other places.[v]

In some cases, authoritarian leaders attempt to protect themselves from domestic crises by paying off their inner entourage. Most people power movements succeed because security forces, economic elites, business elites, civilian bureaucrats, and other regime functionaries conclude that continuing to support the authoritarian leader is no longer in their own personal interest, and they effectively withdraw their cooperation from the powerholder. From the perspective of the incumbent, then, the key is therefore to pay loyalists well and punish defectors visibly.[vi] This may explain why oil-rich countries are less susceptible to such uprisings; their large reserves of sovereign wealth allow them to effectively buy off regime elites in times of crisis, thereby insulating themselves against the possibility that such elites will estimate greater returns from defection.[vii]

Another commonly used measure is to counter-mobilize the authoritarian's own supporters, paying them to set up encampments or turn out in pro-government marches.[viii] This was a common method used by Bashar al Assad during the early days of the Syrian uprising, where tens of thousands of pro-government demonstrators gathered in Damascus to bolster the regime's claim on legitimacy. Often such attempts come in the forms of pseudo-civil society organizations, like the youth movement Nashi (Ours) in Russia. For instance, Hugo Chavez also established the so-called Bolivarian Circles, or pro-government grassroots neighborhood organizations, in the slums of Venezuela.[ix]

In many contexts, authoritarian leaders have been accused of planting plain-clothes police as *agents provocateurs*, who would stoke violence against the police and create confusion in the context of otherwise peaceful demonstrations. Such methods are very hard to verify, since it is often difficult to distinguish between such provocateurs and ordinary protestors reacting to the heat of the moment. Regardless, such behavior allows the regime to justify more extensive crackdowns, lends credibility to propaganda claiming that protestors are really "violent extremists," and diminishes participation.

Because of the fear that regular security forces may not always be loyal in carrying out orders to suppress oppositionists, many authoritarian regimes delegate the dirty work—mobilizing thugs and armed gangs to repress and harass protestors. In Syria, once it became clear that Assad's military was not uniformly willing to repress unarmed activists, he began to dispatch armed gangs, or *shabiha*, to capture, beat up, or kill opposition leaders. Yanukovich apparently attempted a similar method in Ukraine, relying on plain-clothes police officers and thugs to intimidate, beat, and murder activists, including one bizarre case where a Russian activist was tortured and crucified. And when Mubarak became aware that some army units were not equally loyal, he sent in a group of thugs on camelback to break up encampments in Tahrir Square. Such methods give the regime plausible deniability, while also ensuring that those doing the harassment are willing executioners. In some cases, regimes rely on outside forces—as with Saudi troops in Bahrain or Iranian Revolutionary Guard operatives in Syria—to avoid the possibility that the troops begin to sympathize with the protestors.

Many authoritarian regimes have also mastered the arts of censorship, spin, and surveillance. China is the most obvious example, where the government censors a high amount of foreign news and information while relying on internal intranets to control and streamline communication throughout the country.[x] Moreover, the Chinese government pays loyalist bloggers and social media icons to write posts and comments on critical websites, effectively overwhelming these sites with massive amounts of pro-government propaganda. In Sudan, the government has strategically used social media to manipulate activists and dissidents—in one instance entrapping protestors who signed up to attend a fake protest manufactured by the regime. Russia and Iran are known to intercept communications through the Internet or cell phones, quickly arresting activists before planned protests even begin.

In the meantime, authoritarian regimes attempt to keep out foreign journalists, effectively discouraging independent reporting of domestic affairs. The removal of opportunities for witness reduces morale among activists, who may view actions in such a closed information environment as futile. It may also embolden security forces to engage in higher levels of abuse, since they see that they can commit such acts with impunity. Other regimes have barred international observers from monitoring elections, as Egypt, Russia, and Zimbabwe have actively done.

In many instances, authoritarian governments use pseudo-legitimate laws and practices to reinforce their grips on power. In Russia, for example, authorities shut down human rights offices accused of using pirated software or failing health inspections, and in China, the government closes down roads where protestors might march for "repairs." Following the 2011 uprising in Egypt, the transitional government expelled 19 Western NGOs from the country under the pretext of foreign subversion. And in recent months, Russia's highest court ruled as constitutional a law requiring that NGOs that receive funding from foreign entities must be designated as "foreign agents," restricting the degree of autonomy that they possess as well as the range of activities they are allowed to pursue. Moreover, Russia, Venezuela, Iran, and Kazakhstan have reformed electoral laws to favor incumbents or make it virtually impossible for opposition leaders to compete or even participate in the elections.

Finally, authoritarian leaders have assembled a coalition of like-minded allies with whom to share information on how to suppress dissent. In 2005 and 2006, the Chinese government gave the governments of Belarus and Turkmenistan an Internet blocking and filtering technology to prevent outside information from flowing into those countries. China and Russia vetoed a UN Security Council resolution on Burma ahead of the failed 2007 Saffron Revolution—the first time the two countries had both vetoed a resolution since 1989. And the two countries have consistently vetoed resolutions since then, striking down resolutions they saw as undermining sovereignty in Sudan, Kosovo, and Syria. Moreover, the Shanghai Cooperation Organization, Commonwealth of Independent States, and Organization of African Unity have all developed their own "independent" electoral monitoring groups that have approved elections widely thought to be fraudulent, while attempting to restrict the autonomy of OSCE-sent election observer missions so that host governments have greater oversight over the monitoring. It is clear, therefore, that not only have these governments learned effective ways to dismantle opposition movements, but they also cooperate with one another in doing so.

CONCLUSION

Given these recent advances in the authoritarian playbook, does civil resistance have a future in challenging entrenched power in autocratic regimes? I see three reasons for cautious optimism. First, none of the measures in the authoritarian's playbook is foolproof. For example, in the mid-late 2000s, Egypt engaged in bilateral talks with Russia, China, and other countries throughout the Gulf region in an effort to protect itself against domestic challengers. Yet people power removed Hosni Mubarak—a man whom many thought would die in office—as surely as it did in places as diverse as the Philippines, Iran, Poland, and Serbia in the decades before.

Second, research shows that generalized repression is not necessarily a reliable deterrent to collective action. Instead, the vast majority of major nonviolent campaigns throughout history have set up in authoritarian regimes where very little civil society exists.[xi] Even in cases where opponents used violent repression against civil resistance campaigns, these campaigns still succeeded more than twice as often as armed insurgencies that faced repression. Indeed, it appears that sometimes, widely publicized repressive episodes are precisely the sparks that trigger these mass uprisings, seemingly out of nowhere. Mobilization of the Egyptian population in 2011 over the killing of Khaled Said is a case in point.

Third, there are inklings of people power in many repressive places around the world. Protests are still underway in Venezuela, where there is yet hope that the Maduro government and the student-led protests will reach an agreement that satisfies both sides of this deeply polarized society. The central government in China is openly concerned about the rise of localized protests throughout the country. And even in Russia, visible opposition to Vladimir Putin has occurred in the past three years at higher rates than it has in any other years during his tenure. Indeed, perhaps the greatest testimony to the effectiveness of civil resistance is the great lengths authoritarian leaders must go to prevent and subvert it.

Rather than abandoning people power movements, then, the international community should engage in a concerted, coordinated, and urgent effort to understand how, under what conditions, and with which tools international actors can respond to these authoritarian measures. This does not mean that the international community should conspire to sponsor civil uprisings in other countries. Contrary to the rhetoric of many authoritarian regimes, civil resistance campaigns cannot be exported or imported. From 1900 to 2006, campaigns that received funding from a foreign state were no more likely to succeed than campaigns that did not.[xii] Instead, the effectiveness of civil resistance campaigns is fundamentally based on their local roots, because such campaigns must assemble a large and diverse proportion of the population to succeed—an impossible task without a high degree of domestic legitimacy, which cuts across social cleavages and instills confidence in the local population.

But the alternatives to civil resistance—armed struggle or total submission—are not viable in many places. Compared with the status quo, armed struggle, or elite-led transitions, campaigns of civil resistance are associated with longer-term increases in democratic practices, civil peace, and improved quality of life.[xiii, xiv] As such, the international community must take measures to discourage people from resorting to armed struggle and encourage people to use nonviolent methods of political contention—if and when grassroots movements wish to challenge the existing order.

Notes

i.   Erica Chenoweth and Maria J. Stephan, *Why Civil Resistance Works: The Strategic Logic of Nonviolent Conflict* (New York: Columbia University Press, 2011).

ii. Regine Spector, "The anti-revolutionary toolkit." *CACI Analyst*, December 13, 2006.

iii. David M. Herszenhorn, "Xenophobic chill descends on Moscow." *New York Times*, April 13, 2014, A4.

iv. Steven Heydemann, *Upgrading Authoritarianism in the Arab World*. Saban Center Analysis Paper Series 13, Brookings Institution. October 2007.

v.   Erica Frantz and Andrea Kendall-Taylor, A dictator's toolkit: Understanding how co-optation affects repression in autocracies. *Journal of Peace Research* forthcoming 2014.

vi.   Bruce Bueno de Mesquita and Alastair Smith *The Dictator's Handbook: Why Bad Behavior is Almost Always Good Politics* (New York: Public Affairs, 2011).

vii.   Michael Ross, *The Oil Curse: How Petroleum Wealth Shapes the Development of Nations,* (Princeton: Princeton University Press, 2012).

viii.   Thomas Carothers and Saskia Brechenmacher, *Closing Space: Democracy and Human Rights Support Under Fire.* (Washington, DC: Carnegie Endowment for International Peace, 2014).

ix.   Regine Spector and Andrej Krickovic, *Authoritarianism 2.0: Non-democratic regimes are upgrading and integrating globally.* Paper presented at the 49th Annual International Studies Association Conference, San Francisco, CA, March 26, 2008.

x.   William J. Dobson, *The Dictator's Learning Curve: Inside the Global Battle for Democracy,* (New York Anchor 2012).

xi.   Chenoweth and Stephan, *Why Civil Resistance Works.*

xii.   Ibid.

xiii.   Ibid.

xiv.   Judith Stoddard, How do major, violent and nonviolent opposition campaigns, impact predicted life expectancy at birth? Stability: International Journal of Security and Development 2, no. 2 (37):2013, p. 1-11.

CHAPTER 6

The Checklist for Ending Tyranny

Dr. Peter Ackerman
Founding Chair
International Center for Nonviolent Conflict

Mr. Hardy Merriman
President
International Center on Nonviolent Conflict

T ODAY THE MOST DEADLY conflicts in the world are not between states but rather within them, pitting tyrants against the populations they oppress. It is widely believed that these oppressed populations have two choices: acquiesce to tyranny in hopes that it will evolve to something milder or launch a violent insurrection to gain freedom. This limited view is refuted by the fact that civil resistance campaigns (sometimes referred to as "people power" movements or nonviolent conflicts) have occurred far more frequently than generally realized. Beginning in 1900, there has been on average one major campaign of civil resistance challenging an incumbent ruler per year.[i] These citizen-led movements have increasingly defined the outcome of the most geopolitically significant conflicts and democratic transitions since 1972.[ii,1] Yet policy makers, scholars, journalists, and other interested

---

[1] Based on 67 transitions to democracy analyzed between 1972-2005 in the research study *How Freedom is Won: From Civic Resistance to Durable Democracy*. The authors find that: "The force of civic resistance was a key factor in driving 50 of 67 transitions, or over 70 percent of countries where transitions began as dictatorial systems fell and/or new states arose from the disintegration of multinational states. Of the 50 countries where civic resistance was a key strategy (i.e., either countries in which there were transitions driven by civic forces or countries where there were mixed transitions involving significant input from both civic forces and powerholders), none were Free countries, 25 were Partly Free countries, and 25 Not Free countries. Today [in 2005], years after the transition 32 of these countries are Free, 14 are Partly Free, and only 4 are Not Free."

observers consistently underestimate this capacity of ordinary people to undermine tyranny and achieve rights without violence.

AN ANALYTICAL BLIND SPOT

The uprisings in Tunisia and Egypt in 2011, and more recently in Ukraine in 2014, are examples of how grassroots civil resistance can surprise people with its power and transformative potential. No one saw these uprisings coming, but this hardly makes them unique. Few, if any, saw the "Color Revolutions" coming in Serbia (2000), Georgia (2003), and Ukraine (2004). In decades prior, no one anticipated that organized nonviolent resistance would play a decisive role in the fall of Filipino dictator Ferdinand Marcos (1986), Chilean dictator Augusto Pinochet (1988), the Soviet regime in Poland (1989), or the apartheid regime in South Africa (1992).

As international and regional experts struggle to explain these and other nonviolent conflicts, they frequently conclude that successful cases of civil resistance are historical anomalies based on a unique set of circumstances in a given country at a given time. Because their dynamics are seen as case-specific, they are not regarded as evidence of a general strategy by which populations can wield power against a wide variety of oppressors. However, tyrants around the world do not suffer from this blind spot. They have come to recognize people power movements as the greatest threat to their ongoing rule.

With the incidence of nonviolent conflict accelerating over the last decade it is critically important for those who support democratic change to update their understanding of why people power movements succeed. Nonviolent conflict works across many different cases because it exploits two fundamental realities: that authoritarian regimes depend on wide-scale obedience among the populations they oppress in order to maintain their control, and that not everyone in such regimes is equally loyal.

HOW CIVIL RESISTANCE WORKS

Based on these two realities, civil resisters mobilize populations to systematically withdraw their obedience and apply nonviolent pressure—through tactics such as strikes, boycotts, mass demonstrations, and other actions—to disrupt an oppressive system and achieve rights, freedom, and justice. When participation in civil resistance diversifies and grows, repression against resisters is often insufficient to restore tranquility and instead becomes more likely to backfire.

As disruption continues, cracks also begin to appear within the government and other institutions (i.e. police, military, media and political, bureaucratic, and economic entities) critical to the state. These cracks often lead to defections, and as defections cascade, the core capacities that an authoritarian depends on for their rule—control of material resources, human resources, people's skills and knowledge, the information environment, and the capacity to commit sanctions— are devastated. Left with no viable chain of command with which to execute their orders, tyrants ultimately run out of options and are coerced out of their position by sustained nonviolent pressure. Sweeping change has often been the result.

SKILLS VERSUS CONDITIONS

With the increasing incidence and impact of civil resistance, it is important to examine what factors determine its outcomes. Do the conditions prior to the commencement of the conflict determine whether a movement or authoritarian will win? Or is victory for either side determined more by the strategic choices and skillfulness with which they wage the conflict?

A critical facet of the mission of the International Center on Nonviolent Conflict (of which we are a part) is to argue that skills are on balance more important than conditions in determining movement trajectories and outcomes. This point usually invites significant pushback especially focused on the willingness of the adversary to use violence. "Nonviolent resistance only works against benign or mild adversaries" is a frequent refrain, but conveniently forgotten is the defeat of the apartheid regime in South Africa, Pinochet in Chile, Marcos in the Philippines, or the communist regime in Poland. More recent examples include Hosni Mubarak in Egypt and Ben Ali in Tunisia. None of these regimes were mild, benign, or unwilling to use severe repression.

These qualitative examples are supported by quantitative analysis. In 2008 the organization Freedom House issued a research study that examined various structural factors and their influence on civil resistance in 64 transitions from authoritarian governments between 1975 and 2006. Here is an excerpt of its key conclusion:

> ... neither the political nor environmental factors examined in the study had a statistically significant impact on the success or failure of civil resistance movements.... [C]ivic movements are as likely to succeed in less developed, economically poor countries as in developed, affluent societies. The study also finds no significant evidence that ethnic or religious polarization has a major impact on the possibilities for the emergence of a cohesive civic opposition. Nor does regime type seem to have an important influence on the ability of civic movements to achieve broad support.[iii]

The only factor examined in the study that had a statistically significant influence on the emergence and outcomes of civil resistance movements was government centralization. The authors write that:

> The study suggests high degrees of centralization correlate positively with the emergence of a robust civic movement with the potential to challenge regime authority. The reverse also appears to be true: the greater the degree of government decentralization, the less likely it is that a successful movement of civic mobilization will arise.[iv]

Thus, while the study finds one environmental condition that influences the trajectories of civil resistance movements, their overall findings strongly undercut claims that conditions are determinative of the outcome of these conflicts.

Three years later, in their award-winning 2011 book, *Why Civil Resistance Works: The Strategic Logic of Nonviolent Conflict*, scholars Erica Chenoweth and Maria Stephan rigorously analyzed 323 violent and nonviolent campaigns that challenged sitting governments between 1900 and 2006.[v] Their groundbreaking findings showed that nonviolent campaigns succeeded 53% of the time versus 26% of the time for violent campaigns.[vi] They also found that while state repression and other structural factors can influence a civil resistance campaign's prospects for success (though often by less than is commonly assumed—in the case of violent state repression it only reduced success rates by about 35%), they found no structural conditions that were determinative of movement outcomes.[vii] After thoroughly evaluating the data they conclude that "the evidence suggests that civil resistance is often successful regardless of environmental conditions that many people associate with the failure of nonviolent campaigns."[viii]

These results reveal the incorrect premises upon which the conventional wisdom about civil resistance is based. Skills and strategic choice often matter more than conditions in determining the outcomes of these conflicts. This is actually not surprising when we consider that the first strategy-based decision by opponents of tyranny is how to fight. It is reasonable to expect that if external conditions were key in determining the outcome then the strategic choice of how to fight by people challenging tyranny would not matter, and success rates between violent and nonviolent conflicts over time and many cases should be the same.

But that is not what the data indicates. Between 1900 and 2006 people power movements have been twice as successful, and recent case studies show that the differential in success rates has not significantly changed.[ix] Some may counter this by asserting that civil resisters pick battles that are easier to win, but Chenoweth and Stephan anticipated that argument and show that "… the vast majority of nonviolent campaigns have emerged in authoritarian regimes… where even peaceful opposition against the government may have fatal consequences."[x]

Nobel Prize-winning economist Thomas Schelling had it right in an essay he wrote over 50 years ago in the book *Civilian Resistance as a National Defence: Nonviolent Action against Aggression*. He concluded:

> The tyrant and his subjects are in somewhat symmetrical positions. They can deny him most of what he wants—

they can, that is, if they have the disciplined organization to refuse collaboration. And he can deny them just about everything they want—he can deny it by using the force at his command… It is a bargaining situation in which either side, if adequately disciplined and organized, can deny most of what the others wants; and it remains to see who wins.[xi]

According to Schelling the tactics selected by civil resisters have costs and benefits, as do the tactics used by their authoritarian opponent. The winner is the protagonist who distributes these costs and benefits most efficiently for their side. The skillful civil resistance leader wants to create disruption in order to maximize defections, and optimally wants to employ tactics where relatively small disruptions lead to large numbers of defections. The skillful authoritarian needs to enforce obedience, often through violence, and optimally wants to use minimal violence to achieve maximum obedience. The cumulative aggregation of defection vis-à-vis obedience determines who wins.

THE CHECKLIST

If skills and strategic choice are most influential on the outcomes of civil resistance movements then we should be able to identify shared capabilities, skills, and choices across a range of movements that form the common denominators of success. Many aspects of a movement can be analyzed, but when we distill the multitude of variables we find that three key capabilities of successful civil resistance movements are:

1. Ability to unify people
2. Operational planning
3. Nonviolent discipline

When these capabilities are present in a civil resistance movement, it sets the stage for three powerful trends to manifest that are also highly impactful on movement success. These trends are:

1. Increasing civilian participation in civil resistance

2. Diminishing impact of repression, and increasing backfire

3. Increasing defections from a movement's adversary

Taken together, we refer to these three attributes and three trends as "the Checklist." We believe that achieving these attributes and trends significantly increases a movement's probability of success. In this regard, the checklist is not a formula that guarantees an outcome, but rather a framework that helps people organize their thinking and improve their effectiveness.

To this end, one function of the checklist is to cut through the sense of disorientation that can set in during a conflict. Complexity is one of the biggest challenges faced by any civil resistance movement, and in the fog of conflict it can be difficult to discern which factors are most important in decision making. We maintain that if an activist or an external observer wants to evaluate a movement's prospects, asking whether the three capabilities and three trends on the checklist are present will provide a strong basis for evaluating a movement's current state, strengths, weaknesses, and prospects for success.

We elaborate on the checklist below:

1. Ability to Unify People

Authoritarians are adept practitioners of divide-and-rule and those who would challenge them must be more adept at creating unity. Building and maintaining unity is multifaceted, but the foremost aspect of doing so is developing a shared and inclusive vision for a civil resistance movement. Achieving this necessitates that movement organizers have deep knowledge of the grievances, aspirations, culture, and values of the various publics that they wish to mobilize. This knowledge forms the basis of developing and communicating a vision that attracts widespread support and mobilizes people. Effective visions resonate with the personal experience and feelings of ordinary people and summon their participation in collective civil resistance.

Another critical aspect of building unity is the presence of a leadership and organizational structure with legitimacy. Participation in movements is voluntary, and accordingly leaders do not have formal command and control authority over a mobilizing population. This means decisions in a movement must be made and carried out in ways that are felt to be legitimate by the publics that are being asked to mobilize. Each movement develops their own way of doing this— some more hierarchically, some in a more decentralized way, and some a combination of both over time. Regardless of a movement's exact leadership and organizational structure, there are different forms of leadership in movements, and unity involves harmonizing them. For every titular or charismatic national leader, there are many local leaders who need to be highly skillful at developing coalitions, negotiating, and aggregating interests among different groups. It is the ability of different leaders, at different scales (local or national), from different parts of a country, representing different groups, to work together that sustains unity over the long-term.

We can see evidence of both of these aspects of unity in the civil resistance used by the anti-Apartheid movement in South Africa in the 1980s. Hundreds of local civics groups sprouted up during that decade to advocate for municipal demands such as clean water and access to services, while simultaneously uniting under a common vision to end apartheid and to achieve national reconciliation. These civic groups, which coalesced into the United Democratic Front, had local leaders who were able to effectively lead decentralized tactics (i.e. consumer boycotts) for local issues, while simultaneously communicating and collaborating with larger organizing structures and national movement leadership.

2. *Operational Planning*

Waging effective civil resistance is far more complex than commonly assumed. The image that comes to mind when people think of civil resistance is protest, and yet that is only one of literally hundreds of tactics that are available. The most effective movements understand which tactic to choose, when, where, how, by whom it should be executed, at what it should be targeted, and among which other tactics it should be sequenced.

Answering these questions adequately requires planning based on a detailed analysis of a movement's and adversary's strengths, weaknesses, opportunities, and threats, as well as an assessment of the conflict environment and neutral or uncommitted parties (including members of the international community) that could influence the conflict. From this information movements can develop effective short-, mid-, and long-term objectives and corresponding operational plans. While those plans will evolve over time in response to events on the ground (as all plans do), the planning process and mindset are more critical for a movement's participants to develop than any particular plan itself.

Incidentally, it is in operational planning that we see the clearest intersection of skills and conditions in a conflict. The basis of operational planning is an assessment of the conditions—favorable and unfavorable—faced by a movement. The movement then plans to exploit favorable conditions and overcome, transform, or circumvent adverse conditions through skills and strategic choice.

A clear example of operational planning is seen in the Solidarity movement in Poland in the 1980s. Understanding their strengths and capabilities, workers articulated a powerful and politically realistic demand for independent trade unions (but restrained themselves from calling for the then-unachievable goal of ending Communist rule); concentrated their strengths in labor organizing and solidarity among diverse workers against their opponent's economic vulnerabilities and lack of legitimacy; and chose the effective tactic of striking by occupying their workplaces (instead of marching outside of their workplaces, which had made them vulnerable to repression when they had tried this in prior years). This was augmented by the workers' reliance on alternative institutions—particularly printing presses and independent periodicals—that had been developed over the previous decade to facilitate communication between cities. By selecting a strategic objective, an appropriate target, and appropriate tactics (an occupation strike and the use of alternative institutions) that were within their capabilities, the Solidarity movement effectively navigated the conflict environment, overcame adverse conditions, and made progress toward their ultimate goal of a democratic Polish state, which was achieved in 1989.[xii]

3. Nonviolent Discipline

Maintaining nonviolent discipline—which is the ability of resisters to remain nonviolent despite provocation—is core to the functional dynamics of civil resistance. With nonviolent discipline, movements maximize civilian participation, increase the cost of an opponent's repression, heighten the probability that repression will backfire, and are much more likely to induce defections from an adversary's key pillars of support. As Chenoweth and Stephan's research shows, these benefits significantly contribute to the differential in success rates between violence and civil resistance campaigns.[xiii]

Achieving nonviolent discipline requires that movements have confidence that civil resistance is an effective means to prosecute their conflict. Information about how civil resistance works and its historical record can be helpful in this regard, as can an effective strategy that builds incremental victories over time and shows that civil resistance works. Movements also maintain nonviolent discipline by building a culture and norms that enforce it. For example, the Otpor movement in Serbia that ousted Slobodan Milosevic systematically trained new members to understand how civil resistance works and why it is important to remain nonviolent.

Such efforts do not require a movement to make ethical arguments about remaining nonviolent, but people must reinforce in each other the practical benefits of nonviolent discipline, while remembering cases (Syria being the recent tragic example) where impatience or lack of confidence in civil resistance yielded a shift to violent tactics, with predictably disastrous consequences.

4. Increasing Civilian Participation in Civil Resistance

High levels of civilian participation in civil resistance are arguably the single largest predictor of movement success.[xiv] This makes sense since the more people withdraw consent and obedience from an authoritarian, the weaker the authoritarian becomes, and the greater the cost to them of trying to remain in control. Furthermore, we believe that increasing civilian participation also increases the chance that repression will backfire, and quantitative evidence shows that higher civilian participation increases the likelihood that defections among an adversary's supporters will take place.[xv]

Illustrating the importance of high levels of civilian participation, the 2011 revolutions in Egypt and Tunisia galvanized wide support across different demographic groups: men and women; religious and secular groups; young, middle-aged, and older people; lower- and middle-class workers; and urban and rural populations. In contrast, both the 1989 student movement in China and the 2009 Green Movement mobilized millions and grabbed headlines, but neither achieved its stated objectives—in part because neither grew to include widespread civic participation beyond their initial demographic base.

Achieving high levels of participation in civil resistance is an outgrowth of the first three items on the checklist. A unifying vision helps to build cohesion and galvanize mobilization. Operational planning instills confidence and provides an array of tactics to accommodate people's varying risk tolerance, available time, and capacity for sacrifice for the movement. An effective strategy provides options for the poor, the wealthy, the young, the old, and everyone in between to do something, small or large, to support the movement. Nonviolent discipline ensures that everyone can participate (as opposed to only able-bodied men in armed resistance) and nonviolent means are much more likely to appeal to a broad cross-section of society.

5. Diminishing Impact of Repression, and Increasing Backfire

One of the authoritarian's most powerful tools is the capacity to commit repression, and effective movements learn how to reduce the impact of repression while increasing its costs. One way they do so is through accurate risk assessment and tactical choice because not all tactics risk repression equally. While centralized actions such as mass demonstrations are likely to face repression, decentralized tactics such as consumer boycotts, stay-at-home strikes, sick-ins from school, or anonymous display of small symbols in public places are much more challenging for a regime to repress. This is so because the participants in some tactics (i.e. consumer boycotts) are not obvious (you cannot tell by looking at someone whether they are boycotting a product or not) or because the perpetrators are diffuse and have deniability (i.e. a stay-at-home strike requires police to make home visits to every worker and participants in a sick-in can claim that they really are sick that day).

In 1983 in Chile, political dissidents opposed to the dictatorship of Augusto Pinochet had to find a way to circumvent his repression. A decade of mass arrests, executions, torture, and disappearances meant that people were terrified to organize or mobilize together. In April, copper miners called for a strike outside of Santiago, but Pinochet threatened bloodshed by sending his military to surround the mines before the strike was supposed to begin. In the face of such repression, labor leaders called off the strike and called instead for a national day of protest, in which anyone protesting the regime would work slowly, walk slowly, drive slowly, and at 8:00pm bang pots and pans.[xvi] There was unprecedented and widespread participation in these actions, and this led to monthly calls for protests. This was the first major step in breaking through the layer of fear and atomization that was the cornerstone of Pinochet's rule. The actions had an acceptable level of low risk for participants and were also irrepressible—Pinochet's security forces had no answer for such wide-scale decentralized tactics.

Other aspects of reducing the impact of repression, or increasing its costs and the probability of backfire, involve articulating certain grievances in apolitical terms (demonstrators calling for clean water and safe neighborhoods, as opposed to the fall of a regime), building clear lines of leadership succession, and bridging social distance between a movement's participants and domestic and international groups, so that repression against the movement is more likely to backfire. For example, when the Egyptian blogger Khaled Said was pulled out of an Internet café in 2010 and beaten to death by security forces for exposing corruption, the dissident Facebook group "We are All Khaled Said" countered the Egyptian government's attempts to try to devalue Said's life. Through their presence, they made it clear that Said had much in common with everyday Egyptians, thus causing the repression to backfire.

6. Increasing Defections from a Movement's Adversary

As civil resistance progresses over time, it often induces loyalty shifts and defections amongst an adversary's active and passive supporters. For example, reformers and hardliners in government may begin to publicly struggle against each other for control. Economic interests may pressure the state to accommodate a movement's demands so that business will return. Regime functionaries such as soldiers, police, bureaucrats, and others may also begin to shift loyalties, perhaps because they've been persuaded of the movement's demands, disgusted with the regime, or because they have family members and friends who are participating in civil resistance. Even elites who are sympathetic to the regime may begin to doubt its sustainability and become neutral so as not to risk ending up on the wrong side of history if the civil resistance succeeds.

In Ukraine's Orange Revolution in 2004, dissidents intentionally sought out lines of communication with security forces, relying on the military's retired officer corps as intermediaries.[xvii] Over time, the opposition proved through their actions that they were nonviolent and reasonable; called on security forces to serve and protect the public good; bridged social distance through fraternization, slogans, and actions (such giving roses to riot police); revealed the corruption of the incumbent regime; and ultimately fomented loyalty shifts among the security forces. When it came time to engage in repression, many Ukrainian soldiers and police simply became neutral. This happened similarly in Serbia under Milosevic. Without openly defecting, security forces simply stopped enthusiastically carrying out the regime's orders. At the Otpor movement's October 5 climax, the police officer responsible for dropping chemical dispersants from a helicopter on the Belgrade crowds refused to do, claiming that he could not get a clear view of the crowds because the weather was unclear, even though it was sunny. He later commented that he felt he couldn't carry out orders because his family members may have been among the demonstrators that day.[xviii]

Whether driven by persuasion or self-interest, defections such as these are often the result of long-term processes catalyzed by a civil resistance movement. As with the previous two checklist trends, this trend emerges from a movement's embodiment of unity, planning and nonviolent discipline. Data shows that high levels of diverse participation correlate with an increased chance of defection, and unity, planning, and nonviolent discipline all contribute to broad and diverse participation. In particular, nonviolent discipline is important for inducing defections. So long as a movement remains nonviolent and avoids transitioning into violent insurrection (as was the tragic case in Syria during 2011) then the movement can live to fight another day and keeps open the possibility of defections. If the targets for loyalty shifts within a regime are not existentially threatened by a violent insurgency, their potential for defection remains a continuing threat to the cohesion of an authoritarian regime's power structure.

IMPLICATIONS FOR EXTERNAL ACTORS

This checklist is not just useful guidance for dissidents. Other constituencies can apply it as well to improve their performance in relating to these conflicts.

For example, the checklist can help journalists report more perceptively on civil resistance. If journalists want to make penetrating insights into a conflict, the checklist would indicate that placing a reporter in front of the burning target of a Molotov cocktail in Kiev in early 2014 so he can speculate on whether the violence could get worse does not illuminate the driving forces in the conflict. But investigation into the state of a movement's unity and planning, sources of breakdown in nonviolent discipline, increasing civilian participation, the decreasing impact of repression on a movement, and whether or not security forces are fully obeying orders, let alone defecting, would provide cutting edge analysis. Add to this an understanding of lost support in the business community and it becomes clear why Ukrainian president Yanukovych fled on February 21, 2014 hours after the worst regime-perpetrated violence backfired. Such developments are more predictable if one is looking at right indicators beforehand.

If considered by policy makers in the latter half of 2011, the checklist may have indicated greater opportunities for a winning civil resistance against the Assad regime in Syria. Continued loyalty shifts (beyond just Sunni soldiers) in the military away from the regime could have been viewed as the best hope for victory. Withdrawal of support by members of the business community was another indicator. In this light, encouragement of the Free Syrian Army in early 2012 to fight Assad's remaining Alawite military should have been seen as counterproductive if not foreshadowing a tragedy.

The checklist can be especially useful in developing norms governing external assistance for indigenous people power movements. For example, the first three capabilities on the checklist are skills-based and can be augmented through robust information exchange. Under Article 19 of the Universal Declaration of Human Rights, tyrants cannot restrict the flow of information across their borders or punish citizens who re-transmit that information to dissidents. All six items on the checklist can also evoke thought about pathways for technological innovation that can facilitate the cultivation of the three capabilities and three trends.

THE CHECKLIST AND CONFLICTS THAT WILL SHAPE OUR FUTURE

The environments in which nonviolent conflicts are fought are complex, and civil resisters—requiring grassroots coordination to sequence an array of tactics into a strategy for winning—often experience a sense of disorientation. Their natural fear of making the wrong decisions with people's lives and freedom at stake can induce the passivity that a tyrant seeks, and also bolster the illusion of a tyrant's invulnerability.

The checklist can help dissidents cut through this sense of disorientation and navigate a path forward. Some may argue that with so many variables in play a checklist for ending tyranny is too simplistic, and that evaluating critical decision making during future conflicts will require paramount attention on factors unique to that time and place.

However, the checklist does not call for ignoring specific factors in a situation, but rather for understanding those factors in the context of a broader strategic framework that reveals how and why civil resistance movements can win. Atul Gawande, who has researched the importance of checklists in a variety of other contexts, writes:

> Checklists seem able to defend anyone, even the experienced, against failure in many more tasks than we realized. They provide a kind of cognitive net. They catch mental flaws inherent in all of us—flaws of memory and attention and thoroughness...[xix]

> Under conditions of true complexity—where the knowledge required exceeds that of any individual and unpredictably reigns... [effective checklists] ensure the stupid but critical stuff is not overlooked, and... ensure people talk and coordinate... to manage the nuances and unpredictabilities the best they know.[xx]

The checklist may not be the final indicator as to who will prevail: the tyrant or the civil resister. However, the checklist can serve as the critical and continuing set of indicators to understand how citizen demands for freedom can overcome the entrenchment of authoritarian systems.

Notes

i.   Erica Chenoweth and Maria Stephan, *Why Civil Resistance Works: The Strategic Logic of Nonviolent Conflict* (New York: Columbia University Press, 2011), 6. NAVCO 1.1 data available at: *http://www.du.edu/korbel/sie/research/chenow_navco_data.html*.

ii.   Peter Ackerman and Adrian Karatnycky, *How Freedom is Won: From Civic Resistance to Durable Democracy* (Washington, DC: Freedom House 2005), p. 6-7.

iii. Eleanor Marchant, Adrian Karatnycky, Arch Puddington, and Christopher Walter, "Enabling Environments for Civic Movements and the Dynamics of Democratic Transition," Freedom House special report, July 18, 2008, p. 1.

iv.   Ibid.

v.   Erica Chenoweth and Maria Stephan, *Why Civil Resistance Works: The Strategic Logic of Nonviolent Conflict* (New York: Columbia University Press 2011), p. 6.

vi.   Chenoweth and Stephan, *Why Civil Resistance Works,* p. 9.

vii. Chenoweth and Stephan, *Why Civil Resistance Works,* p. 68.

viii. Chenoweth and Stephan, *Why Civil Resistance Works,* p. 62.

ix. Erica Chenoweth, Trends in Civil Resistance and Authoritarian Responses, The Atlantic Council Future of Authoritarianism Project April 15, 2014.

x. Chenoweth and Stephan, *Why Civil Resistance Works,* p. 66.

xi. Thomas C. Schelling, "Some Questions on Civilian Defence," in Adam Roberts, ed., *Civilian Resistance as a National Defence: Non-violent Action Against Aggression,* (Harrisburg, PA: Stackpole Books, 1968), p. 304.

xii. Peter Ackerman and Jack DuVall, *A Force More Powerful: A Century of Nonviolent Conflict,* (London: St. Martin's Press/Palgrave Macmillan 2000), p. 113-174.

xiii. Chenoweth and Stephan, *Why Civil Resistance Works,* p. 30-61.

xiv. Ibid.

xv. Chenoweth and Stephan, *Why Civil Resistance Works,* p. 46-49.

xvi. *A Force More Powerful,* directed by Steve York (2000; Washington, DC: York Zimmerman Inc.). Film.

xvii. Anika Locke Binnendijk and Ivan Marovic. "Power and Persuasion: Nonviolent Strategies to Influence State Security Forces in Serbia (2000) and Ukraine (2004)," *Communist and Post-Communist Studies* 39, no. 3, September (2006), p. 411-429.

xviii. Interview with Nebojsa Covic, *Vecernje Novosti,* Oct. 2, 2010.

xix. Atul Gawande, *The Checklist Manifesto: How to Get Things Right,* (New York: Picador, 2009), p. 47.

xx. Atul Gawande, *The Checklist Manifesto,* p. 79.

CHAPTER 7

People Power Versus the Corruption – Impunity-Authoritarian Nexus

Shaazka Beyerle
Visiting Scholar, Center for Transatlantic Relations, SAIS, Johns Hopkins University
Senior Advisor, International Center on Nonviolent Conflict

CORRUPTION AND AUTHORITARIANISM

The difficult, ongoing battle to achieve governance that is effective, democratic, and responsive to ordinary citizens faces a particularly pernicious obstacle: entrenched corruption.[i]

– Christopher Walker and Sanja Tatic

At its core, corruption involves the impunity and unaccountability of power holders in government, the economic realm, and other parts of society. By their very nature, authoritarian regimes and their state apparatuses are characterized by gross impunity and unaccountability to citizens. In such oppressive systems, rulers and their acolytes thwart or inhibit rule of law and transparency. They actively build ties to or infiltrate nonstate sectors in order to maintain control and consolidate power. They structure economic entities and exploit natural resources to enrich themselves, their families, other elites, and cronies. Taken to an extreme, these regimes become kleptocracies, that is, political systems "dominated by those who steal from the state coffers and practice extortion as their modus operandi."[ii]

Authoritarian regimes depend on the loyalties of various pillars in society to rule, such as the military, police, bureaucracy, business, and media, along with the individuals within them. The support of these pillars is neither monolithic nor unwavering. Corruption is one of the pathways through which loyalties are bought and sustained, or through which state actors in these pillars can themselves gain privileges and benefits to which the rulers turn a blind eye or, often, encourage, as this can strengthen vested interests in maintaining the oppressive system of governance. Rulers also use malfeasance as a pretext to neutralize political adversaries and competitors. Corruption, according to scholar Minxin Pei, becomes "a vital governing tool for authoritarian regimes."[iii] Thus, curbing corruption undermines impunity, a cornerstone of autocracies, and it fosters accountability, a fundamental element of genuine democracy. Successful grass-roots anti-corruption struggles therefore build democracy from the bottom-up.

Corruption can engender outrage and dissent in authoritarian regimes. It constitutes yet another layer of oppression weighing down on citizens. Graft and abuse often impact and harm regular people in their daily lives, from demands to pay bribes or provide favors, to police, judicial, and other power holders, to impunity, organized crime, and paramilitary tyranny, misuse or theft of public funds, and substandard state infrastructure and services that can result in injuries and death. Not surprisingly, corruption is a grievance around which citizens mobilize in many nonviolent movements targeting authoritarian regimes. Examples can be found across the globe, from the People Power I and II revolutions in the Philippines, the nonviolent resistance to Serbian dictator, Slobodan Milosevic, led by the youth movement, *Otpor*, the Rose Revolution in Georgia, to the nonviolent uprisings in Tunisia, Egypt, and Yemen, and the two Orange Revolutions in Ukraine.[iv]

Corruption presents two paradoxes for autocracies. First, while it's a means for authoritarians and their elites to rule and sustain control, it can also lead to their downfall. It can enrich and strengthen competing political elites, who seek to usurp those in power, thereby constituting another threat to the rulers.[v] As well, graft and abuse can erode the legitimacy of authoritarians and rot their venal systems from the inside out. This engenders greater and deeper dissatisfaction and anger among the populace as time goes on, which ultimately can lead to not only popular nonviolent uprisings, but also, tragically, to violent outbursts and conflict. Perceptive autocrats recognize this hazard to their rule. In November 2012, Xi Jinping, then President of China, stated, "A great deal of facts tell us that the worse corruption becomes the only outcome will be the end of the party and the end of the state! We must be vigilant."[vi]

The second paradox concerns the capacity of autocracies to fight graft and abuse. Even if there is some degree of political will at the top, when corruption is endemic, oppressive rulers cannot rein it in, let alone stamp it out. Yet they fear one of the strongest forces against malfeasance: an empowered and active citizenry. A Chinese saying, attributed to a former top leader, encapsulates the dilemma: "Corruption will kill the party; fighting corruption will kill it too."[vii] Not surprisingly, in spite of President Xi's candid and strong words, authorities are cracking down on the "New Citizens Movement" for transparency and fairness, sentencing and jailing activists, including one of its central figures, rights lawyer Xu Zhiyong.[viii]

PEOPLE POWER VERSUS CORRUPTION

Though not widely known, over the past 17 years, citizens around the world have mobilized in nonviolent movements, campaigns, and local community initiatives targeting graft, abuse, and impunity. This chapter is based on an international research project I conducted to identify, study, and extract general lessons learned from such organized civic efforts (Appendix I). The project culminated in the book, *Curtailing Corruption: People Power for Accountability and Justice.*[ix]

Overall, the research found that these organized citizen mobilizations achieved real, tangible outcomes, not only in the short-run, but, in several instances, in the longer term (Appendix II). Secondly, people power targeting corruption is manifested most frequently in societies enduring poor governance, poverty, low levels of literacy, and severe repression, the latter perpetrated by the state, paramilitary groups, or organized crime.[1] The results are in keeping with a 10-year, meta-case study analysis from the development and democracy realm on citizenship, participation, and accountability. It concluded that citizen engagement "can make positive differences, even in the least democratic settings – a proposition that challenges the conventional wisdom of an institution and state-oriented approach that relegates opportunities for citizens to engage in a variety of participatory strategies to a more 'mature' democratic phase."[x]

What is People Power?

In this book, the terms civil resistance and people power are used interchangeably. However, I prefer to draw the following distinctions. *People power* is a positive force that constructively confronts and seeks to challenge injustice, impunity, and oppression while pursuing engagement with both powerholders and the public. It refers to the social, economic, political, and psychological pressure that is exerted by significant numbers of individuals organized together around shared grievances and goals, implementing nonviolent strategies and tactics, such as civil disobedience, noncooperation, strikes, boycotts, monitoring, petition drives, low-risk mass actions, and demonstrations. Gene Sharp, the groundbreaking nonviolent resistance theorist, recorded over 198 types of tactics.[xi] Since his original cataloging, new tactics are constantly generated by movements and campaigns, including those targeting corruption. *Civil resistance*—also called nonviolent resistance, nonviolent struggle, nonviolent conflict, and nonviolent action—is the civilian-based method to fight oppression and injustice through which people power is wielded. It involves strategizing, planning, organizing, communicating, and tactical development, selection, and sequencing.

---

[1] I draw a distinction between the terms people power and civil resistance. *People power* refers to the social, economic, political and psychological pressure that is exerted by significant numbers of individuals organized together around shared grievances and goals, implementing nonviolent strategies and tactics, such as civil disobedience, noncooperation, strikes, boycotts, monitoring, petition drives, low-risk mass actions, and demonstrations. *Civil resistance* – also called nonviolent resistance, nonviolent struggle, nonviolent conflict, and nonviolent action – is the civilian-based method to fight oppression and injustice through which people power is wielded. It involves strategizing, planning, organizing, communicating, and tactical development, selection, implementation, and sequencing.

Re-defining Corruption

In practice, corruption functions as a system of power abuse involving a multitude of relationships. Some are above the surface but most are hidden. Within this system are well-established interests motivated to sustain the venal status quo because of the benefits they derive from it. They use various means ranging from legal and regulatory noncompliance to coercion to violence. Thus, my preferred definition of corruption builds upon traditional notions as follows:

> a system of abuse of entrusted power for private, collective, or political gain – often involving a complex, intertwined set of relationships, some obvious, others hidden, with established vested interests, that can operate vertically within an institution or horizontally cut across political, economic and social spheres in a society or transnationally.[2]

When the experiences of regular people are taken into account, corruption is a form of oppression and a loss of freedom. For Aruna Roy, one of the founders of the landmark "Right-to-Information" movement in India, corruption is "the external manifestation of the denial of a right, an entitlement, a wage, a medicine..."[xii]

People Power Dynamics

In the anti-corruption context, people power produces extra-institutional, nonviolent pressure on corruptors who refuse to change the venal status quo by:

- disrupting systems of graft and abuse, thus interfering in their smooth functioning;

- applying nonviolent pressure through the the "power of numbers," that is, people collectively raising their voice

- over shared grievances and demands to corruptors who have thus far refused to change the malfeasant status quo;

---

[2] This systemic definition was developed by the author, who wishes to credit for inspiration, points made by Maria Gonzalez de Asis, World Bank, in an unpublished, working paper.

- engaging with powerholders and regular citizens in order to pull them toward the nonviolent movement or civic initiative, which in civil resistance theory refers to shifting their positions and loyalties.

Top-down and Bottom-up Synergies

Traditional top-down strategies to combat corruption rest on a flawed assumption that once anti-corruption measures (such as laws, regulations, and institutions)are set in place, venal practices will henceforth change. But how can such technocratic and legal mechanisms bring forth change when they must be implemented by the very institutions that are corrupt? Put another way, those who are benefitting from corruption are expected to be the ones to curb it. Thus, even when political will exists and reformers are present, efforts can be impeded because too many individuals are vested in the venal status quo. As a result, elite-based, state-led efforts alone are unlikely to undermine entrenched systems of corruption.

Civil resistance adds the power of numbers and brings a strategic and complementary dimension to the struggle. It applies extra-institutional methods of action and concomitant pressure when powerholders are corrupt and/or unaccountable and institutional channels are blocked or ineffective.[3]

The cases studied demonstrated that top-down and bottom-up efforts are complementary and synergistic. People power civic initiatives were found to:

- shake-up corrupt practices and relationships;

- engender political will;

- promote citizen-friendly, top-down reforms (such as accessible Right to Information Acts);

- reinforce new patterns of administration and governance centered on accountability to regular people;

---

[3] This conceptualization is based on the definition of social movements by Kurt Schock: Kurt Schock, "People Power and Alternative Politics," In *Politics in the Developing World*, Peter Burnell and Vicky Randall eds., (New York: Oxford University Press, 2008), p. 202-276.

- bolster and even protect integrity champions, reformers, and honest individuals within venal systems who on their own are outnumbered by corruptors with deep-set vested interests, as well as honest state and nonstate powerholders who do not want to engage in corrupt practices, and provide a way out of the corrupt system for individuals who refuse to be a part of it, that is, in civil resistance terms, who wish to engage in noncooperation.

People Power Indicators

Taken together, the research points to five indicators for the potential emergence of organized, strategic nonviolent action in autocracies and semi-democracies:

- realization among civic groups and citizens that they share serious grievances and problems in common that are linked to the government's impunity, denial of freedoms, corruption, mismanagement, and responsibility for economic and social injustice;

- collective sense of being affronted by blatant powerholder (state and nonstate) graft, abuse, and impunity;

- cooperation and new alliances at the grass-roots;

- growing loss of fear to collectively express dissent;

- implementation of small-scale or even low-risk, larger-scale nonviolent tactics (both on the ground and digitally).

CASE STUDIES

Past Cases: Egypt and Turkey

> *When elections are corrupt, we're watching you. When you rig votes, we're watching you. When you torture prisoners, we're watching you. This is our mission statement.*[xiii]

> Bothaina Kamel,
> co-founder, shayfeen.com

Egypt. In the first decade of the 21st century, several grass-roots civic mobilizations began to harness public discontent and anger in Egypt over the rampant corruption and unaccountability of Hosni Mubarak's dictatorship. Each constituted a river of dissent and empowerment that fed into the 2011 "January 25 Revolution." The most sustained was shayfeen.com. A play on words meaning "we see you" in Arabic, it was founded by three Egyptian women in 2005. In spite of threats, intimidation, and judicial proceedings, the savvy, volunteer-based campaign increased public awareness about corruption. It also proved that its nonviolent activities were valid under the United Nations Convention Against Corruption (UNCAC), to which Egypt was a signatory, as the campaign fostered citizen participation, actively monitored the government, and broadcast presidential and parliamentary election fraud in real time via the Internet. The US Department of State used the presidential data for its 2005 annual human rights report.[xiv] Out of the campaign emerged the Egyptians against Corruption movement. Together, these two civic initiatives reframed the anti-corruption struggle—taking it out of an abstract discourse to the tangible ways it harms regular people.[xv]

They created a series of simple, low-risk, mass actions to raise awareness, visibility, and support for the campaign that did not put average citizens at the hands of the regime. For instance, approximately 100,000 tea glasses with the shayfeen.com logo were distributed, bringing the campaign into homes and tea houses around the country. They printed more than 250,000 plastic bags with the slogan, "We see you, and at the elections we are observing you," (which rhymes in Arabic). The bags were used and re-used so much that the minister of trade called those using them, "the supermarket activists."[xvi] Shayfeen. com also launched a popular anti-corruption contest on December 9, International Anti-Corruption Day via an Arabic satellite television station. Regular people voted in the thousands for anti-corruption heroes via SMS, essentially activating the power of numbers to honor and support integrity champions within the government.

They also developed communication strategies directed at the public and various pillars of support for the corrupt, authoritarian status quo, including parts of the government, political and policy elites, and the media. After the fraudulent December 2010 parliamentary elections, Egyptians Against Corruption joined forces with other streams of dissent in the January 25 Revolution, including the April 6 youth movement, the We are All Khaled Said campaign, the youth wing of the El Ghad party, and labor, democracy, and women's rights activists.

Turkey. In 1996, Turkey could be described as a semi-democracy with authoritarian practices and links to the "crime syndicate" consisting of paramilitary entities, mafia, drug traffickers, government officials, members of Parliament, and parts of the judiciary, media, and private sector. The government was elected, but repression against citizen dissent was severe. Extrajudicial murders were commonplace, either political in nature or related to organized crime. Corruption was endemic.[xvii] In February 1997, a few months after a particularly outrageous scandal, the "One Minute of Darkness for Constant Light Campaign" mobilized approximately 30 million Turkish citizens in synchronized low-risk mass actions to pressure the government to take specific measures to combat the crime syndicate, and curtail corruption and powerholder impunity.

Strategic choices were made from the beginning; the campaign would be apolitical and people should feel a sense of ownership in order to counter smear attacks, pull together a large coalition of nonstate organizations, and attract widespread public participation. The civic organizers created a low-risk, mass action designed to overcome real obstacles, including fear, detention, and violent crackdowns. On February 1, 1997 at 9:00 p.m., citizens began to turn off their lights for one minute, with many soon embellishing upon the tactic by banging pots and pans, gathering in neighborhoods, and blaring car horns. In the midst of the campaign, the military forced the coalition government to resign. Prime Minister Necmettin Erbakan remained in power until a new government was approved by the parliament six months later. Organizers ended the campaign after six weeks. It shook the country's competing loci of power and broke the taboo over confronting the problem of government impunity. Although it did not succeed to remove parliamentary immunity, it nonetheless empowered citizens to fight corruption, pushed the government to launch judicial investigations yielding verdicts, and uncovered crime syndicate figures and relationships.

Recent Cases: Kenya and Russia

We are fighting a legacy of corruption and bribery among government officials, law enforcement and industry that has allowed this project to move forward.[xviii]

Yaroslav Nikitenko,
Movement to Defend Khimki Forest

Kenya. Freedom House's 2013 and 2014 Freedom in the World survey classifies Kenya as partly free.[xix] Human Rights Watch reports that new laws introduced in 2013 will, if enacted, "impose draconian restrictions on the media and on nonprofit organizations…"[xx] Overall, civil society is facing a crackdown and activists are facing threats and violence, the latter a common experience in spite of the country's precarious transition to democracy. In 2007, Muslims for Human Rights (MUHURI), a civil society organization in Mombasa, embarked on a radical new approach to gaining human rights, namely fighting powerholder corruption linked to poverty.[xxi] It catalyzed grass-roots civic initiatives to access information about constituency development funds allocated annually to all Members of Parliament (MP). Hussein Khalid, then the organization's Executive Director stated: "If people are able to be encouraged to go out, today it's CDF, tomorrow it's something else, and another day it's another thing. So CDF is an entry point to the realization of so many rights that people are not getting."[xxii]

In an innovative collaboration with the International Budget Partnership and veterans from the successful "Right to Information" movement in India, MUHURI developed the six-step social audit, consisting of:

1. *Information-gathering* – of records from the local CDF office;

2. *Training local people* – men and women, to become community activists.

3. *Educating and mobilizing fellow citizens* – through a variety of tactics, about the CDF and their rights to information and accountability of power holders.

4. *Inspecting* – the CD project site;

5. *Holding the public hearing* – attended by citizens, CDF officials, often the MP, district administrators, and even the media;

6. *Following-up* – with officials.

MUHURI and citizens faced intimidation on more than one occasion. The group proactively took measures to maintain nonviolent discipline. In 2009, after an unidentified gang ransacked its office and stabbed the guard during the Likoni constituency social audit, they made the violence backfire by avowing on a popular radio program that they would continue and present their findings at the public hearing. An International Budget Partnership report concluded:

> Both the MKSS [Mazdoor Kisan Shakti Sangathan/ Union for the Empowerment of Peasants and Laborers] and MUHURI have held social audits in hostile environments. Their experiences show that individuals that would otherwise feel intimidated to speak out against public officials are willing to do so in the context of a well-attended social audit forum – perhaps due to the strength they perceive from being part of a collective evaluation process.[xxiii]

Over the course of three years, MUHURI and slum-dwellers conducted ten social audits in the Coast province, uncovered graft, and rectified the transgressions. The organization has taken strategic steps to sustain overall momentum and empower others to launch social audits. It trains civil society organizations (CSOs) and citizens to conduct their own civic initiatives, and designed a mini-social audit, in which residents monitor a single project in their immediate locality, rather than a set of projects throughout a constituency.[xxiv] Not only is people power devolved to one of the most basic levels of society, each small victory builds confidence and yields a visible outcome that benefits residents in their daily lives. Finally, the CSO is exploring the possibility of conducting social audits in cooperation with authorities in some government departments.[xxv] At the national level, activists from eight constituencies conducting social audits joined together in a campaign to change the CDF law. The Kenyan government set up a task force to review it. The report, finally released in July 2012, outlined a number of reforms.[xxvi,4]

Russia. The Movement to Defend Khimki Forest originated in 2007 when Evgenia Chirikova discovered that the government planned to run the new Moscow–St. Petersburg motorway through the revered, federally protected Khimki forest, when several other, less circuitous routes existed.[xxvii] She disseminated homemade leaflets; locals contacted her, out of which a group formed to save the forest. In 2009 the government awarded the multi-billion dollar highway construction contract to a shell company owned by Vinci, the French multinational company, while President Putin signed a decree changing the forest's protected status.[xxviii] Investigations by Chirikova, journalists, and European and international NGOs (INGOs) found evidence of corruption.[xxix] Chirikova testified to the European Parliament that Vinci "has constructed a complicated network of companies from various tax haven jurisdictions. These companies have no experience in construction at all—but one of them belongs to Mr. Putin's close friend, Mr. Arkady Rotenberg…"[xxx]

The movement is based on four grievances: bisection and irreparable harm to Khimki Forest; local, national and international corruption and impunity; the Russian state's disregard of its own laws; and the interests of oligarchs and money over the interests of citizens and the nation. The demands are to re-route the highway and stop destruction of the forest, end Vinci's involvement until an alternative route is selected, and investigate all violations of laws related to the road project. Over the years, it developed several strategies:

- Disrupt the venal status quo by exposing the threat to Khimki forest, the corruption embedded in the project, and powerholder impunity;

---

[4] The delay was due to the ground-breaking new constitution ratified by voters in 2010, which enshrines the right to information and "the right to petition for enacting, amending and repealing legislation under Article 119." For information about the new Kenyan constitution, see: "Countries at the Crossroads: Kenya," Freedom House, 2012, *http://www.freedomhouse.org/report/countries-crossroads/2012/kenya*.

- Thwart on-the-ground construction;

- Build unity and increase "numbers" to wield people power by forging alliances and/or cooperating with other Russian civil society groups (for example, World Wildlife Fund–Russia and Ecological Watch of the North Caucasus) and grass-roots initiatives (April 10, 2011 "Days of Wrath"), mobilize citizens, and take the struggle to the global arena (with CEE Bankwatch Network, Sherpa, avaaz.org, and other groups).

- Win support from the Russian public, well-known personalities (such as Bono, Alexei Navalny, Ksenia Sobchak), opposition political parties, Members of the European Parliament, and even the Moscow chapter of the Russian Federation of Motorists.[xxxi]

Activists have faced brutal repression, but those entities and actors behind the violence have failed to crush it. The movement has three advantages: its grass-roots nature, the credibility of the leaders and activists, and the public legitimacy of the grievances and demands. Organizers have engaged in a wide variety of nonviolent tactics, including: gathering 50,000 signatures; e-petitions; letter-writing to powerholders; protests; leafleting; graffiti, unfurling banners; Khimki camps; cultural expressions; nonviolent intervention; hunger strikes; Tweeting; and digital exposure of repression. Citizens unable or too scared to take part in on-the-ground actions took on support roles, such as bringing food to the forest camps and gathering information. International solidarity yielded on-the-ground and digital actions in European capitals. Chirikova delivered a 20,000-name petition to Vinci's headquarters, submitted a blacklist to US Senators, and met with President François Hollande.

The movement is achieving interim victories. The European Bank for Reconstruction and Development and the European Investment Bank pulled out of the project. Activists nonviolently disrupted and delayed the project through Khimki forest on a regular basis. In 2010, then-President Dmitry Medvedev temporarily suspended the project. In June 2013, Sherpa, the French human rights legal organization, together with other European NGOs, filed a formal complaint of corruption against Vinci with the Paris Prosecutor. In October 2013, the Prosecutor announced the opening of a preliminary enquiry into financial crimes, which is ongoing at this time.[xxxii] Chirikova reports that while 70 hectares of trees (out of a total 2000 hectares) have been cut down in the forest, felling is presently at a standstill.

The movement has been also connecting with and supporting other civic initiatives around Russia. It joined forces in the post-December 2011 parliamentary election demonstrations. She reports that in 2014 the movement organized solidarity actions in over 30 cities across the country for the "Arctic 30" Greenpeace detainees, and for Evgeni Vitishko, the jailed activist with the "Environmental Watch for the North Caucuses." According to Chirikova, he is serving a three year sentence for writing graffiti on the perimeter wall of a luxury villa built by Krasnodar region governor, Alexander Tkachev, on land protected from construction under Russian law.

POLICY IMPLICATIONS AND RECOMMENDATIONS FOR THE INTERNATIONAL COMMUNITY

> *Citizens are active subjects in the political sphere, not objects of intervention by government programs or passive choosers in the marketplace.*[xxxiii]
>
> John Ackerman

These four cases underscore, along with the others in the aforementioned study, several policy and practical implications for external actors.[5]

First, anti-corruption movements and campaigns were found to be precursors to broader democracy movements, as illustrated in

---

[5] An in-depth treatment of lessons learned and policy implications for civil society, activists, policy makers, and anti-corruption, development, good governance and peacebuilding practitioners may be found Chapters 11 and 12 in my above-mentioned book, *Curtailing Corruption: People Power for Accountability and Justice,* (Boulder, CO: Lynne Rienner, 2014).

Egypt and Russia. "Our first step," said Bothaina Kamel, co-founder of shayfeen.com and Egyptians Against Corruption, "was to open our eyes, to see where we are now and where we are going next, to see where what our government is doing to us, and to understand what we are doing to our country."[xxxiv] In other cases, such as Kenya and Turkey, they can move citizens from acquiescence to agency, and push for practices, laws, and mechanisms that challenge authoritarian currents and strengthen democracy. For external actors, this research demonstrates that democracy-building is not singularly an elite-to-elite exercise; in addition to casting votes, citizens can play vital roles to directly exact accountability and justice. Thus, there are multiple, complementary pathways to gain or maintain genuine democracy, that include but are not limited to representative democracy.

Second, civic anti-corruption initiatives can help build a culture and practice of democracy from the bottom-up, both in terms of their goals, which disrupt corruption, empower honest officials and heighten powerholder transparency and accountability, as well as through direct citizen experiences. The latter includes such activities as informal elections, surveys, reporting to other community members, and a variety of interactions with powerholders, including direct and digital engagement, joint community-official meetings, negotiations, and public forums. Summarizing this organic process, the International Budget Partnership referred to MUHURI's social audits as "exercises in participatory democracy that challenge the traditional 'rules of the game' in governance."[xxxv] Reflecting on the Movement to Defend Khimki Forest, Chirikova said: "We make citizens out of people. We are trying to use our own example to show that it is possible to fight for one's own rights, despite everything."[xxxvi]

Third, in contrast to formulaic, citizen engagement projects propagated by external actors, four central qualities characterize grass-roots, nonviolent civic initiatives: volunteerism, dynamism, strategic thinking, and legitimacy. These can help counter efforts to discredit the mobilizations, thwart intimidation, make attacks backfire, weaken the resolve of corruptors to maintain the status quo, and cumulatively gather support from the public as well as from within malfeasant systems. Civic leaders, activists, and citizens displayed creativity, ingenuity, and adaptability to changing circumstances, thereby maximizing opportunities, large and small, arising from such occurrences, and countering difficulties, such as intimidation and even violence.

Fourth, corruption was not framed in the abstract, but linked to everyday concerns and widely shared grievances, upon which civic leaders identified fairly tangible goals and clear demands in spite of tackling overall systems of graft and abuse in repressive, unaccountable settings. Thus, citizens are most likely to embrace and act upon an anti-corruption agenda based on their realities and what matters to them, rather than priorities set by domestic elites or external actors. Chirikova echoed this dynamic: "This is our homeland, we like our way of life and don't want to lose it because of some officials and their corrupt interests."

Fifth, successful bottom-up, civic initiatives targeting corruption are built upon the existing "social infrastructure"—the social structures, social relationships, prevailing culture, and even history of the struggle context. Effective and credible strategies, tactics, messaging and discourse emanate from these homegrown elements, not from the international community. Civil resistance theorist Hardy Merriman defines the latter as the narratives, cognitive frames, meanings, and language of a movement.[xxxvii] It is encapsulated in the "One Minute of Darkness for Constant Light" Campaign's call to action, which binds the struggle against endemic corruption and impunity to the overarching goal of genuine, responsive democracy:

> 1 Minute of Darkness for Constant Light! To show my determination to bring to justice the ones who assembled crime organizations and the ones who hired their services; to support the persons and authorities who investigate the events in question; to make my yearning for a democratic, contemporary, and transparent state of law be heard... This is a call from CITIZEN TO CITIZEN.[xxxviii]

Lastly, the overriding conclusion is that citizen engagement and action cannot be manufactured and duplicated en masse through externally-developed, standardized projects initiated by international institutions, donors, and their subcontractors. There is no formula or replicable set of objectives, actions, and outcomes. Such attempts can potentially divert grass-roots civic efforts from more effective paths.

While the international community cannot stimulate home-grown, bottom-up movements and campaigns targeting corruption and impunity, there still are positive ways it can support citizen empowerment and action. The following recommendations highlight a few such policies and measures.

What the grass-roots wants

In my research, civic leaders and activists called on external actors to:

1. Look beyond elitist nongovernmental organizations (NGOs) and conventional civil society organizations (CSOs) when soliciting views from and funding civil society entities. Some people power leaders reported anecdotally to me that they were ignored by international actors, even when they directly attempted to contact them.

2. Refrain from efforts to institutionalize bottom-up, anti-corruption campaigns by turning them into conventional NGOs and CSOs.

3. Provide donor support for self-organization and capacity-building in the civic realm that: involves home-grown holistic approaches based on the intrinsic overlap of anti-corruption, good governance, development, human rights, peace-building, and environmental protection; and taps pre-existing social networks and relationships.

4. Make available solidarity and legal, technical, and other support to people power initiatives if they want it. Attention from international figures and civil society, and investigations and legal measures from INGOs were particularly valuable for the Movement to Defend Khimki Forest.

5. Provide protection to anti-corruption activists, when requested. There are wider strategic benefits to international attention and condemnation of crackdowns. Protecting a few can serve to empower many and can make repression backfire by hampering oppressor aims to:

    a. Paralyze civic dissent by inculcating fear, despair and apathy among anti-corruption advocates and citizens

    b. Hinder unity among anti-corruption networks and organizations

    c. Impede alliances with other nonviolent struggles, for example, democracy, labor, women, minorities, land rights, and the environment.

Flexible funding. Citizen empowerment and action doesn't require large amounts of funding because civil resistance is essentially a voluntary endeavor. In instances where bottom-up civic initiatives seek external financial contributions, external actors can provide flexible, modest grants directly or through NGOs that enable experimentation, pilot efforts, an expansion of outreach and activities, and peer-to-peer learning exchanges among grass-roots organizations, social movement organizations (SMOs), activists, and citizens.[6] Financial and practical support to MUHURI in Kenya is an example.

Access to information. Information is often a critical asset for anti-corruption civic initiatives, as was demonstrated in the profiled cases. After the Mubarak regime fell, Engi El Haddad of Egyptians Against Corruption, along with other activists, embarked on a quest to freeze its corrupt gains and recover stolen assets. One of the biggest obstacles they face is gaining needed information. The international community (including economic and financial actors) can generally facilitate access to information through: national and multilateral policies and practices, as well as the direct provision of information about development aid, and domestic budgets; spending in aid-recipient authoritarian countries; resource extraction contracts; stolen assets; illicit financial

---

[6] Social movement organizations (SMOs) are entities that provide a legal and/or administrative identity for social movement activities and fundraising.

flows; shady cross-border deals involving shell companies; money laundering; and assets held in third countries.

Media exposure. In instances of regime censorship or even self-censorship among the media, alternative sources can be vital. In Kenya, MUHURI reached both citizens and corruptors through community radio. In Egypt, Kamel was a regionally popular TV-show host on an Arab satellite station who openly discussed corruption. In the Turkish case, one of the campaign leaders, Ersin Salman, had close ties to the media as a result of his public relations company. Where such options don't exist, funding for in-country civic entities investigating corruption and support for or access to other information/news outlets, both domestic and multi-lingual international broadcasting can potentially help to fill the gap (for example, Radio Liberty, Deutsche Welle).

Top-down responsiveness. Top-down multilateral instruments and democratic mechanisms in third-party countries can both directly and indirectly support grassroots, nonviolent movements and campaigns targeting corruption and impunity. Illustrated in this chapter by the Egyptian and Russian cases, judicial systems (for example, the Paris Prosecutor), international mechanisms (such as UNCAC), governance bodies (for example, the European Parliament), and multilateral institutions (including the European Investment Bank and European Bank for Reconstruction and Development) can disrupt and expose corruption targeted by grass-roots civic initiatives, protect civil society, and undermine malfeasance by withdrawing support from dubious transactions and investments.

In conclusion, even in the harshest of settings, grass-roots struggles against corruption and impunity have generated extraordinary nonviolent pressure on venal, unaccountable rulers and other state and non-state powerholders. Their struggles and triumphs, whether at the local or national level, are an inspiration and lesson to all of us who value, cultivate, and strive to preserve genuine democracy throughout the world.

APPENDIX I: OVERVIEW OF RESEARCH CASE STUDIES

Form of corruption	Type of collective action	Country	Organizers
Reconstruction and development projects	Civic initiative/social accountability	Afghanistan	Integrity Watch Afghanistan (CSO)
State public services	Civic initiative/social accountability	Bangladesh	Transparency International – Bangladesh chapter (CSO)
Overall endemic corruption	Campaign within broader social movement	Bosnia-Herzegovina	DOSTA! (Enough) nonviolent youth movement
Political corruption	Ficha Limpa (Clean Slate/Record) – social movement	Brazil	MCCE (Movement to Combat Electoral Corruption) and avaaz.org
Overall endemic corruption/impunity	shayfeen.com (We're watching you)/ Egyptians Against Corruption – social movement	Egypt	shayfeen.com/ Egyptians Against Corruption (SMOs)
Organized crime (narco-traffickers)/ local state capture/ impunity	Social movement	Guatemala	Community
Overall endemic corruption/bribery	5th Pillar – social movement	India	Fifth Pillar (SMO)
Efforts to neutralize the anti-corruption commission	CICAK (Love Indonesia, Love Anti-Corruption Commission) Campaign	Indonesia	Informal network of civic leaders, activists and CSOs
Cosa Nostra mafia	Addiopizzo (Good-bye protection money) social movement	Italy	Addiopizzo (SMO)

(continues on next page)

Parliament Constituency Development Funds	Civic initiative/social accountability	Kenya	MUHURI (Muslims for Human Rights) (CSO-CBO)
Overall endemic corruption	DHP* (*Dejemos Hacernos Pendejos/* Quit Playing Dumb) – social movement	Mexico	Informal network of civic leaders and activists
Primary school corruption/textbooks	Textbook Count/ Textbook Walk campaigns/social accountability	Philippines	G-Watch, PSLINK (Public Services Labor Independent Confederation), Boy Scouts/Girl Scouts, CSOs, citizen groups, communities
Environment, illegal development	Movement to Defend Khimki Forest	Russia	Informal network of civic leaders and activists
Political corruption	CAGE (Citizens Alliance for the General Election) 2000 campaign	South Korea	Coalition (1,104 NGOs, CSOs, citizen groups, YMCA/YWCA, religious organizations)
State-organized crime-paramilitary groups linkages	One Minute of Darkness for Constant Light campaign	Turkey	Informal network of civic leaders and activists
Police	Civic initiative/social accountability	Uganda	NAFODU (National Foundation for Democracy and Human Rights in Uganda) (CSO-CBO)

APPENDIX II: CASE STUDY DESCRIPTIONS AND OUTCOME HIGHLIGHTS[7]

Afghanistan: Integrity Watch Afghanistan is empowering villagers in community monitoring of internationally and domestically funded projects, in order to curb corruption and improve reconstruction and development. By 2013, 400 civic initiatives had been conducted in seven provinces. In approximately one-third of the cases, problems were found and solved as a result of community pressure. In another third of the cases either project implementers were cooperative with efforts to resolve problems or none were found. Among the final cases, there was no "success" in that irregularities weren't discovered during the monitoring, site access was blocked to citizens, or the communities weren't sufficiently mobilized.

Bangladesh: The "Social Movement against Corruption," launched in 2009 by Transparency International-Bangladesh in 34 districts, empowered citizens to hold public officials accountable for health, education, and local government services through citizen committees, youth groups, and a variety of nonviolent actions, such as information tables outside targeted hospitals and volunteer monitoring of their services, cleanliness, and medical staff attendance.

Bosnia-Herzegovina: *Dosta!* (Enough!), a nonviolent youth movement, promotes accountability and government responsibility to citizens and seeks to foster civic participation across religious and ethnic groups in the country. In 2009 it launched a digital and on-the-ground campaign that pressured Prime Minister Branković to resign over his acquisition of an upscale, state-owned apartment through a series of administrative maneuvers, for approximately EUR 500. He left office a year and a half before his term was over.

Brazil: The Movement against Electoral Corruption coalition (MCCE) collected 1.6 million signatures to introduce the *Ficha Limpa* (Clean Slate/Record) legislation to the Brazilian Congress,

---

[7] The achievements of these nonviolent civic initiatives cannot be adequately encapsulated in 1-2 sentences per case study. This table presents very brief highlights of their outcomes. In-depth information can be found in my book, *Curtailing Corruption: People Power for Accountability and Justice,* (Boulder, CO: Lynne Rienner, 2014).

which would prohibit candidates from taking office if they have been convicted of specific crimes by more than one judge (misuse of public funds, drug trafficking, rape, murder, or racism). Following a sustained campaign of street actions, and later, digital civil resistance coordinated by avaaz.org, the bill was passed both in the Chamber of Deputies and the Senate. It subsequently was approved by then-president Luis Ignazio da Silva in June, 2010, and in February 2012, the Supreme Court ruled that *Ficha Limpa* was constitutional and would be enforced.

Egypt: The women-led watchdog and anti-corruption movement, *shayfeen.com* ("we see you"), launched in 2005, and its sister movement, Egyptians Against Corruption, initiated in 2006, cumulatively put corruption into the domain of public discourse and sparked a nonviolent campaign for judicial independence. They fostered citizen participation, monitored the government, broadcast election fraud in real time via the Internet, and proved their nonviolent activities were valid under the UNCAC. Thousands of citizens expressed dissent against the corrupt regime of Hosni Mubarak through low-risk mass actions and supported integrity champions within the state through a satellite broadcast award where the public voted for anti-corruption heroes.

Guatemala: A local citizens' movement emerged in Santa Lucia Cotzumalguapa, after the cessation of the civil war in 1996. Over the years it has fought to recover the community from drug lords and organized crime, foster social and economic development, provide youth recreation, and challenge the climate of impunity by exposing electoral fraud, supporting honest candidates in local elections, and monitoring criminal activities as well as the activities and spending of power-holders. It maintained resilience in the face of violent repression. Human rights activists expanded the struggle to the international arena, garnering on-the-ground solidarity from external actors.

India: 5th Pillar is a social movement with long-term transformative goals to change the culture of corruption in the country. In the short-run, it targets bribery with innovative low-risk actions such as passing out "anti-corruption" Zero-Rupee Notes in public places, conducting Right to Information workshops, petitioning, holding citizen anti-bribery pledges, and leafleting queues outside state offices. Since 2007, over 2.5 million Zero-Rupee Notes have been distributed, and the campaign has received numerous reports of success. The movement conducts outreach to rural populations, is building voluntary, student-led chapters in higher education institutions across Tamil Nadu state, is engaging the business community, and is experimenting with a local television talk show.

Indonesia: The 2009 CICAK (Love Indonesia Love Anti-Corruption Commission) campaign mobilized well over a million citizens around the country, digitally and on-the-ground, to defend the Corruption Eradication Commission (KPK) and two falsely imprisoned deputy commissioners. As a result, the officials were released, President Susilo Bambang Yudhoyono established an independent fact-finding team, and Deputy Attorney General Abdul Hakim Ritonga and Police Chief Detective Susno Duadji later resigned. The latter official subsequently testified that the police force had a special team designed to target senior KPK officials.

Italy: Addiopizzo (Good-bye Protection Money) is a youth anti-mafia movement in Palermo that empowers businesses to publicly refuse to pay pizzo, educates schoolchildren about integrity, and mobilizes citizens to resist the Cosa Nostra crime group through simple, everyday acts, such as patronizing pizzo-free stores and businesses (reverse boycott). By 2012, 1,000 businesses joined the pizzo-free network, and a new civic group, *Libero Futuro* (Future with Freedom), was formed by the older generation of anti-mafia advocates to complement the youth movement. It encourages and helps businesses go through *denuncia*, the denunciation process of testifying to the police and courts about mafia extortion.

Kenya: MUHURI (Muslims for Human Rights) is empowering communities to conduct comprehensive social audits of constituency development funds and projects in order to fight poverty and curb misuse of these resources. Within three years, comprehensive citizen-led social audits were conducted in 10 constituencies. Corruption was uncovered and problems were addressed by the authorities. In 2010, the civic organization made a strategic decision to empower others by training CSOs and citizens to launch their own social audits. It also developed a new "mini-social audit" in which citizens monitor a single development project in their community, rather than multiple projects throughout their respective constituency.

Mexico: DHP★ (Dejemos de Hacernos Pendejos/Let's quit being an ass/Quit playing dumb) is an emerging civic movement that seeks to alter public apathy, foster civic responsibility, and win accountability, using humor (evident from their name), street actions, stunts, and social networking. In 2009, through digital resistance and on-the-ground actions such as a signature drive, it wielded pressure on incoming members of XLI Legislature to stop giving themselves a tax refund on their Christmas bonuses. It also launched the *Diputómetro*, an interactive digital monitoring platform about legislative activities that is maintained by volunteers, mostly university students.

Philippines: In 2003, a consortium (comprised of CSOs, local community groups, the Public Services Labor Independent Confederation/PSLINK) coordinated by the G-Watch program at the Ateneo School of Government launched a nation-wide campaign in cooperation with the Department of Education to stamp out corruption in the production and delivery of school books. The Textbook Count/Textbook Walk campaign annually mobilized about one million boy and girl scouts to count books. Between 2003 and 2008, textbook prices were reduced by 50 percent, the procurement process was shortened from 24 to 12 months, and ghost deliveries ceased.

Russia: The Movement to Defend Khimki Forest is targeting corruption and impunity, and is employing both nonviolent action and legal efforts to prevent the bisection of an old-growth, state-protected woodland outside Moscow for a large highway and illegal development involving the French firm, Vinci. The European Bank for Reconstruction and Development (EBRD) and the European Investment Bank (EIB) pulled out of the project. In 2010, then President Dmitry Medvedev temporarily suspended the project. In June 2013, Sherpa, the French human rights lawyers' group, along with other European NGOs, filed a formal complaint of corruption against Vinci with the Paris Prosecutor. In October 2013, the Prosecutor announced the opening of a preliminary enquiry into financial crimes.

South Korea: A coalition of 1,104 civic networks and groups launched the "Civil Action for the General Election 2000" (CAGE 2000) campaign to tackle political corruption. It identified malfeasant and ineligible candidates in the general election and pushed for their defeat through a blacklist based on publicly-documented assessments of all initial nominees and final candidates in the National Assembly elections. They held street rallies, petitions, phone and email campaigns, and launched youth websites that included celebrity endorsements. Sixty-nine percent of blacklisted candidates (59 out of 86) lost the elections.

Turkey: In 1997, the six-week "One Minute of Darkness for Constant Light" campaign pressured power-holders to tackle the crime syndicate, which refers to a nation-wide network of politicians, parts of the police, paramilitary groups linked to state security institutions, mafia, and parts of the private sector. Through low-risk mass actions based on turning off lights for one minute every evening at 9:00 p.m., approximately 30 million people mobilized around the country. In the midst of an unanticipated military intervention, it shook up a convoluted system of impunity and corruption. It broke the taboo of exposing the country's crime syndicate, and succeeded in pressuring power-holders to take specific measures, such as trials of some mafia leaders, security forces, and business people.

Uganda: The National Foundation for Democracy and Human Rights in Uganda (NAFODU)-Police-Community Partnership Forum initiated a community-monitoring mobilization that targeted local police intimidation and extortion. Marginalized people exposed police graft through radio call-ins and SMS texts while efforts were made to win elements of law enforcement toward the community, for example through local integrity trainings. Over the course of one year organizers reported a change in police behavior based on citizen input during the weekly radio shows, SMS monitoring, and direct communications with NAFODU's district offices. Toward the end of

the civic initiative officers asked for the help of NAFODU and citizens
to help overcome the problems they faced within the institution.

Notes

i.   Christopher Walker and Sanja Tatic, "Corruption's Drag on Democratic States," *Christian Science Monitor*, August 2, 2006.

ii. "Glossary," U4 Anti-Corruption Resource Centre, accessed March 30, 2014, *http://www.u4.no/glossary/kleptocracy/*.

iii. Minxin Pei, "Government by Corruption," *Forbes*, January 22, 2009.

iv. For research on civil resistance and the history of nonviolent social movements, see the following: Peter Ackerman and Jack DuVall, *A Force More Powerful: A Century of Nonviolent Conflict* (New York: Palgrave, 2000); Howard Clark, ed., *People Power: Unarmed Resistance and Global Solidarity* (London: Pluto Books, 2009); Adrian Karatnycky and Peter Ackerman, *How Freedom is Won: From Civic Resistance to Durable Democracy* (New York: Freedom House, 2005); Adam Roberts and Timothy Garten Ash, eds., *Civil Resistance and Power Politics: The Experience of Non-violent Action from Gandhi to the Present* (Oxford: Oxford University Press, 2009); Kurt Schock, *Unarmed Insurrections: People Power Movements in Nondemocracies* (Minneapolis: University of Minnesota Press, 2005); Stephen Zunes, Lester Kurtz and Sara Beth Asher, eds., *Nonviolent Social Movements: A Geographical Perspective* (Malden: Blackwell, 1999). For additional information, see: Mary King, *A Quiet Revolution: The First Palestinian Intifada and Nonviolent Resistance* (New York: Nation Books, 2007); Maria Stephan, ed., *Civilian Jihad: Nonviolent Struggle, Democratization and Governance in the Middle East* (New York: Palgrave, 2010).

v.   Kanybek Nur-tegin and Hans Czap, "Corruption: Democracy, Autocracy and Political Stability," *Economic Analysis and Policy* 42, no. 1, March 2012.

vi. "China's Xi Warns of Unrest if Graft not Tackled," *Reuters*, November 18, 2012.

vii. Pei, "Government by Corruption."

viii. Andew Jacobs and Chris Buckley, "Chinese Activists Test New Leader and are Crushed," *New York Times*, January 15, 2014.

ix. Shaazka Beyerle, *Curtailing Corruption: People Power for Accountability and Justice*, (Boulder, CO: Lynne Rienner Publishers, 2014).

x.   John Gaventa and Gregory Barrett, "So What Difference Does it Make? Mapping the Outcomes of Citizen Engagement," Institute of Development Studies Working Paper 2010, no. 347, October 2010, accessed November 18, 2014 *http://opendocs.ids.ac.uk/opendocs/bitstream/handle/123456789/902/Wp347.pdf?sequence=1*.

xi. Gene Sharp, *Waging Nonviolent Struggle* (Boston, MA: Porter Sargent Publishers, Inc. 2005).

xii. Aruna Roy, "Survival and Right to Information," Gulam Rasool Third Memorial Lecture. MKSS website, accessed November 18, 2014, *http://www.mkssindia.org/node/42*.

xiii. Sherief Elkatshas, *Shayfeen.com: We're Watching You, Independent Television Service International film, 2007,* accessed November 18, 2014, *http://www.itvs.org/films/shayfeencom.*

xiv. Robin Wright, *Dreams and Shadows: The Future of the Middle East* (New York: Penguin, 2008).

xv. Shaazka Beyerle and Arwa Hassan, "Popular Resistance against Corruption in Turkey and Egypt," in *Civilian Jihad: Nonviolent Struggle, Democratization and Governance in the Middle East,* ed. Maria Stephan (New York: Palgrave Macmillan, 2009), p. 265 – 280.

xvi. Ibid., p. 271.

xvii. This section on the "One Minute of Darkness for Constant Light Campaign" is based on: Shaazka Beyerle, *Curtailing Corruption.*

xviii. Yaroslav Nikitenko, "Save Khimki Forest: Stand with Russia's Human Rights and Environmental Activists," Change.org petition, accessed April 3, 2014, *https://www. change.org/ru/%D0%BF%D0%B5%D1%82%D0%B8%D1%86%D0%B8%D0%B8/ save-khimki-forest-stand-with-russia-s-human-rights-and-environmental-activists.*

xix. Freedom House, "Freedom in the World 2013," accessed November 18, 2014, *https://freedomhouse.org/report/freedom-world/freedom-world-2013#.VGxP51ffNhA;* Freedom House, "Freedom in the World 2014," accessed November 18, 2014, *https:// freedomhouse.org/report/freedom-world/freedom-world-2014#.VGxQEFffNhA .*

xx. Human Rights Watch, "Kenya," *World Report 2014,* accessed November 18, 2014, *http://www.hrw.org/world-report/2014/country-chapters/kenya.*

xxi. This section on the MUHURI social audits is based on: Shaazka Beyerle, *Curtailing Corruption.*

xxii. "It's Our Money. Where's It Gone," International Budget Partnership documentary film. *http://www.youtube.com/watch?v=z2zKXqkrf2E&feature=player_embedded.*

xxiii. "Social Audits as a Budget Monitoring Tool," International Budget Partnership. 2012, 6.

xxiv. Rocio Campos, "Kenya's Muslims for Human Rights (MUHURI) Takes Its Success with Social Audits to the Next Level," International Budget Partnership newsletter, 58 (January-February 2011), accessed November 18, 2014, *http://internationalbudget.org/ wp-content/uploads/2011/04/newsletter58.pdf.*

xxv. Ibid.

xxvi. "It's Our Money. Where's It Gone,"; Faith Muiruri, "New law guarantees right to information, representation," Special Report, *The Link,* November 2012, *http://www. kas.de/wf/doc/kas_32744-1522-1-30.pdf?121115081109.*

xxvii. This section on the Movement to Defend Khimki Forest is based on personal communications with Evgenia Chirikova and other members who wish to remain anonymous.

xxviii. "Evgenia Chirikova," The Goldman Environmental Prize, 2012, accessed April 3, 2014, *http://www.goldmanprize.org/recipient/evgenia-chirikova.*

xxix. "Vinci – A Cover for Oligarchs and Tax Havens in Russia's First Road PPP," CEE Bankwatch Network, April 30, 2011.

xxx. "Hearings on Khimki Forest in the European Parliament – First Step Towards Changes?" khimkinews, June 27, 2012, accessed April 3, 2014, *http://www.khimkiforest. org/news/hearings-khimki-forest-european-parliament-%E2%80%93-first-step-towards-changes*.

xxxi. "Evgenia Chirikova," The Goldman Environmental Prize; J.Y., "Russian Politics: Yevgenia Chirikova," *The Economist*," October 13, 2012.

xxxii. "NGOs Welcome Enquiry by Paris Prosecutor Into Financial Crimes Related to the VINCI CONCESSIONS RUSSIE SA Moscow-St. Petersburg Motorway," CEE Bankwatch Network, October 4, 2013, accessed November 18, 2014, *http:// bankwatch.org/news-media/for-journalists/press-releases/ngos-welcome-enquiry-paris-prosecutor-financial-crimes-rel*.

xxxiii. John Ackerman, "Human Rights and Social Accountability." *The World Bank Social Development Papers: Participation and Civic Engagement* no. 86, May, 2005, p. 3.

xxxiv. Sherief Elkatshas, Shayfeen.com.

xxxv. *Manuela Garza, "Social Audits as a Budget Monitoring Tool," International Budget Partnership, 6, October 2012, accessed November 18, 2014, http://internationalbudget.org/ wp-content/uploads/Social-Audits-as-a-Budget-Monitoring-Tool.pdf.*

xxxvi. Leon Aron, "Talking to the Vanguard," *Foreign Policy*, February 7, 2012, 3, accessed November 18, 2014, *http://www.foreignpolicy.com/articles/2012/02/07/talking_to_the_vanguard*.

xxxvii. Hardy Merriman, "Forming a Movement" Presentation, Fletcher Summer Institute for the Advanced Study of Strategic Nonviolent Conflict, Tufts University, June 20, 2011.

xxxviii. Ezel Akay and Liam Mahoney, *A Call to End Corruption* (Minneapolis: Center for Victims of Torture, 2003), p. 2.

PART THREE

CASE STUDIES OF CIVIL RESISTANCE

It's All About the Strategy: Civil Resistance in Bahrain and Challenges Facing Nonviolent Activism in the Gulf

Nada Alwadi
Bahraini independent journalist and researcher

INTRODUCTION

Influenced by the waves of the Arab Awakening, the Gulf region has been witnessing some major tremors since the year 2011. The claims for more democratic systems in Bahrain, Kuwait, Saudi Arabia, Oman, UAE, and even Qatar have been increasingly raised not only by activists and democracy fighters, but even by intellectuals and officials who are known for their loyalty to existing regimes. The idea of having a more democratic Gulf is becoming more popular in the region; however, democratic transition seems to remain a remote possibility. Challenges for the transition to democracy arise from the concentration of absolute monarchies and wide range of entrenched, interest-based networks in the region. Nonetheless, the emerging Gulf youth movements, especially the one which began in Bahrain in early 2011, are starting to break the rules in this region which has been politically stuck for decades. The most surprising result of the Bahraini movement for many in the West was the unforeseen activism of its Gulf neighbors, above all Saudi Arabia. Many believed that the Arab awakening movements had somehow bypassed the Gulf, but the sustained movement in Bahrain, as well as other organized efforts across the region proved the Gulf is not immune to change. In fact, democratic transition in the Gulf region is an old goal; people in the Gulf have been demanding more rights from the state and organizing themselves since the beginning of the last century. What they have always been lacking is a long-term strategy which takes into account the challenging factors in their environment and provides a new vision for the future in this part of the world.

TRANSITION TO DEMOCRACY IN THE GULF REGION: BIG CHALLENGES

There are several challenges limiting the chances for a smooth democratic transition in the Gulf region. The civil society in the Gulf is generally weak and divided; the economies are rentier in nature due to depending on petroleum industries, with the traditional mentality of ruling families which mainly control the petroleum industry. The economic interests of the major players in the international community are tied to the political economy of this region, which is why the international powers are in favor of keeping the status quo.

Weak and Divided Societies

One of the major challenges facing the Gulf societies now and in the near future is what is called *"the demographic imbalance"*; this definition refers to the "societies which have big percentages of foreigners living in their land and participating in the economic, social and cultural welfare for extended periods of time."[i] Based on recent statistics, the percentages of foreigners to citizens in the Gulf region are between 25 percent to 85 percent, and they represent between 54 percent to 94 percent of the total percentage of residents of the Gulf countries.[ii] The demographic imbalance has an impact on Gulf societies; citizens in this region are no longer a majority in some cases; they have become one minority among many other minorities in many of the Gulf States.

While some Gulf States such as Bahrain and Kuwait have very well established and strong civil society organizations, others have not been able to build a strong civil society outside of a government umbrella. These states are less likely to witness organized efforts to democratize their societies.

While the middle class in the Gulf States is large (between 26 percent to 40 percent of the population in the Gulf), the youthful majority (between 42 percent to 52 percent)[iii] is facing serious challenges with issues like unemployment, lack of political participation, and the weak civil society. This has been the perfect opportunity for radical Islamist groups to recruit young people from the Gulf region in the past decade.

Sectarian tension in the Gulf region has been the focus of many studies and books in recent years. In his book *Sectarian Gulf: Bahrain, Saudi Arabia and the Arab Spring that wasn't*, Toby Matthiesen argues that "when faced with rising political challenges in early 2011, the Gulf states – Bahrain and Saudi Arabia in particular – mobilized sectarianism in order to suppress domestic calls for reform... I saw first-hand how the invention of a Shiite threat narrative unfolded standing on the now demolished Pearl Roundabout in the Bahraini capital Manama in mid–February 2011."[iv] Matthiesen was one of very few observers who looked at the role played by regimes in the Gulf in escalating the sectarian tensions. Authoritarian regimes raise sectarian tensions in order to divide populations, especially when faced with popular demands. It's evident that publics in the Gulf have been systematically divided into sectarian and tribal groups, unable to reach one strong national identity.

Rentier State and Traditional Mentality

The biggest group to oppose any change in the region has been comprised of members of the ruling families as well as those who hold power around them. They would be the first to lose if a new democratic system was introduced in the region, which would require sharing power and wealth with the people. Recent events in the Gulf suggest that the regimes have no intention to introduce any real change; most of what have been offered in the past few years have included cosmetic changes and gratuities given to citizens. None of the regimes can support a sustainable solution and a real transition to democracy.

Members of the ruling families in the Gulf are technically a minority but make up the majority of those holding leading positions in ministries and state institutions. They receive monthly allowances and enjoy legal immunities.[v] This traditional mentality sustained itself within a rentier economic system, and was encouraged when the oil prices went up during the 70s and the 80s. Oil revenues flooded to the Gulf and increased the financial ability of these regimes to sustain their traditional system, reinforcing their ability to hold on to power.

This kind of system opens the door to corruption and exploitation of authority. In fact, the popular uprising of Bahrain in 2011 was partly fueled by evidence showing involvement of members of the Bahraini ruling family in corruption dealing with land ownership.[vi]

International Interests – External Actors

Since independence from the British in the early 70s, Gulf States developed powerful alliances with the West; strong economic, political and military ties were built between the GCC countries and the United States as well as other Western countries. The US military has bases in several countries in the region, and Gulf States rely heavily on Western countries for implicit security guarantees against any threats. These strong alliances have always been essential in supporting the status quo in this region and strengthening the position of the regimes, which has resulted in their continuous repression of any pro-democracy movement or activity in the past.

A new U.S approach to Gulf security has been called for by many researchers and political scientists in Washington DC over the past few years in reaction to the Bahraini crisis and the human rights violations in the whole region. This new approach propounds the idea that a more democratic and sustainable Gulf is in the interest of the United States.

In an article published for the Carnegie Endowment for International Peace, political scientist Frederic Wehrey argues, "The United States must focus more on promoting political and security sector reforms in the Gulf that are critical to long-term regional stability by better integrating its use of military and diplomatic tools."

He recommends making Bahrain the focus of US reform promotion in the Gulf, and that the US administration should empower government and opposition moderates to reconcile, using a road map of political and institutional reforms. He even suggests that "If the situation deteriorates, Washington should prepare a contingency plan for moving the US Fifth Fleet headquarters out of Bahrain."[vii]

NONVIOLENT RESISTANCE IN THE GULF REGION – BAHRAIN AS AN EXAMPLE

It is hard for those who have been following the pro-democracy movement unfolding in Bahrain since 2011 to miss one of the most popular phrases used by protesters and supporters of the movement: "Somood" which means "steadfastness." After three years of repression the idea of "Somood" remains popular among activists and freedom fighters in Bahrain and many supporters in the general public alike; many people don't miss any chance to use this catch phrase on social media platforms, on the streets, and even in their day-to-day conversations, raising their hands with the victory sign.

Analysts argue that Bahrain and Kuwait witnessed the peak actions of civil resistance in recent years compared to the rest of the countries in the Gulf region. However, one can't overlook the organized efforts in countries like Saudi Arabia which witnessed three major movements in recent years: the Shia movement in the eastern province; the movement of the families of prisoners; and the Saudi women's movement for the right to drive. Several movements appeared in other Gulf countries such as the movement against corruption in Oman, and petitions presented by the intellectual elites in UAE and Qatar requesting constitutional amendments. All of these organized efforts argue against the assumption that the Gulf countries—unlike other Arab countries—are going to be stable based on factors including oil rents, small and homogeneous populations, robust security forces, and high levels of wealth. Even if we don't see those changes in the Gulf on a formal political level, pressures exist at informal political and social levels, which can be seen in the activist work in several countries in the Gulf region.[viii] Furthermore, technology and social media have played a great role in rallying youth in this region, creating a space for them to interact and share ideas about change in their communities, even if their actions do not directly challenge existing regimes. For example, one of the slogans used by the movement in Kuwait is addressed to the Amir himself, and says, "We will not allow you," which is a bold and unprecedented statement for people in this region.

These recent movements in the Gulf countries are a reminder of the year 1938 during which this region witnessed a remarkable development. Three movements emerged in Bahrain, Dubai, and Kuwait that year—all then under British "protection"—calling for a greater say in ruling matters, even daring to ask for a representative assembly. Although this was not the first political initiative in Bahrain,[ix] it was up until then the most coherent and organized. The movements in Bahrain and Dubai were put down, and only in Kuwait did an elected assembly emerge for a few months before being disbanded. This set the tone for future political activities in Bahrain, swinging between regime overthrow and reform, clandestine and public activity, and broad-based coalitions and factional movements.[x]

Political movements in Bahrain faced great repression by the state since the 1950s; therefore it was not surprising to the Bahrainis to witness the great repression against political activists following the popular "Feb 14" movement in 2011. Authorities in Bahrain increased their internal repression to the maximum, imprisoning and torturing activists and political leaders, muzzling outspoken bloggers and journalists, and enacting draconian censorship laws. The Bahraini movement in 2011 was unique in many ways; it was viewed as part of the Arab awakening and therefore was joined by many supporters (both Shia and Sunni) before the state media started using the sectarian card portraying the movement as violent, Shia-centered and allied to external powers: Iran and Hezbollah.

Repression and state media were not the only problems facing the movement in Bahrain in 2011. The lack of a unified strategy for the movement led to premature actions being taken by the activists and protesters on the ground; these actions were later viewed as the main factors responsible for the weakening of the movement. In an interview published at the popular website "Bahrain Mirror"[xi] a few months after the crackdown in 2011, prominent Bahraini opposition figure and anthropology Professor Abdulhadi Khalaf analyzed the strategic mistakes made by the movement and said, "the 'Feb 14' movement achieved a lot in a short period of time, especially in mobilizing people to protest and persuading new groups to join, however, two strategic mistakes were committed: the first one was calling for civil disobedience at a very early stage when the people were not ready, and the expansion of the protests to include crucial areas like the Bahrain harbor before all political groups agreed on this step." Khalaf, who published a book[xii] on "civil resistance" in 1986 and introduced the idea of "nonviolent actions" to the Bahrainis, argues that the movement in Bahrain needs to get organized, draw a detailed map of the pillars of support behind the current system in Bahrain, and strategize their actions for the long term. During the past three years after the 2011 crackdown on the movement in Bahrain the political society has become more fragmented than ever. The pro-democracy movement still has no defined public leadership; it has made some activists into public heroes, such as famous hunger striker Abdulhadi Alkhawaja, and human rights defender Nabeel Rajab (both currently in prison), but these are icons who are influential in the movement rather than leaders who command it. Political parties and civil society organizations have been working together organizing protests and public events, lobbying international media, and speaking at global outlets to keep the discussion on the Bahraini crisis alive. Their demands were explained in the "Manama Document" issued in 2012. However, every day the gap widens between these efforts and the situation on the ground, where villages witness frequent clashes between police and youth groups, who increasingly use more extreme measures such as Molotov cocktails or metal rods. These groups, such as the youth of "Feb 14" and coalition of "Feb 14," decided to "defend themselves" against state repression, believing that other efforts will not be fruitful. Their discourse and statements included more religious terms in recent years, revolving around "resistance" and "self-defense."[xiii]

Even though the situation doesn't look very promising, strategic nonviolent actions could still prove to be effective in this tiny island.

One of the ongoing success stories is the campaign to rebuild the destroyed mosques in Shia villages. During the crackdown in 2011, the Bahraini authority backed and supported by the GCC countries (Saudi Arabia in particular) demolished around 38 mosques in many Shia villages—one of them believed to be over 400 years old. This repression was seen by the Shia majority as an attack against their beliefs and cultural identity. According to Sheikh Maytham Al Salman, Chairman of the Bahrain interfaith center, a spontaneous action by many people took place right after the state demolished 38 mosques. [xiv] People started gathering at the sites of each demolished mosque to perform their prayers. This collective action was taken by the people and then encouraged by religious leaders. The issue of demolished mosques went viral, and US President Barack Obama mentioned it in a speech in 2011. According to Al Salman, joint prayers—*jamaat*—are held in some of the demolished mosques daily while the majority of the 38 demolished mosques hold prayers every Saturday. He said: "crowds attending the prayers are from different lifestyles, ages and social backgrounds. They insist on continuing prayers in the demolished mosques to convey a message to the regime, stating that Shias are still there after the crackdown. They believe they are not only praying but preserving their national and religious identity; they believe they are safeguarding their cultural heritage." This action played a major role in driving the government of Bahrain to announce the rebuilding of 30 of the 38 demolished mosques.

CONCLUSION

Minor and cosmetic changes are not enough to lead the Gulf countries to be more democratic. It is time for major changes to be implemented, offering a more sustainable democratic system in the Gulf. Those major shifts require civic mobilization and strong and well-organized efforts from the grassroots of Gulf societies. Countries like Bahrain and Kuwait witnessed major movements and civic mobilization, but interest-based networks are challenging the shift toward a more democratic Gulf and a just society. Movements in the Gulf need to revisit the power map in their region and draw a long-term strategy for their actions to be more effective in bringing change to this region.

Notes

i.   Omar Alshehabi, "Demographic imbalance in the GCC countries. Its history, causes and how to face it," Development Forum, Feb 8, 2013, accessed November 18, 2014, *https://www.gulfpolicies.com/index.php?option=com_content&view=article&id=1280:2013-01-29-21-58-20&catid=145:2011-04-09-07-47-04* .

ii. Ibid., 22, table 6, based on: Martin Baldwin-Edwards, "Labor Immigration and Labor Markets in the GCC Countries: National Patterns and Trends", Kuwait Programme on Development, Governance and Globalization in the Gulf States, London School of Economics, No. 15 (2011), p. 17, Table 9.

iii. Dr. Hassan Alaali, "Middle Class in GCC countries," Aljazeera Center for Studies, July 22, 2013, accessed November 18, 2014, *http://studies.aljazeera.net/repor ts/2013/07/201372272619767829.htm*.

iv. Toby Matthiesen, "The Sectarian Gulf vs the Arab spring," *Foreign Policy*, August 10, 2013, accessed November 18, 2014, *http://www.tobymatthiesen.com/wp/newspaper_ articles/the-sectarian-gulf-vs-the-arab-spring/*.

v.   Abdulhadi Khalaf, "Plunder narratives and the Bahraini Spring," *Alsaffir*, July 11, 2012, accessed November 18, 2014, *http://arabi.assafir.com/article.asp?aid=85&refsite=arabi&ref type=leftmenu&refzone=authorarticles* .

vi. Sara Chayes and Matar Matar, "Bahrain's shifting sand," Carnegie Endowment for International Peace, Feb 13, 2013, accessed November 18, 2014, *http://m.ceip. org/2013/02/13/bahrain-s-shifting-sands/fgn1?lang=en*.

vii. Fredrik Wehrey, "A new US approach to Gulf Security," Carnegie Endowment for International Peace, March 10, 2014, accessed November 18, 2014, *http:// carnegieendowment.org/2014/03/10/new-u.s.-approach-to-gulf-security/h30d*.

viii. For more information on youth activism in the Gulf, refer to Kristin Diwan, "Breaking Taboos: Youth Activism in the Gulf States," Atlantic Council, March 2014, accessed November 14, 2014, *http://www.atlanticcouncil.org/publications/issue-briefs/ breaking-taboos-youth-activism-in-the-gulf-states*.

ix. For more information refer to Hassan Radhi, "Events in Bahrain: the Crisis and the Way Out," Development forum, Feb 8, 2013, accessed November 18, 2014, *https:// www.gulfpolicies.com/index.php?option=com_content&view=article&id=790:2012-02-20-16-06-10&catid=147:2011-04-09-07-47-31*.

x.   Omar Alshehabi, "Political Movements in Bahrain, Past, Present and Future," Jadaliyya, Feb 14, 2012, accessed November 18, 2014, *http://www.jadaliyya.com/pages/ index/4363/political-movements-in-bahrain_past-present-and-fu*.

xi. Abdulhadi Khalaf, Interview with Abdulhadi Khalaf, *Bahrain Mirror* staff, "Nonviolent Resistance in Bahrain Now," *Bahrain Mirror*, June, 1, 2011, accessed November 18, 2014, *http://www.bahrainmirror.com/news/1029.html*.

xii.   Abdulhadi Khalaf, "Civil Resistance," IAR (RAWAFED Ltd), 1986, accessed
        November 18, 2014, *http://zaaherrr.files.wordpress.com/2014/04/almouqawma.pdf.*

xiii.   Jane Kinninmont, "Bahrain: Beyond the Impasse," Chatham House, June 2012,
        accessed November 18, 2014, *http://www.chathamhouse.org/sites/default/files/public/
        Research/Middlepercent20East/pr0612kinninmont.pdf.*

xiv.   Shaikh Maytham Alsalman, Chairman of the Bahrain Interfaith Center. Interview by
        Nada Alwadi. Skype, April 22, 2014.

CHAPTER 9

Politics as Trojan Horse

Howard Barrell
Senior Lecturer, School of Journalism, Media and Cultural Studies
Cardiff University

P OLITICS AND ARMED STRUGGLE have conventionally been seen as mutually reinforcing in conflicts in which the weak take on the strong. This certainly was the case in most Marxist and anti-colonial struggles, and appears again to be so in a number of current conflicts involving jihadis. Recent research suggests, however, that armed struggle might have needed such a relationship far more than politics has. This research shows that struggles for maximal outcomes such as regime change that are waged by civil resistance movements—that is, by those employing only nonviolent, *political* tactics—are, for all practical purposes, neither helped nor hindered if others choose to conduct armed struggles in parallel to them. It shows, moreover, that struggles that use only nonviolent, political tactics are twice as likely to succeed as those that resort to armed struggle. Politics, it would seem, is sufficient. Armed struggle, by comparison, begins to look as if it might be rather needy.[i]

This article explores how a number of groups that have pursued armed struggle—groups that Chenoweth and Stephan term 'radical flanks'—have wanted political activities to complement their own violent projects. There has been no single view across all such armed groups. Perspectives have differed. But they have generally seen nonviolent, political mobilization as being capable in some degree of redressing the early asymmetries of force with which insurgent movements usually have to contend. In the case of jihadi armed struggles the corresponding form mobilization takes is conceived of as religio-political.

The approach taken by this article entails looking at how radical flanks view political activity or civil resistance movements, rather than the other way round. Doing so from this rather unusual point of view does, however, offer a set of insights. First, the article explores the different ways in which the relationship between armed struggle and civil resistance has been cast by various proponents of armed struggle. Second, and more important, this approach should enable us to see how mobilization by nonviolent, political means can help achieve the encirclement of a regime—encirclement, that is, not merely from without but also *from within*. Moreover, as will become apparent further below (and at the risk of mixing a mess of metaphors), it will show how encirclement of a regime can induce a tipping point in a civil resistance struggle.

To reach that point, the article briefly surveys the perspectives developed in four armed struggles, each of which marks out a different way of seeing the politico-military relationship in asymmetric contests. The examples do not pretend to offer a full typology; they do, however, mark out some of the poles in the debate. The first case is the Bolshevik Revolution in Russia in 1917. The second is the perspective developed by Mao Zedong in China's communist revolution that lasted some 28 years to 1949. The article then remarks upon an influential though disputed historical account of the Cuban revolution between 1953 and 1959. And finally it turns its attention to some of the paradoxes that unfolded in the struggle against apartheid in South Africa after the adoption of armed struggle in the name of the African National Congress (ANC) in 1960. These paradoxes then return the focus of the article to Mao and the issue of encirclement.

Any armed struggle for regime change can, and usually does, claim to be in service to a political objective. But a paradox seems invariably to follow. Once the resort to arms is decided, all subsequent political organizing is considered by the leadership in question to be, to some degree, subject to the imperatives of armed struggle.

Russia's World War I revolution was the product of a quite exceptional set of circumstances in its then capital, Petrograd. Economic crisis and agitation by a range of leftist and liberal political factions had driven workers, the unemployed, women, and children into the streets. Thousands of Russian soldiers had deserted the long front against Germany. Sailors at the Kronstad base near the city were openly seeking a revolutionary outcome. And in August the country's provisional government, a coalition of liberals and socialists that had taken power after Tsar Nicholas's abdication in March, distributed arms to various leftist factions to help it defeat an anticipated military putsch by the army. Recipients of these arms included V. I. Lenin's small Bolshevik caucus within the Russian Social Democratic and Labor Party.

In October, the Bolsheviks used these same arms to mount their armed insurrection—in the Marxist lexicon, that is a quick-fire, convulsive uprising comprising basically three kinds of tactics: armed attacks on the citadels of state power, popular demonstrations, and defections from the ranks of state security forces.[ii] During the event, strikes and demonstrations involving ordinary citizens played a minor role; this resulted in the Bolsheviks' seizure of power more closely resembling a coup d'etat by a small conspiratorial group taking advantage of popular unrest than a popular revolutionary act.

Without the creative intervention of Mao, who was a rising star in the Chinese Communist Party by the late 1920s, Russian communists might have succeeded in their attempts to make the narrow conspiracy and armed insurrection that characterized the events of October 1917 in Petrograd *the* model that communists elsewhere in the world had to follow in the forthcoming class and anti-colonial wars of the 20th century. The Bolsheviks energetically promoted the approach through the Communist International (or Comintern), formed in 1919. The chronic and costly failure of armed insurrections that followed across Europe and China in the 1920s[iii] prompted Mao to challenge this Russian attempt to impose strategic orthodoxy.

Through the 1930s, Mao put together an alternative strategic vision on how to fight—and win—asymmetric wars.[iv,1] His key

---

[1] What follows is my summary of Mao Zedong's strategy.

innovation was the part he saw ordinary people playing in revolutionary struggle, and the role he saw for nonviolent, political organization in equipping them for that struggle. The emphasis Mao placed on political organization was, however, always intended primarily to help deliver *military* victory.

Four themes developed in Mao's thinking. The first centered on the best use of geographic space. Insurrectionary strategy alone had succeeded in the circumstances of Petrograd in 1917, where the state had been exceptionally weak, but not elsewhere. Whereas the challenge before revolutionaries was to reverse asymmetry, in most cases the strategy of armed insurrection exacerbated its effects. It was madness to choose to face better trained and equipped forces within a confined urban space—as armed insurrection seemed to demand. Doing so invited encirclement and annihilation. Being the weaker force in a war—the position in which revolutionary forces almost always found themselves in the early phases of a conflict—required that forces be capable of mobility if they were to survive and fight effectively. That meant revolutionaries had to contrive to fight on more expansive terrain, not within a few city blocks. They often needed large, open spaces. A second theme in Mao's thinking was that training revolutionary forces to the required level took a great deal of time. Traditionally, military theorists had argued a war was best fought quickly. But Mao now suggested that it could be to the weaker side's advantage to fight a long war—the better to be able to train up and blood its forces, and to attenuate and exhaust its enemy. In this sense, time too was a form of space. The third theme was that the most important factor in reversing asymmetry entailed winning the participation of ordinary people. This mobilization should be achieved primarily by political means. Doing so could provide one's military forces with fresh recruits, intelligence, shelter, and the means to fight behind enemy lines. Mao was conjuring up a notion of what we can usefully call 'political space'—a space created by *political* means but serving *military* imperatives. Together, these three themes supported a fourth in Mao's thinking: the possibility for counter-encirclement of an opponent. As with encirclement in Mao's thinking so, too, counter-encirclement meant encirclement from both without and from within—an insight brilliantly captured by Yale's Scott Boorman using the metaphor of *wei-ch'i*, an East Asian board game in which two players try to capture each other's territory.[v]

The very antithesis of Mao's approach found voice in two dubious accounts of the Cuban revolution—one by Che Guevara, the other by French philosopher Regis Debray.[vi] Their books largely wrote out of history the importance of nonviolent, political work that had been done mainly in the cities in the latter 1950s by variegated socialists and trade unionists in support of the armed struggle in the rural areas waged by Fidel Castro's 26th of July Movement. Starkly in the case of Debray, less so Guevara, the two men suggested that Cuba showed that redressing asymmetry did not require nonviolent, political organization. Rather, the mere commencement of armed struggle itself could and would adequately organize revolutionaries' popular support base. This point of view, influential in the 1960s and early 1970s, would come to be considered partly responsible for the arrival of terrorist groups such as the German Red Brigades and Palestinian Black September and, so, as a disaster for the militant Left.[vii]

Attempts by the ANC of South Africa to arrive at what it considered an appropriate relationship between military and political forms of struggle produced a series of paradoxical outcomes. Having spent 48 years using Gandhian civil resistance, in 1960 sections of its leadership and of the outlawed communist party decided to embark upon armed struggle after a massacre of 69 unarmed protestors and the outlawing of the ANC. Those ANC and communist party leaders still at liberty deployed their best activists into armed roles. This undermined the prospects of reorganizing their political base in the new circumstances. Some ANC leaders active at that time attributed this emphasis on armed struggle partly to the influence of Guevara's book.[viii] By 1965, the ANC and its allies had been completely suppressed inside South Africa. The organization's very focus on armed struggle had, paradoxically, undermined its ability to sustain armed struggle.

Four years later, the ANC declared in a contradictory formulation of strategy that armed struggle was now the 'the only method left open' to it.[ix] Yet that same year in 1969, radical nonviolent black political organization re-emerged openly inside South Africa among black students. A few years later radical political organization also re-emerged among black workers. The ANC's initial response from exile was suspicion: it argued that no legal space existed for open, authentic black political organization. When in 1976 this domestic black political resurgence prompted a series of uprisings, the exiled ANC received a new generation of younger recruits. It quickly resumed armed infiltration after 10 years of being unable to do so. As it had in the early 1960s, the ANC again deployed almost all of its new recruits to military tasks. Resources deployed to nonviolent, political organizing were minuscule. By 1978, the ANC worried that its armed struggle remained at an extremely low level of intensity. A delegation of its leadership visited Vietnam to seek advice. Senior veterans of the Vietnamese struggle blamed the ANC's lack of political organization. Again, the ANC's very emphasis on armed struggle had undermined its capacity to wage armed struggle.[x]

Over the following five years, the ANC played political catch-up inside South Africa. Despite some leadership obstruction, others in exile succeeded in developing close relations with popular political organizations formed independently of the ANC inside South Africa. Gradually, ANC aligned as an autonomous political organization cohered inside South Africa and, in 1983, formed the United Democratic Front (UDF), an umbrella confederation that aggregated the demands of hundreds of pre-existing organizations representing millions. The UDF used only nonviolent political means despite sustained and acute pressure on it from apartheid security forces, survived, and grew. By the mid-1980s, it and the black trade unions had become the most important domestic forces for change.

For the ANC's exiled leadership, the main significance of the resurgence of popular political organization inside the country was the opportunity it was thought to provide for the escalation of armed struggle. If such an opportunity indeed now existed, the ANC failed to exploit it. By the late 1980s, the armed struggle was residual. The UDF organizations and their members had not submitted to military imperatives. There was very little incentive to do so. Politics by nonviolent means were considerably more effective than armed struggle had been or seemed capable of ever being. It was a twist some ANC leaders found difficult to accept: the radical flank had been outflanked.

The outcome in South Africa was a demonstration of the power of politics by nonviolent means in a situation of acute conflict. Civil resistance methods had demonstrated in South Africa what Chenoweth and Stephan call their 'participation advantage'[xi]: they involved millions in confronting the apartheid regime across a wide variety of tactics. These included strikes, boycotts, marches, rallies, petitions, and representations. Pressure "from without"—applied by the black majority on the regime—was rapidly approaching a tipping point. This rise in civil resistance pressure in South Africa is quite plausibly explained by the model suggested by American economist Timur Kuran to describe the growth of contemporaneous challenges to communist rule in Eastern Europe.[xii] Kuran argues that each individual has a tipping point at which fear of the cost of opposing an oppressive government is trumped by revulsion for it. He calls this point an individual's 'revolutionary threshold.' Until that threshold is breeched, an individual is likely to hide his personal desire for change. How is this threshold calculated? It is that percentage of the population that must be active in the opposition for an individual to feel he, too, can relatively safely participate. For example, Mr A may feel it is safe to participate when 1 percent of the population is involved. (In reality, A's judgment of whether the proportion participating meets his threshold is more likely to be made intuitively. But Kuran's desire to put a figure to it is defensible.) If many others have the same threshold as Mr A they, too, will also be drawn into active opposition when 1 percent of people are seen to be participating. The addition of Mr A and other one-percenters to the ranks of those active in the opposition may, in turn, drive the proportion participating up to 2 percent. This then draws in people whose threshold is 2 percent. This new group of participants may then drive the proportion involved in the opposition to 3 percent, drawing in yet another cohort, this time with a 3 percent revolutionary threshold. And so on, in exponential fashion. This process can be accelerated further by a lowering of the revolutionary threshold, resulting from, perhaps, increased sympathy for the opposition or a decline in government efficiency.

Kuran's model prompts the question: at what level of participation in a civil resistance movement might a target government topple? Estimates differ. Mark Irving Lichbach, reckons active participation by just 5 percent of a population is often adequate for revolutionary success. [xiii] Chenoweth and Stephan report that no civil resistance struggle is known to have failed where it achieved the active and sustained participation of at least 3.5 percent of the population.[xiv] That's all. That's not to say 3.5 percent participation in opposition activity is a condition sufficient to guarantee regime change; nor that achieving that level of involvement is a necessity for success. Rather, their research shows a strong correlation between this minimum level of active participation in opposition activity in a civil resistance struggle and regime change.

By the time the apartheid government began negotiating with the black opposition after 1990, *political* pressures and persuasion had convinced a critical mass of apartheid's intelligence, security and military chiefs, white businessmen, intellectuals, and many others that an accommodation with black aspirations was, if they were to serve their own self-interest, necessary. Persuasion included a series of open, but also sometimes undisclosed, meetings between the ANC and white establishment figures outside South Africa. In the course of these meetings they were persuaded, also, that a mature accommodation with the ANC was possible. Although the *wei-ch'i* metaphor Boorman has applied to explain Mao's strategy and tactics cannot be transferred to the strategic use of nonviolent action in civil resistance, the end of apartheid seemed to show that one rule of both the board game and Maoist strategy was relevant to civil resistance. It was that encircling an opponent effectively involved not only surrounding and pressurizing him from without; it involved also penetrating and undermining his political programme and support —and persuading him—from *within*. South Africa also showed that this need to encircle from within was particularly well catered to by civil resistance's stress on political engagement with an opponent, his allies and the instruments of his power.

Notes

i.   Erica Chenoweth and Maria Stephan, *Why Civil Resistance Works: The Strategic Logic of Nonviolent Conflict.* (New York: Columbia University Press, 2011).

ii. Harold Walter Nelson, *Leon Trotsky and the Art of Insurrection, 1905-1917,* (London: Frank Cass and Company, 1988). See also: A. Neuberg, *Armed Insurrection,* (London: New Left Books, 1928/1970). A. Neuberg was a collective pseudonym used by a number of agents of the Communist International (Comintern). *Armed Insurrection* was originally published in German in 1928 and then in French in 1931 as a primer for communist parties across the world. It was first published in English in the edition cited here.

iii. Neuberg, *Armed Insurrection.*

iv. See Mao Zedong, *Selected Military Writings of Mao Tse-Tung,* (Peking: Foreign Languages Press, 1967); Mao Tse-Tung, *Selected Works of Mao Tse-Tung, Volume II,* (Peking: Foreign Languages Press, 1975); Mao Tse-Tung, *Selected Works of Mao Tse-Tung, Volume III,* (Peking: Foreign Languages Press, 1975); Mao Tse-Tung, *Selected Works of Mao Tse-Tung, Volume IV,* (Peking: Foreign Languages Press, 1977).

v.   Scott A. Boorman, *The Protracted Game: A Wei-ch'i Interpretation of Maoist Revolutionary Strategy,* (New York: Oxford University Press, 1969).

vi. Che Guevara, *Guerrilla Warfare,* (Harmondsworth: Pelican, 1961/1969); Regis Debray, *Revolution in the Revolution? Armed Struggle and Political Struggle in Latin America,* (New York: Grove Press, 1967).

vii. Oral debates the author has witnessed in Left circles.

viii. Howard Barrell, "Conscripts to Their Age: African National Congress Strategy, 1976-1986," (doctoral thesis, Oxford University, 1993), accessed November 18, 2014, *http://www.nelsonmandela.org/omalley/index.php/site/q/03lv02424/04lv02712/05lv02713.htm.*

ix. African National Congress, "First National Consultative Conference: Report on the Strategy and Tactics of the African National Congress," 1969, accessed April 16 2014, *http://www.anc.org.za/show.php?id=149.*

x.   Barrell, "Conscripts to Their Age."

xi. Chenoweth and Stephan, *Why Civil Resistance Works.*

xii. Timur Kuran, "Sparks and Prairie Fires: A Theory of Unanticipated Revolution," *Public Choice,* Vol. 61, No. 1, (1989); see also: Timur Kuran, "Now out of Never: The Element of Surprise in the East European Revolution of 1989," *World Politics.* Vol. 44, No. 1, (1989).

xiii. Mark Irving Lichbach. *The Rebel's Dilemma,* (Ann Arbor: University of Michigan Press, 1998), p. 11-13, p. 16-19.

xiv. Chenoweth and Stephan, *Why Civil Resistance Works;* see also Erica Chenoweth, "Civil Resistance and the 3.5% Rule," (presentation, TEDxBoulder, September 21, 2013), accessed November 18, 2014, *http://rationalinsurgent.com/2013/11/04/my-talk-at-tedxboulder-civil-resistance-and-the-3-5-rule/.*

CHAPTER 10

Myopia of the Syrian Struggle and Key Lessons[1]

Maciej J. Bartkowski
Director for Education and Research at the International Center on Nonviolent Conflict

Julia Taleb
Independent Journalist with a focus on the Middle East.

FAILURE OF THE ARMED RESISTANCE

By any measure the armed struggle against the Assad regime has been a failure. The armed struggle failed to topple the Assad government, protect civilians, or bring more rights and freedoms to Syrians. Although Assad's government is primarily responsible for the atrocities, the opposition's militarization of the resistance has contributed significantly to what is considered to be the worst humanitarian crisis in the last two decades, which—as of August 2014—has left more than 190,000 people dead, 6.5 million internally displaced, and close to 3 million as registered refugees. Among other things, the armed resistance invited an influx of foreign fighters, decreased the chances of possible reconciliation among various ethnic groups, and made the

[1] We would like to acknowledge that analytical and narrative text in an unpublished article on Syria written by Peter Ackerman, Mohja Kahf and Maciej Bartkowski provided important source material for this article. We would also like to thank Stephen Zunes for his recommendations and suggestions on improving the content of this article.

prospect of a democratic outcome highly unlikely. A number of the 'liberated areas' in Syria are now experiencing deep tensions and open conflicts among various armed groups[i] that vie for power and control while endangering the lives of civilians.

Achievements of nonviolent resistance have not been fully assessed and little consideration has been given to possible strategic gains that could have been accomplished had the resistance remained nonviolent. The myopic strategies of the Syrian resistance paralleled a general failure of the international community to provide effective assistance to the Syrian nonviolent movement.

RISE AND FORCE OF THE SYRIAN CIVIL RESISTANCE

The Syrian nonviolent resistance, manifested in mass demonstrations that began on March 15, 2011, created the gravest challenge to the Syrian Baathists in more than 40 years of their rule. The threat was greater than all combined armed uprisings by the Muslim Brotherhood or Kurds in recent Syrian history and more effective than any other opposition toward the Assad regime, including the so-called "Damascus Spring" in 2005. During the first six months—March to August 2011[ii]—the vibrant nonviolent movement was reminiscent of nonviolent and cross-sectional mobilization of Syrians during the 60-day general strike in 1936, which forced France to grant formal independence to Syrians a year later.[iii]

During this period, the regime's brutality backfired and the number of protests and participants steadily increased. Corteges honoring killed activists soon became rallying venues. What started as peaceful demonstrations of tens of thousands of people in a few cities and towns turned to massive protests of hundreds of thousands of people across the country by the end of July 2011. People from diverse ethnic, social, and religious backgrounds were participating. Solidarity among various sects was evident in that Ismaeli Shia from Salamiya donated blood to injured Sunnis that were supporters of the Muslim Brotherhood in Hama. Druze and the Greek Orthodox minority in Al-Suwayda organized protests to support Sunnis in Daraa—the bedrock of the revolution. Alawites in Jableh and other coastal cities hit the streets by the thousands to protest, chanting "Christians, Alawites and Sunnis, we are one!" and calling for the trial of Daraa's governor who was responsible for the arrest and torture of children — the event that triggered the uprising. One of the activists remarked, "no one was thinking of religion, ethnicity, or status. It was all about demanding freedom and supporting each other." Demonstrators held Christian and Muslim signs and chanted "peaceful, peaceful, peaceful— neither Sunni nor Alawite, we want national unity."[2] The nonviolent discipline of protesters was a strategic goal to increase the participation. "We were careful not to use force," emphasized a Syrian activist and an organizer of peaceful demonstrations. "From day one we chanted 'peaceful, civic,' and used signs, music, and caricature images [not guns], which attracted people's attention and generated sympathy." While the Syrian nonviolent resistance was predominantly characterized by protests, it used other tactics involving art, music, public theater, graffiti, and caricatures to promote their cause. The movement also established "local coordination committees" that spearheaded nonviolent campaigns and opposed militarization of resistance.[3]

With increased demonstrations the movement was winning government concessions that included the dismissal of the governor of Daraa, the release of hundreds of political dissidents, the grant of citizenship rights for Kurds, and the removal of the 48 year-old emergency law. Defection from the bureaucracy, Ba'ath party, diplomatic corps, business community, and the security forces was a growing movement. Prominent intellectual figures such as Muntaha al-Atrash, a Druze and the daughter of the late renowned nationalist leader Sultan Pasha al-Atrash, and famous Alawites actors like Fadwa Soliman and Jamal Suleiman joined the revolution. Security defections including high-level army defections, though limited to Sunnis, accelerated. By the summer of 2011 it was estimated that around 30,000 soldiers had left the Syrian army.

At a time when civil resistance was gaining public support, and both government concessions and a limited yet growing number of defections, the monumental decision was announced on July 31 to form the Free Syrian Army (FSA) to protect civilians and topple the

---

[2] The video footage of the protest: *https://www.youtube.com/watch?v=zCjLWBfaYCg&feature=results_video&pl aynext=1&list=PL4ECF881C5FC322BC%20*

[3] On August 29, 2011 the LCC warned and accurately predicted that "militarizing the revolution would minimize popular support and participation in the revolution (...), undermine the gravity of the humanitarian catastrophe involved in a confrontation with the regime [and] would put the revolution in an arena where the regime has a distinct advantage and would erode the moral superiority." Cited by Ignacio Alvarez-Ossorio, The Syrian Uprising: Syria's Struggling Civil Society, *Middle East Quarterly*, Spring (2012), 27.

regime with arms. This, however, played into the regime's hands as it led the rebels to engage the government on military terms where the Assad rule remained at its strongest. The FSA attracted a motley group of secular and religious types, each with its own goals and agenda. As a result, it failed to deploy a more organized force with an effective strategy. Finally, rebels were also responsible for mass killing, executions of minorities and looting, which further deepened sectarian tensions[iv] and undermined solidarity that the nonviolent resistance built.

ADVENT OF OPPOSITION VIOLENCE DRIVEN BY EMOTIONS AND MISCALCULATIONS

With an increase in regime assaults and brutality against protesters including detention and torture of activists, the leadership of the civil resistance movement was decimated and the consensus around nonviolent tactics weakened. This was accompanied by a growing desire for revenge among ordinary people. According to an activist from Hama, the regime "would purposefully capture children and torture them to trigger violence among protesters." In one of the rare surveys conducted recently in Aleppo and Idlib, almost half of polled Syrians identified revenge as the single most important factor behind their decision to join the armed resistance.[v]

Unlike Egypt and Tunisia, which saw sudden mass refusals of the militaries to follow regimes' orders thus helping civil resistance win, the gradual defections from the Syrian military undermined the nonviolent resistance. While the regime managed to maintain its capacity to repress, activists were left unprepared to integrate defecting soldiers into nonviolent protests. Eventually, soldiers organized alternative armed resistance, a tactic they knew best. Tragically, nonviolent actions were undermined by the same armed soldiers who responded early on to the appeal of the nonviolent movement and defected from the regime. To some extent nonviolent resistance became the victim of its own success.

Nonviolent resistance was seen as an unsuitable and weak strategy to face Assad's repression given the level of violence. Consequently, it was seen as impossible to bring the regime down with only peaceful means. Skeptics spent much less time than needed assessing the level of risks of armed struggle, the resources required to sustain it and the probabilities involved in removing the regime with arms. In this way, civil resistance confronted a much higher burden of proof in persuading others it could be effective against the brutal regime compared to its armed counterpart.

Resorting to arms was also dictated by another misguided assumption. An interviewed FSA member noted that "we did not think for a second that we are going to end up fighting for real and long. We thought we would put on a show, so the international community will come and save us the way it was in Libya. They will bomb Bashar Al Assad's Palace and bring the government down." He added, "when this did not happen, we found ourselves stuck in an armed struggle that we were not prepared for. "An expectation that the international community would intervene meant there was no incentive to consider at any depth how well the armed resistance was prepared to take on the Assad regime. After all the very weakness of the armed resistance — as in Libya — could be crucial to its rescue as it increased pressure on the international community to intervene and salvage what was left of the revolution.

Militarization of the resistance has given the Assad government a pretext to use indiscriminate firepower, including warplanes and chemical weapons that were not deployed when the resistance was peaceful. Arming the resistance also meant that Syrians themselves lost control over the trajectory of the struggle. Armed rebellion helped foreign extremist elements to establish their footing in Syria and start competing with FSA for battlefield-derived legitimacy and outside military assistance. Syrians became dependent on foreign states' sponsorship for arms and money to fuel the armed struggle. A lawyer and activist from Hama acknowledged, "the moment there were arms in the hands of some, we knew we lost our battle. It is what the government wanted us to do. They wanted a reason to fire and we were careful not to give them that excuse. Once the resistance became armed, we had to go home. The dynamic of the conflict changed and it was not our fight anymore."

Armed struggle in Syria reinforced divisions among religious and ethnic groups, hardening extreme views. The regime's divide-and-rule tactics, including the use of sectarian militias, have been very effective in further undermining opposition unity. Syrian civil resistance also experienced a significant decline in the weekly protests at the onset of violent struggle.[vi] Violent resistance undermined the solidarity that nonviolent resistance managed to build as long as it lasted. The armed resistance jeopardized any attempts to develop a more unifying and inclusive vision of a future Syria. By choosing to shoot its way to freedom, the opposition squandered its chance to make all ethnic groups stakeholders in the political change—the idea originally advanced by the civil resistance movement.

CIVIL RESISTANCE PERCOLATING ON THE SURFACE OF CIVIL WAR

Although overshadowed by the armed resistance, nonviolent resistance remains visible and active despite ongoing civil war — a testimony to the endurance of peaceful struggle and its deep roots that were developed during the first few months of the resistance. This is evident in the work of grassroots committees that sprang up across Syria to provide humanitarian assistance and basic services. It is also expressed in civic actions such as the "Stop the Killing" campaign organized by minority women[4] to monitor the work of the local councils and promote the culture of rights and justice,[vii] the peaceful protests in various Syrian towns against the Islamic State in Iraq and Syria (ISIS) and its authoritarian practices and the establishment of an alternative schooling system, including volunteer-run baccalaureate exams. The Karama ("dignity") Bus—a mobile center for addressing trauma in children—was organized by women in Kafr Nabl outside the regime controlled area but with the intention to expand to other places.[viii] In the same town, a group of young activists called 'Sharaa' (Arabic for "street") deploys graffiti as a way "to gain back the public space that was stolen from us by the militias,"[ix] according to one of its members. The proliferation of local newspapers and political magazines is another example Syrian civic groups' self-management. The number of publications available went from less than a dozen that were tightly controlled by the regime to more than sixty independent outlets run by popular groups.

---

[4] For more information about the Stop the Killing campaign and each of its actions check its Facebook page: *https://www.facebook.com/media/set/?set=a.309765662466852.67278.220124418097644&type=3.*

If nonviolent organizing and mobilization is still blooming in a predominantly violent environment, then how much more could be achieved if the opposition violence was taken out of the conflict and the resources committed to supporting armed groups were instead used to strengthen the Syrian nonviolent resistance?

For instance, the return to nonviolent resistance could be highly disruptive for the Assad regime and prove to be a more rational choice with more realistic chances of success than its violent counterpart. Media reports point to growing dissatisfaction among the members of the Alawite community from which the Assad regime draws its main power and support.[x] Members of the Alawite sect feel they are bearing an unusually large burden of sacrifice to keep Assad in power and receive relatively few benefits in return. But they remain unwaveringly loyal to him and his family because they are genuinely terrified of violent insurgents. The moment this fear is assuaged, Alawites would be ready to challenge Assad by asking for a "payback" for the costs they endured. Thus, the internal dissent and strife among Alawites would be much more likely to result in political action if the current violent insurgency would cease and open the way for the return of unarmed resistance.

KEY LESSONS FROM THE SYRIAN CONFLICT

An Extremely Violent Adversary Wants Civil Resistance to Turn Violent

It is widely thought that a regime that rules with brutal violence can only be stopped by another more powerful violent force. However, violent regimes are often caught off balance when challenged by the unarmed resistance. The British historian B.H. Lidell-Hart, who interrogated the German generals after the World War II, noticed that Nazis were bewildered by nonviolent resistance. Therefore, "it was relief to them when resistance became violent and when nonviolent forms were mixed with guerrilla action thus making it easier to combine drastic repressive action against both at the same time."[xi] The

Syrian regime brutalized its people with the goal of suppressing the resistance. When this did not succeed the regime used indiscriminate violence to force people to abandon peaceful resistance in favor of armed uprising. According to an activist who later joined the FSA, the Syrian security forces were leaving caches of weapons in public areas to encourage the use of arms. If brutal regimes are interested in facing a violent rather than peaceful challenge, activists must develop a plan to thwart that desire.

Fewer Civilian Casualties in Civil Resistance Campaigns

For civilians the cost of armed struggle will always be higher than the costs of civil resistance even in cases where violent resistance succeeds. A study that examined violence against civilians in wars between 1989 and 2004 showed that civilians' risk of dying in conflicts that did not devolve into armed struggles was less than one percent.[xii] During the relatively low intensity armed resistance in South Africa, a former African National Congress (ANC) operative noted that ANC's own intelligence assessed the survival rate of an ANC armed insurgent to be between three and seven days on average. Despite the risks involved in suffering from years of imprisonment, the death rate among nonviolent resisters was much lower. As for Syria, the probability of dying in the conflict became three times higher once the opposition abandoned nonviolent resistance in favor of the armed rebellion.[5]

Developing a Mindset for a Protracted, Five to Ten Year Long Struggle Against a Brutal Regime

Two factors contributed to the failure to develop a collective mentality and strategies for a protracted struggle and led to a premature

---

[5] "During the first five months of nonviolent civil resistance (mid-March to mid-August, 2011), the death toll was 2,019 (figures exclude regime army casualties). In the next five months (mid-August 2011 to mid-January 2011) mixed violent and nonviolent resistance saw the death toll climbed to 3,144, a 56 percent increase. Finally, during the first five months of armed resistance (mid-January 2012 to mid-June 2012) the death toll was already 8,195, a staggering 161 percent increase in comparison with the casualties during nonviolent struggle." See Maciej Bartkowski and Mohja Kahf, "The Syrian Resistance, Part 2."

·abandonment of the nonviolent resistance: the impatience of the opposition mixed with the belief shared by policy makers in other capitals that Assad would step down as quickly as his counterparts in Egypt and Tunisia.

The research on nonviolent and violent campaigns concludes that it takes on average three years for nonviolent resistance to run its course (whether it succeeds or fails) while a violent uprising requires at least nine years.[xiii] In practice, Syrians allowed for only one-fifth of the average lifespan of a nonviolent movement before they turned to arms.

Winning the Loyalty Contest

Unlike other autocrats in the region, Assad had initially a larger social base of support that included minority groups, business entrepreneurs, religious figures, military, and middle-income citizens across various ethnic groups. The loyalties of some of these groups were shaken with the onset of nonviolent resistance. However, the regime made a concerted effort to keep the loyalties intact and attract neutrals with financial and political incentives. It was relatively effective in preventing major loyalty shifts within its pillars of support—a strategy that the opposition was unable to counter successfully.

Ultimately, it was degeneration of the conflict into a civil war that offered a major boost for the government. Opposition violence combined with the influx of extremists allowed the regime to consolidate the rank and file people who until then sat on the fence. They did not necessarily support Assad's policies but they did favor him over radical Islamist groups that hijacked the armed struggle and whose presence they associated with the interference of foreign powers, including Saudi Arabia, Qatar, and Turkey, backed by the West, in the affairs of their own country.[xiv]

Devising a Viable Strategy to Shift from Armed Toward Nonviolent Resistance

South Africa, Nepal, Egypt, Palestine, West Papua, Western Sahara, and East Timor have all seen the reduction of emphasis on armed struggle replaced by an emergence of mostly nonviolent campaigns after re-evaluating their goals and means, taking stock of the costs, and weighing the risks and probabilities of the success of civil resistance. Syrians can rely on existing citizens' councils and the ongoing nonviolent organizing in localities, which is also extending mutual aid networks and developing cross-sectional coordinating bodies. All of these efforts are developing the foundations of future "peace communities." Examples of resistance-driven and self-managed nonviolent local communities abound in countries that experienced high level of violence including Colombia,[xv] the Philippines,[xvi] Mexico,[xvii] Kosovo,[xviii] Afghanistan, Rwanda, and Bosnia.[xix] They offer encouraging lessons for Syrians. Their local populations rose up and defied violent state and nonstate groups, establishing zones of peace where organized citizens expelled or kept at bay violent perpetrators. In violence-torn places like Liberia, the emergence of women-run networks helped launch anti-civil war campaigns and forced the warring parties to negotiate and sign a peace accord.

Reinventing the Role of the International Community

From the beginning of the conflict in Syria the international community resorted to traditional instruments of pressuring the government. In May 2011 the European Union and the United States introduced a series of targeted political and economic sanctions against the Assad regime. What became clear is that the international community lacks instruments to protect and assist nonviolent uprising when it lasts. There is an urgent need to reinvent the role of the international community in helping nonviolent movements.

THE INTERNATIONAL COMMUNITY AND THE SYRIAN NONVIOLENT MOVEMENT

No amount of external assistance can substitute for an authentic grassroots movement to achieve its civic and political goals. Unlike violent resistance, nonviolent struggles are owned and won by the indigenous population alone. However, international aid could support these grassroots movements in achieving their goals more effectively. The Syrian tragedy showed that the international community has yet to develop effective mechanisms to support civil resistance movements, at least with the same energy and material aid that it devotes to finding diplomatic solutions, reaching peace accords, or intervening militarily.[6] When, in early 2012, senior US policymakers were asked why the international community had not encouraged a sustained civil resistance, their response was: "Why should we bother? Assad will be gone in a couple of months." Although Western governments were not enthusiastic about backing armed resistance and probably wanted civil resistance to succeed, their support for nonviolent movement was modest.

Lessons from Syria show that there is a genuine urgency to develop new international norms or understandings (e.g. in the form of a universal right to help) designed to refocus international efforts to assisting nonviolent resistance movements and preventing them from turning to arms. A global normative framework for helping nonviolent movements could also benefit from the establishment of an international rights-based institution devoted entirely to supporting civil resistance movements around the world. In the Syrian case, such an institution could have deployed small teams of veteran nonviolent volunteer-activists from the Arab-speaking region and more broadly from across the world to meet their younger, more inexperienced Syrian counterparts to share lessons from their respective struggles. The extended "train-the-trainers" program in different localities across Syria could have been devised to share practices and experiences among activists. When strict security measures made it difficult to facilitate the entry of trainers, commonly used and accessed online technology could have been used to disseminate information and address the bedeviling problem of how to plan a *protracted* nonviolent struggle. Other activities undertaken by a specialized international

---

[6] As for the latter, the bill for a relatively short-lived NATO military intervention in Libya (limited to 8 months of air campaign) was estimated to reach at least $2 billion. See Jessica Rettig, "End of NATO's Libya Intervention Means Financial Relief for Allies," *U.S. News and World Report*, October 31, 2011, accessed November 18, 2014, *http://www.usnews.com/news/articles/2011/10/31/end-of-natos-libya-intervention-means-financial-relief-for-allies*.

institution could include in this case distribution of Arabic-language educational toolkits that highlight aspects of civil resistance movements and explain what makes them historically more successful than their violent counterparts.

Providing technology and communication equipment including laptops, portable printers, satellite phones, and cameras without the usual bureaucratic red tape could support nonviolent movements in spreading their messages faster and more effectively. Such assistance, according to a young Alawite female activist who was part of the 2011 uprising, would have been extremely helpful. "We were too poor to afford to buy computers, toners, printers that were needed to produce informational brochures to break government propaganda." During the government's nationwide shutdowns of the Internet, the availability of inexpensive, subsidized, and secure satellite technology to coordinate protests among activists inside the country and communicate with the outside world would be particularly useful. Other valuable support from the international community would include access for activists to mainstream media or support in setting up local radio or TV broadcasts so that activists could beam information about the achievements, progress, and challenges on the nonviolent battlefield. Provisions of such technology and resources would benefit from greater discretionary powers given to diplomats on the ground by their own capitals. A major impediment that Robert Ford, the former US ambassador to Syria, found in his work was a lack of autonomy in decision-making. He recalled, for example, spending time in "long meetings to debate small issues, such as which Syrian opposition members he could meet with and whether it was okay to give cell phones, media training and management classes to a local Syrian government council controlled by the opposition."[xx]

Finally, benchmarks of the progress of civil resistance could be set up to assess levels of defections, increases in civic mobilization and participation, and government responses including any concessions as well as the toll from repression, and costs to society. These benchmarks could be used to compel those advocating military solutions to explain and show how they could achieve more and with lower costs. In the Syrian case, millions of small handheld radio and TV devices could have been distributed to the public, making it easier to reach out to hesitant minorities with messages of unity and cooperation.

On the military front, the international community could have facilitated exchanges between activists inside and outside Syria on how best to prepare for gradual defections from the security forces so as to prevent defected soldiers from undermining the nonviolent nature of the resistance, including effective ways of integrating them into the civil resistance movement. If that would not have been feasible, the international community should have developed strategies to keep defecting soldiers and their arms away from the urban centers where civil resistance was thriving.

The establishment of large military camps in remote places closer to the border with Turkey or Jordan and Iraq where soldiers could receive stable salaries, training, and modern equipment would have attracted fighters and, in turn, encouraged more officers to defect. Arguably, the existence of such camps could have incentivized foreign countries in the region that transferred weapons and fighters into Syria without much coordination and strategic planning to channel their material and human resources to the established military camps. Containment of defected soldiers in camps protected against regime's air-strikes could have kept them safe and occupied until such time when a capable, vetted, and professional force was ready for deployment. By then, however, civil resistance might have already won the struggle and a military force could have been used to perform a policing function and provide security for all segments of the Syrian population regardless of religious affiliations to win them over to support the common fight against violent foreign extremists.

Today, local councils and civil administrations in both liberated and conflict areas are in a need of more decisive international support. For example, according to UN staff, the administration of the city of Homs is taking great risks in trying to implement water projects benefitting both sides of the conflict. Local administrations need to be trained in governance, rule of law, and civil liberties, including inclusive policies for women and minorities. Local administrations should be funded so they can rebuild critical infrastructure such as water and sewage systems, and electric power infrastructure. Setting up local police forces would require help in re-training and equipping policemen that defected from the Assad regime.

Both the international community and mobilized local population have yet to acknowledge that they are engaged in a genuine race with extremist groups such as ISIS not to determine who can deploy the most capable fighting force but who can be most effective governance manager. This is because ISIS secures local support not purely by military conquest and brutal repression but also—if not mainly—by restoring damaged infrastructure, delivering water and electricity to the population in the territories they govern, and by providing basic social services as well as jobs and salaries. The communities with the experience of nonviolent mobilization and organizing will be better prepared than violent groups to establish and run more effective governance while, at the same time, staying stronger to defend their autonomy. This understanding could help international community develop appropriate tools to assist these communities become more skilled governance managers.

With extremist Islamic practices taking place in many liberated areas, outside support for civil institutions such as schools and courts is needed to counter views and actions of radicals that are despised by most Syrians. Various protests contesting the authoritarian and brutal practices of ISIS[7] took place in Aleppo and Raqqa. More than 40 percent of Syrian children are out of school, mainly in conflict zones but also in some liberated areas, where Islamic teaching is becoming the only alternative to nonfunctioning public education. Support for building schools and developing curricula that promote self-expression, critical thinking, and basic democratic and civic concepts would be invaluable for a democratic future of the country. Similarly, in areas where *Sharia* Islamic courts are functioning and sentencing people to public flogging, civic courts and local councils need to be supported to counter religious courts. International funding could also

---

[7] Islamic State of Iraq and the Levant. For more on the foreign fighters in Syria see Aaron Y. Zelin, "Who Are the Foreign Fighters in Syria?" *The Washington Institute*, December 5, 2013.

aid defected judges and lawyers who are now working to establish civic courts in places like Harem and Atareb to counter *Sharia* law.

Most valuably, the international community could work to ensure that external sponsorship for armed extremist groups dries up, incentivizing armed groups to disengage and providing space for civil resistance groups to reemerge and renew nonviolent conflict.

Despite the ongoing civil war, threats from the regime and Islamist reactionary groups, hatred combined with a lust for revenge, and seemingly insurmountable divisions among Syrians, nonviolent activism and mobilization remain the most realistic alternative for achieving social and political change in Syria. The Syrian resistance movement failed to plan for a prolonged confrontation while the actions of the international community were less than adequate to strengthen the Syrian nonviolent resistance and prevent it from becoming violent. It is time that both learn from their short-sightedness. In the current humanitarian crisis, a number of opportunities might emerge to build solidarity and mutual aid-networks across divided ethnic communities affected by the war. Nonviolent activists must identify and utilize such opportunities while the international community must remain ready to step in to support activists' efforts.

Notes

i. Mohammed Al Attar, "Al Raqqa: The reality of the military brigades, the administration of the liberated city and the revolutions to come," September 16, 2013, accessed November 18, 2014, *http://therepublicgs.net/2013/09/16/al-raqqa-the-reality-of-the-military-brigades-the-administration-of-the-liberated-city-and-the-revolutions-to-come/*.

ii. Maciej Bartkowski and Mohja Kahf, "The Syrian Resistance: A Tale of Two Struggles," Part 1 and Part 2, *openDemocracy*, September 24, 2013, accessed November 18, 2014, *https://www.opendemocracy.net/civilresistance/maciej-bartkowski-mohja-kahf/syrian-resistance-tale-of-two-struggles* and *https://www.opendemocracy.net/civilresistance/maciej-bartkowski-mohja-kahf/syrian-resistance-tale-of-two-struggles-part-2*.

iii. See, for example, Philip Khoury, *Syria and the French Mandate: The Politics of Arab Nationalism 1920-1945*, (Princeton NJ: Princeton University Press), 1987.

iv. "Syria: Executions, Hostage taking by rebels," *Human Rights Watch*, October 11, 2013.

v. See Vera Mironova Loubna Mrie and Sam Whitt, *Voices of Syria Project*, February 2014, accessed November 18, 2014, *http://vmironova.net/voices-of-aleppo/papers-and-reports/*.

vi.   Stephen Zunes, "Supporting Nonviolence in Syria," *Foreign Policy,* December 20,
      2012, and see the graph that shows the raise of death toll and a decline in a number of
      protests since the resistance turned violent, Freedom Days's Facebook Page, accessed
      November 18, 2014, *https://www.facebook.com/photo.php?fbid=495042097174752&set
      =a.288141837864780.82005.287684561243841&type=1&theater.*

vii. Ibid.

viii. Ibid.

ix.   Adrian Hartrick, "Syria's graffiti revolution," *Al Monitor,* March 23, 2014, accessed
      November 18, 2014, *http://www.al-monitor.com/pulse/originals/2014/04/syria-graffiti-
      revolution-kafr-nabl.html#.*

x.   Anne Barnarda, *If Assad Wins War, Challenge From His Own Sect May Follow,* NYTimes,
      April 24, 2014.

xi.   Kurth Schock, "Nonviolent Action and Its Misconceptions: Insights for Social
      Scientists," *Political Science and Politics* 36, no. 4, (2003), p. 708.

xii. Kristine Eck and Lisa Hultman, "One-Sided Violence Against Civilians in War:
      Insights from New Fatality Data," *Journal of Peace Research,* vol. 44, no. 2 (2007), p. 237,
      accessed November 18, 2014, *http://www.pcr.uu.se/digitalAssets/147/147088_eck.
      hultman.jpr.pdf.*

xiii. Erica Chenoweth, "Why Sit-Ins Succeed--Or Fail," *Foreign Affairs,* August 11, 2013.

xiv. "Assad Winning the War for Syrians' Hearts and Minds," *World Tribune,* May 31, 2013.

xv.   Oliver Kaplan, "How Communities Use Nonviolent Strategies to Avoid Civil War
      Violence," ICNC Academic Webinar, January 20, 2013.

xvi. Ibid.

xvii. Lilian Palma, "The Courage of Cheran: Organizing against Violence," *openDemocracy,*
      December 14, 2011.

xviii. Howard Clark, *Civil Resistance in Kosovo,* (London: Pluto Press, 2000).

xix. All three last cases are discussed in Mary B. Anderson and Marshall Wallace, *Opting
      Out of War: Strategies to Prevent Violent Conflict.* (Boulder, CO., Lynne Rienner
      Publishers, 2012).

xx.   David Rohde and Warren Strobel, "Special Report: How Syria policy stalled under
      the 'analyst in chief'," *Reuters,* October 30, 2014.

PART FOUR

OUTSIDE ACTORS'
ROLE IN CIVIL
RESISTANCE

CHAPTER 11

Influencing Armed Forces to Support Democratic Transitions

Admiral Dennis Blair (Ret.)
US Navy
Former PACOM Commander and Director of National Intelligence

T HE ARMED FORCES ARE one of the most powerful institutions in any country. They have weapons and disciplined personnel and are organized for taking action. To an extent that is hard for those in mature democracies to understand, the military leaders of new countries and new governments believe they have both the right and the responsibility to play a decisive role in the political development of their countries. Their independence wars are more recent, military coups have often been frequent and not that long ago, and few other established institutions have their power and influence within the country. They will often assume or be thrust into a decisive role in a political crisis, and large sectors of society will look to them for leadership and action.

Rarely will a country's armed forces be in the vanguard of a popular movement for democratic reform. It is true that many military coups are proclaimed to have been made in the name of the people and that their leaders often announce that their goal is to restore or establish democracy. Once in power, however, they generally then announce that it will take a period of time to deal with the country's immediate problems before power can be turned over to a democratic government. As that period of time becomes longer and longer, the rulers may exchange their uniforms for business suits, but they generally convince themselves they do not need an election to confirm their own conviction that they are the most qualified candidates to lead the country. This has been the pattern in many African countries when anti-colonial military revolutionaries became long-serving dictators. Often it takes another coup or political crisis to force them from power. However, power has not always corrupted absolutely, and there have been examples of military governments voluntarily relinquishing power: the military regimes in Chile and Brazil in the 1980s sensed growing popular demands for democracy and led the transition process themselves. In South Korea, it was a group of military leaders who realized that their military academy classmate President Chun should turn the office over to a freely elected successor. More recently, the Thai military government in 2007 turned over power to the political party led by the sister of the leader they had deposed months earlier.

The armed forces have the power to suppress most armed revolts against authoritarian regimes if they decide to support the dictator or party in power. Numerous Latin American armies successfully defeated armed insurgent groups during the 1970s and 1980s. In 1989 the People's Liberation Army cleared Tiananmen Square. In 2009 armed forces of Iran obeyed orders to quell popular protests against the clerical regime. At this writing the Syrian armed forces continue to follow orders from President Assad to fight rebels.

However, the armed forces do not always support authoritarian leaders when their power is challenged. Contrary to much conventional wisdom, relations between a dictator and the armed forces are fragile and tense. Dictators fear military leaders as potential rivals, and use many means to keep them loyal, under observation and politically weak. Military officers for their part often resent promotions based on personal loyalty rather than merit, corruption, and possibility of orders to suppress popular opposition. When there is a political crisis, military leaders make decisions on what they believe is best for their country, their services, or their personal interests. It is not rare for the armed forces to play a positive role in allowing popular movements to overthrow dictators, even if they have been in power for a long time and have assiduously courted and controlled their military leaders. In the Philippines in 1983, Indonesia in 1998, Serbia in 2000 and the

Ukraine in 2004, the armed forces refused to suppress protestors, in some cases even cooperating with them, and allowed dictators to be overthrown. In 2011 the Tunisian and Egyptian army leaders decided not to support the Ben Ali and Mubarak regimes against popular protests, and those dictators fell.

Decisions by the armed forces to suppress opposition to an autocratic regime or withdraw support from it are made for complex reasons. So long as a regime maintains social order and security and delivers economic prosperity, its armed forces are not likely to support opposition movements. If opposition is armed and violent, employing terror tactics, and especially if it is either supported or perceived to be supported by an outside country, then the army will generally obey orders to restore order and defeat the insurgents. This was the case in Latin America in the 1970s and 1980s, when armies successfully and often brutally defeated left-wing groups. These groups were considered to be inspired by Cuba and the Soviet Union, and were observed to have been assisted by them as well. Military leaders will also make decisions based on the ethnic and tribal composition of the regime and its opposition. It is a rare senior military officer in Africa who will support democratic reform if he believes his ethnic group or tribe will be oppressed or disadvantaged under an unproven democratic system potentially run by a rival group. Religious, tribal and family loyalties have governed the decisions of Syrian officers in supporting the regime. Finally, many military officers believe that their countries are simply not ready for democracy. They feel that the necessary institutions for representative government do not yet exist in their countries: an informed citizenry that will elect competent political leaders, an honest and functional legal system that will protect minority rights and tame corruption, a capable civil service, and a responsible legislature. They believe that until these components of democracy are present, some form of authoritarian government that earns popular support is best for their countries.

The combination of circumstances that causes military leaders to withdraw their support from dictatorships is also complex. Sometimes it is a logical part of the maturing of a country. Such was the case in the Republic of Korea and Taiwan. In both countries, the growth of powerful, capable groups of politicians, civil servants and businessmen, the lessening of outside threats, and the example of democratic governance in other advanced friendly countries led to the development of representative governance. In both cases dominant political parties that had cultivated close relations with military leaders lost power, and the military leaders let them go. Similarly, in some Latin American countries – Brazil and Chile – military-supported regimes handed over power peacefully through elections as other groups in society gained the capability and self-confidence to challenge them, economic progress seemed stable and external threats receded. In other cases such as Indonesia in the 1990s, or Tunisia in the 2000s, the armed forces recognized that aging dictators were losing touch with their countries, had become corrupt and unpopular. These dictators either had in the past, or were expected to call on their military leaders to suppress popular protests, to turn their weapons against their own peacefully protesting citizens. Military leaders have a well-developed sense of legacy. Although they can take pride in defeating armed and violent revolutionaries who kill their soldiers and kill and maim innocent citizens, it is a rare military officer who wants to go down in his country's history as the man who gave the orders to fire on citizens who were protesting peacefully.

Finally, individual leaders do make a difference. Time and again, democratic transitions have been moved forward by the decisions of individual military officers who understood what was right for their countries and their military services. In the early years of the United States, George Washington declined a proconsulship and supported a constitutional form of government. A century and a half later in Turkey, Mustafa Kemal Ataturk used his enormous prestige as the military victor in a war of independence to support the establishment of a democracy in his country. In Senegal, General Jean Alfred Diallo in the 1960s established a positive role for the army in his newly independent country that has continued to the present. In Spain in the 1970s, General Gutierrez Mellado was the "irreplaceable initiator of reform" in Spain's transition from the Franco dictatorship. In the 1980s, General Prem Tinsulanonda, as prime minister of Thailand, voluntarily left the premiership for an elected successor. General Fidel Ramos stepped down after a constitutionally mandated single term as president of the Philippines, declining to change the constitution or to declare martial law. In the 1990s Staff General Ferenc Vegh, the Hungarian chief of defense, led the reform of the armed forces to assume a new democratic role. In Tunisian in 2011, General Rachid Ammar refused orders to use military force to suppress peaceful protests, leading to the end of President Ben Ali's dictatorship.

Internal factors are decisive in the success or failure of democratic transitions in autocratic regimes. They are fundamentally contests for power in which the interaction of groups including political parties and factions, the armed forces and the police, business leaders and popular organizations will determine whether an authoritarian ruler stays or is replaced. Military leaders will make their decisions whether to support or turn on a dictator in alliances and struggles among these groups.

However, outside influences on military leaders can have an effect on their thinking about the best political system of their country, and the actions they take in political crises. Their attitudes are formed by their training, thinking and experiences over their careers in the armed forces. Even in closed dictatorships, they will have some knowledge of democratic countries, their armed forces and civil-military relations.

There are many opportunities for the armed forces of the established democracies to affect the thinking of their counterparts in authoritarian regimes. With the exception of a few closed countries like North Korea and Iran, the armed forces of the world are in frequent contact in many different settings. They attend each other's military colleges and training centers; they operate together in peacekeeping forces; they have frequent bilateral and multilateral training exercises; they gather in international conferences; they visit back and forth. These are all touch points during which the officers and noncommissioned officers from the established democracies can influence their counterparts to appreciate the advantages of democratic systems of government.

In their interactions with counterparts from authoritarian regimes, the armed forces of the democracies have important advantages. The most professionally advanced, skilled, and respected armies, navies, air forces, and marine corps are in the democratic countries; the pay is better in democratic armed forces, their promotion systems are fairer and based on merit, they retire from their service with honor, and they will never be ordered by their government to fire on their own citizens. Some of these advantages are self-evident, but they can be accentuated through the personal appearance, bearing, conduct, and conversational approaches of military representatives of the democratic countries.

One of the most effective and important opportunities for influencing officers from autocratic countries occurs when they participate in military education and training courses in democratic countries, from Canberra and Tokyo to London and Paris. These are often the most promising officers, who will go on to higher ranks in the course of their careers. Forty international students who attended the Army War College in Carlisle, Pennsylvania, went on to become the highest ranking general in their own armies, and over 600 of the international students of the Navy War College in Newport, Rhode Island, have become admirals. There is an opportunity for these international students to learn not only military strategy, but to absorb the principles and practices of civil-military relations in democracies.

The armed forces of democratic countries conduct a wide range of exercises with the armed forces of authoritarian countries, from seminars on professional subjects through war games and field training exercises. While it is not appropriate to conduct seminars on democratic transformation in every international exercise, there are many opportunities to introduce relevant democratic civil-military concepts – subordination of military units to civilian government leadership, effective cooperation with civilian government and international nongovernmental organizations, and the importance of media transparency during military operations.

There is a well-developed schedule of conferences among the world's armed forces. Some of them, on topics such as peacekeeping operations, military law, defense budgeting and procurement, by their nature lead to discussions of the characteristics of defense forces in democracies. The participants from democratic countries can ensure that these characteristics are discussed and highlighted as best practices. Some of the most valuable opportunities offered by these kinds of activities are in the interactions that take place outside the formal sessions.

Bilateral visits are the most common points of contract between the more senior officials of advanced democratic countries and officers and officials of authoritarian countries. Generally the representatives of authoritarian countries are well prepared in their formal meetings with talking points including a justification for their authoritarian form of government and the roles of their armed forces in supporting those governments. While a meaningful exchange of real ideas is not likely in such settings, there are opportunities for real dialogue in more informal settings that form a large part of these visits – in cars between meetings, during dinners, or in waiting rooms when travel plans are changing.

Finally, when political crises occur in authoritarian governments, military leaders in the democracies can communicate directly with their counterparts to try to influence them to support democratic transitions. With the frequent rotation of assignments in the armed forces, senior officers will often not know their counterparts. It is much more effective if officers in the democracies who have known or worked with officers currently in the leadership positions in autocratic countries can communicate with them. During a crisis, communication is best with a familiar voice.

Every point of contact between officers and officials of the advanced democracies with an officer, official or counterpart in an autocratic country is an opportunity for influence. Individuals sometimes seize these opportunities, and make a positive difference. However the official policies and practices of the democratic armed forces are haphazard and not well developed. There is room for great improvement. This is true for the US Department of Defense which directs the most widespread programs of military engagement around the world. It is also true for the ministries of defense of the other established democracies, which have unique influence with different countries, and often have more relevant experiences from their own democratic development.

While there are many short-term imperatives and benefits from military engagement with other countries around the world, there is no more important long-term objective than helping them make a successful transition to democracy.

CHAPTER 12

International Legal Basis of Support for Nonviolent Activists and Movements

Elizabeth A. Wilson
Assistant Professor for Human Rights Law, School of Diplomacy and International Relations, Seton Hall University

T HE LEGAL BASIS FOR support to nonviolent activists and movements ("NV actors") can be thought of as having primary and secondary aspects, both of which are grounded in international human rights law. The right to engage in nonviolent activism is the primary right, while the right to provide support derives from that right and is in some sense secondary to it. The distinction is important because the right to provide support does not include the right to support individuals or groups that use violence. Support is protected by the rights to expression and association and may include a variety of resources, e.g., training programs, small grants, educational materials, and even technologies to circumvent surveillance, Internet filters, or censorship. This paper outlines the general legal basis for support to NV actors and applies it to the question of funding for NV actors in circumstances where national laws restricting civil society organizations (CSOs) have been adopted by governments in an effort to suppress dissent.

THE RIGHT TO ENGAGE IN NONVIOLENT PROTEST

The primary right to engage in nonviolent protest implicates political participation rights; the rights to opinion, information and expression; and rights of peaceful assembly and association. It has been suggested that the right to NV protest is "a supporting or instrumental freedom that [goes] together with and facilitate[s] the realization of other rights and freedoms."[i] Some of these primary rights are transitive with respect to the secondary right to provide support to NV actors. The right to receive information is transitive with respect to the right to impart information. The right to associate with those willing to provide support is transitive with the right to associate with those who wish to receive support. In addition to the primary rights that are transitive, discussed at greater length below, the primary rights of NV actors are protected by, *inter alia*, the right of self-determination,[ii] the right of peaceful assembly,[iii] and various political participation rights.[iv]

INTERNATIONAL HUMAN RIGHTS LAW

International human rights law derives from the Universal Declaration of Human Rights (UDHR), a General Assembly Resolution adopted in 1948. The UDHR gave rise to two core, binding treaties: the International Convention on Civil and Political Rights (ICCPR) and the International Conventional on Economic, Social, and Cultural Rights (ICESCR). Of these two, the ICCPR is the most relevant source of law on the question of aid to NV actors. Specialized treaties like the Convention on the Elimination Against All Forms of Discrimination Against Women (CEDAW) also articulate related human rights, as do various regional treaties like the European Convention on Human Rights and Fundamental Freedoms (ECHR), the American Convention on Human Rights ("American Convention"), and the African Charter on Human and People's Rights ("African Charter"). International treaties are binding on States Parties and, together with regional treaties and UN and regional mechanisms, can also form evidence of customary international law. International treaties also create International Organizations, such as the International Labor Organization (ILO), with an important role in setting international standards.

The ICCPR is implemented by means of the Human Rights Committee ("HRC"), a body created by the treaty that prepares country reports and observations on a periodic basis, hears individual complaints in accordance with the Optional Protocol, and issues

"General Comments" interpreting substantive and procedural issues related to the treaty. Although its jurisprudence is technically nonbinding, the HRC has increasingly been regarded as authoritative in regards to interpretation of the ICCPR.

In addition, the United Nations Human Rights Council ("Council") oversees the implementation of human rights generally through the "universal periodic review" process and the creation of "special procedures" to investigate particular themes or country issues. Through the "special procedures" mechanism the UN has created Special Rapporteurs on the situation of human rights defenders, on the promotion and protection of the right to freedom of opinion and expression, and on the rights of peaceful assembly and association, all of which have issued a number of reports relevant to the legal basis of aid to NV actors. The United Nations General Assembly ("UNGA") also plays a role in monitoring human rights and establishing standards.

THE RIGHT TO SUPPORT NV ACTORS

The international human rights that form the legal basis for aid to NV actors are set out in the main international and regional treaties:

> *Right to Freedom of Expression (ICCPR Article 19):*
> *1. Everyone shall have the right to hold opinions without interference. 2. Everyone shall have the right to freedom of expression…*

The right to freedom of expression includes speech and press, freedom of information, and, more recently, freedom to access the Internet or social media. The ICCPR, the African Charter on Human and Peoples' Rights, and the American Convention on Human Rights all contain explicit protections of the right to receive information, including transnationally.[v] The ICCPR and the American Convention further elaborate this right as including the "freedom to seek, receive and impart information and ideas of all kinds, *regardless of frontiers*, either orally, in writing or in print, in the form of art, or through any other media of his choice"(italics added).[vi] In a General Comment interpreting Article 19, the HRC affirmed that access to information extends to the new "global network for exchanging ideas and opinions that does not necessarily rely on the traditional mass media intermediaries."[vii] Relatedly, the European Court of Human Rights has held that the right to freedom of expression "applies not only to the content of information but also to the means of transmission or reception since any restriction imposed on the means necessarily interferes with the right to receive information."[viii]

In 2011, the UN Special Rapporteur on the promotion and protection of the right to freedom of opinion and expression stated the "right to freedom of opinion and expression is as much a fundamental right on its own accord as it is an 'enabler' of other rights, including... the rights to freedom of association and assembly....Thus, by acting as a catalyst for individuals to exercise their right to freedom of opinion and expression, the Internet also facilitates the realization of a range of other human rights."[ix]

> *Right to Freedom of Association (ICCPR Article 22): 1. Everyone shall have the right to freedom of association with others, including the right to form and join trade unions for the protection of his interests.*

Though it has not yet issued General Comments specifically on the rights of association and peaceful assembly, the HRC has taken a broad view on the right to freedom of association, stating, "[t]he right to freedom of association, including the right to form and join organizations and associations concerned with political and public affairs, is an essential adjunct to the [political participation rights protected by Article 25],"[x] which in turn "[lie] at the core of democratic government based on the consent of the people and in conformity with the principles of the Covenant."[xi] The HRC has also held that the protections of Article 22 of the ICCPR extend "to all activities" of a CSO, which includes the right to receive support.[xii] Furthermore, the right to assist NV actors does not depend on whether those actors have formally incorporated into associations under law.[xiii]

Other regional and specialized treaties protect the rights to freedom of expression and association. A nonexhaustive list includes the following: the European regional human rights regime recognizes the rights protected in ICCPR Articles 21 and 22 in Article 11 of the ECHR (protecting "the right to freedom of peaceful assembly and to freedom of association with others, including the right to form and to join trade unions for the protection of his interests"). Freedom of association and peaceful assembly are also protected by the African Charter[xiv] and the American Convention on Human Rights.[xv] The Elimination of All Forms of Racial Discrimination prohibits discrimination based on "race, colour, descent, or national or ethnic origin" from inhibiting the exercise of the rights of political participation, freedom of opinion and expression, and freedom of peaceful assembly and association.[xvi]

The rights in question are not absolute and may be subject to derogation and limitation, e.g., for reasons related to "national security or public safety, public order, the protection of public health or morals for the protection of the rights and freedoms of others."[xvii]

GENERAL ASSEMBLY RESOLUTIONS AND REGIONAL SUPPORT

The UN General Assembly has been active in supporting NV actors. In 1998, the UNGA adopted the Declaration on the Right and Responsibility of Individuals, Groups and Organs of Society to Promote and Protect Universally Recognized Human Rights and Fundamental Freedoms (Declaration on Human Rights Defenders or "HRD").[xviii] Technically not a binding legal document, the HRD was adopted by consensus by the UNGA, making it evidence of *opinio juris*[1] in customary international law.

Inter alia, the HRD protects the right of "everyone, individually and in association with others"[xix]

1. "to promote and to strive for the protection and realization of human rights and fundamental freedoms at the national and international levels."[xx]

2. "to participate in peaceful activities against violations of human rights and fundamental freedoms."[xxi]

---

[1] The sense of legal obligation.

The HRD clarifies that freedom of association extends to international and transnational associational networks.[xxii] It guarantees the "right, individually and in association with others, to *solicit, receive, and utilize resources* for the express purpose of promoting and protecting human rights and fundamental freedoms through peaceful means" (italics added).[xxiii] No geographical limitation is put on the right to receive aid. The Office of the High Commissioner for Human Rights has explicitly interpreted the Declaration's protections to extend to the "receipt of funds from abroad."[xxiv]

The UN has been moving rapidly to develop initiatives that support the HRD. In 2000, the then-Human Rights Commission asked Secretary-General Kofi Annan to appoint a special representative to monitor and support the implementation of the HRD. In 2008 the Council directly appointed the Special Rapporteur.

The European Union is also taking action to support the HRD. In 2004, the Council of the European Union adopted Guidelines based on the HRD providing practical suggestions for EU bodies, institutions and missions (Embassies of EU Member States and European Commission Delegations in third party countries) among other things "to effectively work towards the promotion and protection of human rights defenders in non member states." Suggested support and ways of engagement include:

- capacity-building activities and public awareness campaigns;
- access to resources, including funding from abroad;
- visible recognition and support through publicity, visits and invitations, attending and observing trials;
- support for UN special procedures.

HUMAN RIGHTS COUNCIL RESOLUTIONS AND SPECIAL PROCEDURES

Other United Nations charter mechanisms also provide a legal basis for support to NV actors and are strongly affirming the view that domestic restrictions on funding to CSOs violate international law. At its 24th session in September 2013, the Human Rights Council passed a resolution on Civil Society Space: Creating and Maintaining, in Law and Practice, a Safe and Enabling Environment, in which it:

1. expressed concern that *inter alia* domestic restrictions on funding to civil society "have sought to or have been misused to hinder the work and endanger the safety of civil society *in a manner contrary to international law*;"

2. recognized "the urgent need to prevent and stop the use of such provisions, and to review and, where necessary, amend any relevant provisions in order to ensure compliance with international human rights law and, as appropriate, international humanitarian law."[xxv]

Other special procedures provide a legal basis for support to NV actors as well. In 2010 the Human Rights Council appointed a Special Rapporteur on the Rights to Freedom of Peaceful Assembly and of Association.[xxvi] In the Second Report, the Special Rapporteur called the ability of associations to access financial resources "a vital part of the right to freedom of association" and, even more broadly, stated, "The right to freedom of association not only includes the ability of individuals or legal entities to form and join an association but also to seek, receive and use resources – human, material and financial - from domestic, foreign, and international sources."[xxvii]

UN agencies also support NV actors. In 2006 the United Nations launched the UN Democracy Fund mainly to support CSOs engaged in pro-democracy activities.[2] In the first five years of its operation, the fund received \$106,466,154 from UN member states and allocated \$77,751,597 in small grants.[xxviii]

OTHER INTERNATIONAL ORGANIZATIONS

The practice of other international organizations also provides evidence of customary international law. Trade unions and employers'

---

[2] 85% of the funds are required to go to CSOs.

organizations are particular types of CSOs, protected internationally by the rights set out in the Constitution of the International Labor Organization (ILO). Though ILO law is not directly binding on states with respect to other types of CSOs, the decisions of ILO mechanisms represent state practice pertaining to freedom of association and the principles underlying ILO jurisprudence inform by analogy the customary law applicable to other CSOs.

Freedom of association has been called "the bedrock principle" of international labor law.[xxix] It was protected in the Treaty of Versailles, from which the Constitution of the ILO was drawn.[xxx] The Preamble of the ILO Constitution includes "recognition of freedom of association" among the conditions necessary for improving labor conditions. In 1948, the ILO adopted the Convention Concerning Freedom of Association and Protection of the Right to Organize (No. 87), Article 2 of which declares: "Workers and employers, without distinction whatsoever, shall have the right to establish and, subject only to the rules of the organisation concerned, to join organisations of their own choosing without previous authorisation."[xxxi] Article 4 of Convention No. 87 protects workers and employers' organizations from being "dissolved or suspended by administrative authority." Article 5 gives labor organizations the right to "affiliate with international organizations of workers and employers," as well as the right to create and join federations and confederations. Article 7 stipulates that any conditions on legal personality shall not restrict basic rights.

The ILO established a Committee on Freedom of Association (CFA) which is mandated to receive complaints against a state party by another state party or qualified organizations of workers or employers. The FCA can hear complaints against any state party that has ratified the ILO Constitution; its decisions are binding for states that have ratified Convention No. 87. The practice of the CFA supports a broad interpretation of freedom of association, including internationally or transnationally: e.g., "[p]articipation by trade unionists in international trade union meetings is a fundamental trade union right."[xxxii] "[P]rovisions governing the financial operations of workers' organizations should not be such as to give the public authorities discretionary powers over them";[xxxiii] and "[u]nions and confederations should be free to affiliate with international federations or confederations of their own choosing without intervention by the political authorities."[xxxiv]

TREATY BODY JURISPRUDENCE ON SUPPORT TO NV ACTORS

Since treaties are binding legal documents, jurisprudence by the "treaty bodies" (like the HRC) created to oversee compliance is strong evidence that support to NV actors is consistent with international law. State practice in recent years has seen a rise in domestic legislative restrictions on CSOs.[xxxv] These restrictions can take a variety of forms, including bans or limitations on international funding or onerous conditions placed on registration. Many of the laws target CSOs that receive foreign funding. When these legislative restrictions have been litigated before international human rights bodies or addressed in state reports to treaty bodies, they have invariably been found to violate human rights norms.

Ethiopia's 2009 Charities and Societies Proclamation prohibited CSOs getting more than 10% of their funding from foreign sources from engaging in human rights activities.[xxxvi] The African Commission on Human and Peoples' Rights condemned the Proclamation as "denying human rights organizations access to essential funding" and called on Ethiopia to amend the law in accordance with the UN Declaration on Human Rights Defenders.[xxxvii] Indonesia has adopted a Law on Mass Organizations which imposed on international CSOs the obligation to refrain from activities that might disrupt the "stability and oneness" of Indonesia, or interfere with "diplomatic ties."[xxxviii] The HRC criticized the law for its "undue restrictions," *inter alia,* on the freedoms of "association [and] expression…of both domestic and 'foreign' associations," and urged Indonesia to bring the law into compliance with the ICCPR.[xxxix] The Economic, Social and Cultural Rights Committee said it was "deeply concerned" that Egypt's Law no. 153 of 1999 "gives the Government control over the right of NGOs to manage their own activities, including seeking external funding," and stated that the law violated Article 8 of the ICESCR.[xl] In Concluding Observations to the Fourth

Periodic Report of Belarus in 2011, the Committee Against Torture instructed the state party to "enable [NGOs] to seek and receive adequate funding," not limited to domestic sources. [xli] In reviewing the Russian Federation's sixth Article 40 periodic report, the HRC found that the 2006 Non-Profit Organizations Act enacted by the Russian Federation, even after being liberalized in 2009, continued to "pose a serious threat to the enjoyment of the rights to freedom of expression, association, and assembly."[xlii] The Committee also noted "with regret" additional measures taken by the Russian Federation to limit tax exemptions available to international donors to NGOs and made recommendations to bring the Russian Federation into compliance with IHRL standards.[xliii] This jurisprudence upholds the right of NV actors to receive support from "foreign" sources.

THE QUESTION OF COMPLIANCE WITH RESTRICTIVE NATIONAL LAWS

Providers of support for NV actors face the question of whether to operate in states with restrictive national laws and whether to comply with those laws if they do.[xliv] The question of the legal basis for support of NV actors involves the institutions used to provide the aid, about which there is considerable debate for policy reasons. A variety of institutions may be involved in providing aid to NV actors, such as foreign embassies, bilateral aid agencies such as USAID, foundations affiliated with political parties, specialized democracy organizations such as the National Endowment for Democracy or the European Endowment for Democracy, private foundations, and CSOs. In considering the question of whether providers of aid are entitled to disregard national laws restricting CSOs, the legal analysis differs depending on whether the provider of aid is deemed to be a state or nonstate actor. Thus, in addition to the policy considerations, legal consequences must be considered as well.

The case law described above concerning the HRC involves national laws limiting CSOs that have been found to violate the ICCPR. The effect of such laws in preventing individuals within the state from realizing their rights under the ICCPR creates a *delict* under international law that engages the state's responsibility.[xlv] The state is in breach of a treaty.

It is well-settled that a state may not rely on national law in failing to meet an international obligation; less well-settled is what other states are entitled to do in response. Most human rights treaties set out procedures to be followed in the event of a conflict among states. [xlvi] Yet enforcement procedures for human rights treaties are often weak, and may not be automatic; in the ICCPR, a state must declare that it is willing to have the HRC receive communications that it is not fulfilling its obligations under the treaty brought by another state. In practice, state-to-state complaints are rarely made. Even so, some authorities argue that when a treaty provides for enforcement, those procedures are exclusive.[xlvii]

Given the weakness of human rights treaties enforcement regimes and nonexclusivity provisions in some treaties, including the ICCPR, the better argument is that general rules governing state responsibility are available as a fallback to treaty enforcement mechanisms.[xlviii] The rules governing state responsibility are customary in nature, though a draft treaty – the Draft Articles on State Responsibility (DASR) – purporting to codify them exists. Under these rules, an injured state is entitled to resort to countermeasures, defined as "the nonperformance for the time being of international obligations of the State taking the measures toward the responsible State."[xlix] Countermeasures are acts by a state that would be unlawful but for the retaliatory circumstances under which they are being taken. They are also referred to as "self-help." Thus, if State A breaches an obligation to State B, State B may respond in turn by breaching an obligation to State A, subject to a rule of proportionality.

As applied to human rights treaties, the rules governing state responsibility are less clear. The traditional view is that international law creates obligations only between states; and only states and their actors (as defined under international law) can breach these obligations.[1] International human rights treaties and customary law differ from general international law, because they create two different kinds of obligations – obligations that run between or among states and between states and individuals under the jurisdiction of those states. Thus, human rights treaties create obligations among states that benefit individuals, but the benefitted individuals do not have legal duties toward each other or toward the state.[li] While most rules pertaining to state responsibility presume the bilateral nature of the obligation in question, basic international human rights obligations are obligations *erga omnes* – that is, obligations owed to the international community as a whole.[lii] When a state breaches its obligations to its own citizens, a bilateral model of state responsibility provides no means of redress for the individuals injured and no means of enforcements for other state parties, who are not directly injured by the breach but who have an interest in its remedy.

The DASR treats the question raised by human rights treaties in two ways. In what must be regarded as progressive development of the law, the DASR sets out rules in relation to violations of peremptory (*jus cogens*) norms of international law[liii] and also in relation to the broader category of breaches of obligations owed *erga omnes*.[liv] In the face of "a serious breach by a State of an obligation arising under a peremptory norm of general international law," Article 41 provides that a state is obliged to cooperate with other states in bringing about an end to the violation.[lv] A state is also permitted – indeed it is obligated – not to recognize the lawfulness of such a breach *delict*.[lvi] With respect to obligations owed *erga omnes* that do not amount to serious breaches of a peremptory norm, Article 54 provides that a third state may claim from the responsible state "cessation of the internationally wrongful act, and assurances and guarantees of non-repetition,"[lvii] as well as "reparation...in the interest of the injured state or of the beneficiaries of the obligation breached."[lviii]

Article 41 might be interpreted as providing a basis for an argument that third states should not comply with restrictive national laws that are in violation with international norms, but even if it represented codification of customary law (which is debatable), it is not clear it would apply to provide a legal basis for noncompliance with national laws restricting the activities of CSOs. Freedom of association and expression are generally not considered peremptory norms, like norms against genocide, slavery, and aggression,[3] and even in the case of the latter, Article 41 only applies if the breaches are "serious."[4]

Thus, under normal circumstances, in addition to whatever mechanisms were available through the relevant treaty, only the provisions in Art. 48 would be open to a third state wishing to enforce the human rights norms of freedom of association and expression – demands for cessation, guarantees of nonrepetition, and reparations. The DASR does not explicitly give third states a right to resort to normal countermeasures.[5] Article 54 (discussing countermeasures in regard to obligations *erga omnes*) is regarded as a savings clause and the Commentary describes the use of unilateral countermeasures to enforce international human rights or humanitarian law as "limited and rather embryonic."[lxix] At the same time, meaningful state practice of countermeasures in response to human rights violations can be found, and it is possible that in the future a customary norm will crystalize.[lx] A recent analysis has examined the question of whether interested or so-called third states are entitled to resort to countermeasures in response to a *delict* of an obligation *erga omnes* has found that, though the question is not definitively settled, "human rights law is complemented by the enforcement regime outlined in the draft articles."[lxi]

Even if countermeasures enforcing *erga omnes* norms were permissible, however, it is doubtful that in the specific case at issue here – national laws breaching the obligation to respect, protect, and

---

[3] This is not to say that peremptory norms are never implicated in NV protest. If a state responds with violence on a large scale, as has happened in Syria, the threshold of Art. 41 may well be reached.

[4] Art. 41(2) provides that "[n]o state shall recognize as lawful a situation created by a serious breach within the meaning of Article 40, nor render aid or assistance in maintaining that situation." While the Commentary to Art.41 indicates that a wide "diversity of circumstances" may be implicated in this article, most of the examples of state actions entailing non-recognition mentioned in the Commentary involve acquisition of territory. Commentary to Art. 41, at para. 2. A difficulty in applying this Article to the question of not complying with restrictive laws is that the precise language used in Article 41 says that states should not recognize as lawful "a situation created by" a serious breach. In legal writing, laws are not usually referred to as "situations." Moreover, while laws restricting CSOs might be used to *create* a serious breach of a peremptory norm (e.g., genocide or torture), it is difficult to see them as *created by* a serious breach.

[5] A draft provision explicitly permitting countermeasures in the case of human rights violations was proposed by the ILC but rejected by the Sixth Committee of the General Assembly. Simma & Pulkowski supra n. 48, at 528. The rejected provision was replaced by the current Art. 54, a general savings clause ("This chapter does not prejudice the right of any State, entitled under article 48, paragraph 1, to invoke the responsibility of another State, to take lawful measures against that State to ensure cessation of the breach and reparation in the interest of the injured State or of beneficiaries of the obligation breached").

fulfill the right to freedom of association and expression – lawful countermeasures would include the disregard of national laws. Codifying international law, the DASR states that countermeasures "are limited to" the nonperformance of an international obligation, subject to proportionality. For example, when Poland imposed martial law in 1981 the United States and other Western countries responded by suspending treaties for landing rights.[lxii] Disregard of a national law that is in violation of an international obligation would likely not be considered an acceptable countermeasure under current international law, because it does not involve nonperformance of an international obligation.[6]

An additional consideration is that states are subject to the norm of nonintervention, which is considered to be the correlate of the principle of state sovereignty.[7] States that have adopted restrictive domestic laws regarding CSOs frequently assert that foreign-funded or foreign-supported activities in their territory violate the norm of nonintervention. Treaty body jurisprudence implies that where states are parties to relevant human rights treaties, the norm of nonintervention does not apply to support to NV actors. International human rights treaty bodies have not differentiated between support coming from state actors as opposed to support coming from nonstate actors. As to states, HRC practice implies that, by ratifying human rights treaties, states have consented to human rights law and to supporting the work of NV actors acting to uphold those norms, including to consenting to their funding by foreign sources, at least to some degree.[8] As Special

---

[6] This conclusion is subject to the caveat that a consistent state practice of disregarding noncompliant national laws could result in new customary law regarding countermeasures, at least with respect to obligations *erga omnes*. Current state practice appears inconsistent. See Carothers & Brechenmacher, at 52 ("Some aid providers… follow a policy of always conforming to local laws. Yet others have opted for a different approach").

[7] The 1933 Montevideo Convention on the Rights and Duties of States, 49 Stat. 3097, 165 L.N.T.S. 19 (Dec. 26, 1933), which sets out the most widely accepted definition of statehood, enunciates a norm against forcible intervention in Article 8 (providing "No state has the right to intervene in the internal or external affairs of another"). Though the UN Charter did not adopt the Montevideo language, the 1970 Declaration on Principles of International Law concerning Friendly Relations and Co-operation among States in Accordance with the Charter of the United Nations (adopted by consensus) is generally accepted, among other things, as an authoritative interpretation of the Charter and states that the "progressive development and codification of…[t]he duty not to intervene in matters within the domestic jurisdiction of any State, in accordance with the Charter…would promote the realization of the purposes of the United Nations." *See* Thomas D. Grant, *Defining Statehood: The Montevideo Convention and Its Discontents*, Colum. J. Int'l L. (1999). The Montevideo Convention is a treaty between the United States and numerous Latin American countries.

[8] The cases examined do not address explicitly the question of whether foreign funding for specific political candidates is permitted under human rights law. *See* Lori Damrosch, *Politics Across Borders: Nonintervention and Non-forcible Influence over Domestic Affairs*, 83 Am. J. Int'l L. 1 (1989).

Rapporteur Maina Kiai points out, "The protection of State sovereignty is not listed as a legitimate interest [serving as a ground for derogation]" in the ICCPR. [lxiii]

Where states have not ratified an international or regional treaty and the law being applied to them is customary international law, the situation is more complicated, because it could be argued that by passing restrictive CSO laws, states are objecting to the formation of custom. By objecting long and often enough, they will be seen as "persistent objectors" to any emerging customary law. Given the considerable legal unclarity that surrounds the norm of nonintervention as it applies to nonforcible means, it cannot be ruled out that states electing to operate where restrictive laws have been passed may be found in violation of international law.

As a consequence, strictly from the perspective of international law, nonstate actors are the preferred vehicles of delivery in states that have passed restrictive national laws. In addition, the rights recognized by human rights treaties – here, the rights of expression and association – do not properly belong to the states parties; they belong to individuals. Nonstate actors are not subject to the customary international legal rules regarding state responsibility. They are entitled to exercise their right to associate with individuals in the restricting state, and the individuals in the restricting state are entitled to exercise their right to associate with individuals in foreign states. Of course the mere lawfulness of acts under international law does not prevent the restricting state from prosecuting such actors for disregarding national laws. The diplomatic immunities available to state actors have to be weighed into the legal analysis. Moreover, the acts of nonstate actors may be *attributed* to the state for the purposes of international law under certain conditions "if the person or group of persons is in fact acting on the instructions of, or under the direction or control of, that State in carrying out the conduct." [lxiv] However, the threshold is high for such attribution. Set down in an ICJ case involving the US funding of the Nicaraguan *contras,* the standard requires more than merely funding and supplying the nonstate actors. The state must have "effective control" over their actions. [lxv]

QUALIFICATIONS AND IMPORTANT PRECEDENT

While the above appears to be the best reading of the law, it is important to note that the DASR is not clear on what Article 41 may entail and the disregard of national laws as a response to breach of peremptory norms is not out of the question. The Commentary refers to the ICJ Advisory Opinion in *Legal Consequences for States of Continued Presence of South Africa in Namibia (South West Africa) notwithstanding Security Council Resolution 276*.[lxvi] That decision dealt with South Africa's refusal to give up a mandate to govern Namibia originally accorded by the League of Nations, even after a Security Council Resolution explicitly revoked South Africa's authority there. In the Namibian case, the serious breach came about as the result of a change in legal status of South Africa's presence in Namibia. Obviously, the South African laws administering the Namibian territory were already in place at the time the Security Council resolution was adopted. Most of the ICJ's analysis regarding the legal consequence for states in this situation concerned ending diplomatic, economic, and treaty relations with South Africa insofar as they involved Namibia. But also implicit in the decision is that states should not recognize South Africa's laws enabling the "serious breach" in question, as the Court qualifies: "while official acts performed by the Government of South Africa on behalf of or concerning Namibia…are illegal and invalid, the invalidity cannot be extended to those acts, such as…the registration of births, deaths and marriages, the effect of which can be ignored only to the detriment of the inhabitants of the Territory."[lxvii]

Along these lines, at least one directly relevant precedent exists for noncompliance with national laws in response to serious breaches of peremptory norms: the Sullivan principles (a code of conduct for corporations operating in South Africa during the apartheid era), as codified in the US Comprehensive Anti-Apartheid Act of 1986 (CAAA).[lxviii] The Sullivan Principles required US companies doing business in South Africa to desegregate their workplaces and eventually to work to end South African Apartheid laws. These requirements brought US companies into conflict with South African laws, and

Sullivan himself referred to them as "corporate civil disobedience." While the Sullivan principles were voluntary and engaged only nonstate actors, the CAAA applied to both state and nonstate actors in South Africa, in addition to enacting other trade and economic sanctions. Furthermore, the CAAA provided for civil and criminal penalties, thus subjecting US nationals to conflicting legal regimes. The CAAA went far beyond countermeasures as described in DASR and is an example of disregard of national laws in response to a serious breach of a peremptory norm.[lxix]

The context for this precedent is important. By 1986, apartheid in South Africa had been the target of concerted, though not completely unified, multilateral action on the part of the international community for more than two decades.[9] Despite the use of the veto in the Security Council by the United States and Great Britain, both the General Assembly and Security Council (though not under Chapter VII) had asked member states to take unilateral measures against South Africa, and the US Congress was eventually able to override a Presidential veto of the CAAA. Even though the CAAA went far beyond the actions requested by the United Nations,[lxx] its actions did not meet with condemnation by the international community, as it was becoming apparent that only unilateral action could overcome the impasse in the Security Council. States contemplating disregard of national laws restricting CSO activities would be advised to seek multilateral support in the form of resolutions by the General Assembly or Human Rights Council calling on states to take unilateral measures to protect NV actors.[10]

---

[9] In the context of the anti-apartheid activities of the United Nations, the Advisory Committee on Questions of Public International Law was asked to assess the lawfulness of sanctions in light of the duty of nonintervention set out in the Declaration on Principles of International Law Concerning Friendly Relations Among States. In an early intimation of the Responsibility to Protect, a 1982 report of the Committee found that "the duty of nonintervention should not be viewed in isolation but, on the contrary, should be examined in the light of other rules of international law. Since apartheid was regarded by an overwhelming majority of states as a flagrant violation of the human rights of the non-white population of South Africa, it could not be protected within the ambit of the rule of non-intervention." Elena Katselli Proukaki, The Problem of Enforcement in International Law: Countermeasures, the Non-Injured State, and the Idea of International Community 173 (2009).

[10] In this regard, it should be noted that the kind of unilateral coercive measures that were also enacted in the CAAA have recently been opposed by many Third World states. *See* Human Rights Council Resolution on Human Rights and Unilateral Coercive Measures, H.R. Council Res. 19/32, 19th Sess., UN Doc. A/HRC/Res/19/32 (opposed by the United States and all European members of the Council).

CONCLUSION

Grounded mostly on the rights of association and expression, a sound legal basis for support for NV actors exists in international and regional human rights treaties and UN mechanisms. In situations where states have passed laws restricting CSOs from associating with "foreign" supporters, nonstate actors are on sounder legal footing than states in disregarding national laws, though this needs to be weighed against the protections of immunity that may be available to state actors. States deliberating how to respond to national laws restricting CSOs should seek multilateral support through international organizations, particularly the United Nations, or try to coordinate a more consistent state practice in order to develop the customary law regarding countermeasures.

Notes

i.   Report the United Nations High Commissioner on Human Rights, Seminar on Effective Measures and Best Practices to Ensure the Promotion and Protection of Human Rights in the Context of Peaceful Protests, UN Doc. A/HRC/25/32/, para. 11 (Jan. 29, 2014). The seminar took place on December 2, 2013.

ii. ICCPR, Art. 1(1) ("All peoples have the right of self-determination. By virtue of that right they freely determine their political status and freely pursue their economic, social and cultural development.").

iii. *Id.* at Art. 21("The right of peaceful assembly shall be recognized").

iv. ICCPR, Art. 25 ("Every citizen shall have the right and the opportunity, without any of the distinctions mentioned in article 2 and without unreasonable restrictions: (a) To take part in the conduct of public affairs, directly or through freely chosen representatives; (b) To vote and to be elected at genuine periodic elections which shall be by universal and equal suffrage and shall be held by secret ballot, guaranteeing the free expression of the will of the electors…").

v.   Art. 19(1), Art. 9(1), and Art. 13(1), respectively.

vi. ICCPR, at Art. 19(2). The language in the American Convention is almost identical and found in Art. 13(1).

vii. Human Rights Comm., Gen'l Cmt. No. 34, UN Doc. CCPR/C/GC/34, at para. 15.

viii. *Autronic AG v. Switzerland*, (May 22, 1990), Application No. 12726/87, at para. 47.

ix. Human Rights Council, 17th Session (May 16, 2011), Report of the Special Rapporteur on the Promotion and Protection of the Right to Freedom of Opinion and Expression, Frank LaRue, UN Doc. A/HRC/17/27, para. 22.

x.   See Human Rights Comm., General Comments Under Article 40, Paragraph 4, of the International Covenant on Civil and Political Rights (Addendum), General Comment 25 (57), UN Doc. CCPR/C/21/Rev.1/Add.7 (Aug. 27, 1996), at para. 26.

xi.   Human Rights Comm., Gen'l Cmt No. 25: The Right to Participate in Public Affairs, Voting Rights and the Right of Equal Access to Public Service (Art. 25), UN Doc. CCPR/C/21/Rev.1/Add.7 (1996), para. 1.

xii.   Human Rights Comm., *Korneenko et al. v. Belarus*, Comm. No. 1274/2004 (Oct. 31, 2004), para. 7.2, UN Doc. CCPR/C/88/D/1274/2004 (Views adopted Oct. 31, 2006).

xiii.   Human Rights Comm., Consideration of reports submitted by States Parties under Art. 40 of the Covenant, Concluding Observations (Lebanon), UN Doc. CCPR/C/79/Add. 78, paras. 27 & 28 (May 5, 1997) (noting while statute governing associations is compatible on its face with Art. 22, *de facto* state practice imposes system of prior control, and urging state to adhere to terms of statute); *see also*, Report of the Special Rapporteur of the Secretary-General on Human Rights Defenders, Hina Jilani, UN Doc. A/59/401, para. 82(a) (Oct. 1, 2004) ("the Special Representative also believes that registration should not be compulsory. NGOs should be allowed to exist and carry out collective activities without having to register if they so wish"); *see also id.*, at 82(b) (encouraging states to adopt regimes of "declaration" or "notification" whereby an organization is considered a legal entity as soon as it has notified its existence to the relevant administration").

xiv.   African Charter, Art. 10 ("Every individual shall have the right to free association provided that he abides by the law") and Art.11 ("Every individual shall have the right to assemble freely with others. The exercise of this right shall be subject only to necessary restrictions provided for by law, in particular those enacted in the interest of national security, the safety, health, ethics and rights and freedoms of others").

xv.   Art. 16(1) ("Everyone has the right to associate freely for ideological, religious, political, economic, labor, social, cultural, sports, or other purposes").

xvi.   Convention on the Elimination of All Forms of Racial Discrimination, Art. 1(1), Art. 5(c), Art. 5(d)(viii) and (ix).

xvii.   ICCPR, Art. 22(2); *see also* Human Rights Comm., Gen'l Cmt 31(6), UN Doc. CCPR/C/21/Rev.1/Add. 13 (May 26, 2004) ("Where such restrictions are made, States must demonstrate their necessity and only take such measures as are proportionate to the pursuance of legitimate aims in order to ensure continuous and effective protection of Covenant rights.").

xviii.   G.A. Res. 53/144, UN Doc. No. A/RES/53/144 (Dec. 9, 1999).

xix.   Ibid. at Art. 1 and Art. 12(1).

xx.   Ibid. at Art. 1.

xxi.   *Id.* at Art. 12 (1).

xxii.   Art. 5(b) ("For the purpose of promoting and protecting human rights and fundamental freedoms, everyone has the right, individually and in association with others, at the national and international levels: ... (b) to form, join and participate in nongovernmental organizations, associations, or groups").

178   IS AUTHORITARIANISM STAGING A COMEBACK?

xxiii. *Id.* at Art. 13.

xxiv. Office of the High Commissioner for Human Rights, Fact Sheet 29, at *http://www. ohchr.org/Documents/Publications/FactSheet29en.pdf.*

xxv. Human Rights Council, 24th Sess. (Sept. 23, 2013), Res. 24/..., Res. on Civil Society Space: Creating and Maintaining, in Law and Practice, a Safe and Enabling Environment, UN Doc. A/HRC/24/L. 24, at preamble.

xxvi. Human Rights Council (Oct. 6, 2010), Res. 15/21, The Rights to Freedom of Peaceful Assembly and of Association, UN Doc. A/HRC/RES/15/21.

xxvii. Human Rights Council, 23rd Sess. (April 24, 2013), Rep. of the Special Rapporteur on the Rights to Freedom of Peaceful Assembly and of Association, Maina Kiai, UN Doc. A/HRC/23/39, at III(A) and para. 8.

xxviii. Audit Report, UN Democracy Fund (2010), at http://usun.state.gov/documents/organization/159739.pdf.

xxix. Steve Charnovitz, *The ILO Convention on Freedom of Association and its Future in the United States*, 102 Am. J.Int'l. L. 90, 90 (2008).

xxx. Treaty of Peace with Germany (Treaty of Versailles), pt. XIII, pmbl., June 28, 1919, 2 Bevans.

xxxi. Convention Concerning Freedom of Association and Protection of the Right to Organize (No. 87), July 9, 1948, 68 UNTS 17.

xxxii. *Freedom of Association, Digest of Decisions and Principles of the Freedom of Association Committee of the Governing Body of the ILO, Fifth (rev.) Edition* (ILO Office, Geneva) (2008), at para. 153 (citing 300th Report, Case No. 1805, para. 421; and 336th Report, Case No. 2328, para. 885).

xxxiii. *Id.* at para. 468 (citing 304th Report, Case No. 1865, para. 248; and 306th Report, Case No. 1865, para. 326).

xxxiv. *Id. at* para. 733 (citing 1996 Digest, para. 623).

xxxv. Civicus, World Alliance for Citizen Participation, Report, *Global Trends on Civil Society Restrictions. Mounting Restrictions on Civil Society: The Gap Between Rhetoric and Reality* (October 2013), available at *http://civicus.org/images/GlobalTrendsonCivilSocietyRestrictons2013.pdf.*

xxxvi. National Legislative Bodies / National Authorities, *Ethiopia: Proclamation No. 621/2009 of 2009, Charities and Societies Proclamation*, 13 February 2009, available at: http://www.refworld.org/docid/4ba7a0cb2.html [accessed 17 September 2014].

xxxvii. African Commission on Human and Peoples' Rights, 51st Ordinary Session (May 2, 2012), Resolution on the Human Rights Situation in the Democratic Republic of Ethiopia, No. 218, at Preamble and iv, available at *http://www.achpr.org/sessions/51st/resolutions/218/.*

xxxviii. CIVICUS, "Indonesian NGO Law a Setback for Freedom of Association," press release, August 19, 2013, *http://civicus.org/media-centre-129/press-releases/1822-indonesian-ngo-law-a- setback-for-freedom-of-association.*

xxxix. Human Rights Comm., Concluding Observations on the Initial Report of Indonesia (Aug. 21, 2013), UN Doc. CCPR/C/IDN/CO/1, para. 24.

xl.   Consideration of Reports Submitted by States Parties under Articles 16 and 17th of the Covenant, Concluding Observations of the Committee on Economic, Social and Cultural Rights (Egypt)(May 23, 2000), UN Doc. E/C.12/1/Add.44, para. 19.

xli. See also Comm. Against Torture, 47th Session (Dec. 7, 2011), Consideration of Reports Submitted by States Parties under Article 19 of the Convention, Concluding Observations of the Comm. Against Torture (Belarus), CAT/C/BLR/CO/4, para. 25(a) (recommending state party enable CSOs "to seek and receive adequate funding to carry out their peaceful human rights activities").

xlii. Human Rights Comm., 97th Session (October 2009), Consideration of Reports Submitted by States Parties Under Article 40 of the Covenant, Concluding Observations of the Human Rights Committee (Russian Federation), para. 26, UN Doc. CCPR/C/RUS/CO/6.

xliii. *Id*.

xliv. Cf. Thomas Carothers & Saskia Brechenmacher, *Report, Closing Spaces: Democracy and Human Rights Under Fire*, Carnegie Endowment for International Peace (2014), at 51.

xlv. For the reasons of space, this paper is not able to consider the question of whether the rights to freedom of association and expression have attained the status of customary international law.

xlvi. The ICCPR sets out these procedures in Arts. 41-43.

xlvii. *See, e.g., Military and Paramilitary Activities in and against Nicaragua* (Nicaragua v. United States of America), Merits, ICJ Reports (1986), at 134 ("[W]here human rights are protected by international conventions, that protection takes the form of such arrangements for monitoring or ensuring respect for human rights as are provided for in the conventions themselves.") But since the ICJ in *Nicaragua* specifically noted that "the mechanisms provided for have functioned," it left open use of general international law state responsibility rules as a fallback. *Cf.* Bruno Simma & Dirk Pulkowski, *Of Planets and the Universe: Self-Contained Regimes in International Law*, 17 Eur. J. Int'l. L. 483, 524 (2006) (noting the Court then "turns to a unitary counter-argument, with a view to preventing a potential 'effectiveness gap' in human rights treaties").

xlviii. *Cf.* Bruno Simma & Dirk Pulkowski, *Of Planets and the Universe: Self-Contained Regimes in International Law*, 17 Eur. J. Int'l. L. 483, 529 (2006)(concluding "general international law provides a systemic fabric from which no special legal regime is completely decoupled"). This approach is reflected in the DASR. *See* Art. 55 ("These articles do not apply where and to the extent that the condition for the existence of an internationally wrongful act or the content or implementation of the international responsibility of a State are governed by special rules of international law").

xlix. DASR, Art. 49(2).

l.   For a critique of the traditional view, see Jordan Paust, *Nonstate Actor Participation in International Law and the Pretense of Exclusion*, 51 Vir. J Int'l L. 977 (arguing that "[f]or centuries, there have been vast numbers of formally recognized actors in the international legal process other than the state").

li.   The African Charter is anomalous among human rights treaties because it does purport to create duties that individuals have against the state.

lii.   *Barcelona Traction, Light and Power Company, Ltd. (Belgium v. Spain),* Judgment, ICJ Reports 1970, at para. 33.

liii.   Art. 41 ("Particular consequences of a serious breach of an obligation under this chapter.") "This chapter" refers to Chapter III ("Serious Breaches of Obligations Under Peremptory Norms of General International Law.") *Cf.* Bird, at 888 ("The duty of cooperation outlined in Article 41 clearly represents the progressive development of international law, since it would be premature to conclude that third states believe they are under an obligation to cooperate to stop serious breaches.").

liv.   DASR, Art. 48 ("Invocation of responsibility by a State other than an injured State").

lv.   DASR, Art. 41(1).

lvi.   DASR, Art. 41(2).

lvii.   Ibid. at Art. 48(2)(a).

lviii.   Ibid. at Art. 48(2)(b).

lix.   DASR, Commentary to Art. 54, at para. 3.

lx.   Ibid.

lxi.   Annie Bird, *Third State Responsibility for Human Rights Violations,* 21 Eur. J. Int'l. L. 883, 900 (2010)(concluding that "unless the Draft Articles become law, future state practice will ultimately determine whether third states act upon the rights and obligations outlined by the ILC"). In this context, "third state" is a term of art designating a state other than the injured state; in many cases involving human rights treaties there will be no injured states, so unless third states can take countermeasures, no countermeasures will be available.

lxii.   Ibid., at 897.

lxiii.   Kaia, supra n. 29, at para. 30.

lxiv.   DASR, Art. 8.

lxv.   *Military and Paramilitary Activities in and Against Nicaragua (Nicaragua v. United States of America), Merits Judgment,* ICJ Reports 1986, at paras. 109 and 115.

lxvi.   ICJ Reports 1971.

lxvii.   Commentary to Art. 41, para. 10.

lxviii. Pub. L. 99-440, 100 Stat. 1086, *codified at* 22 U.S.C. ss 5001.

lxix.   Ibid., Commentary to Art. 54 (describing the suspension of landing rights by the CAAA as an example of state practice regarding countermeasures by a third state).

lxx.   *See, e.g.,* G.A. Res. 1761 (1962) (requesting member states to cut or refuse diplomatic ties with South Africa, close ports and landing ships to South African ships and airplanes, forbid ships from entering South African ports and boycott South African goods); S. C. Res. 569 (1985) (calling on states, *inter alia,* to suspend new investments, prohibit sale of South African coins, restrict sports and cultural relations, and suspend guaranteed export loans).

CHAPTER 13

Bringing Down the Dictators: The Utility of Smart Sanctions

George A. Lopez
Vice-President, US Institute of Peace

THE DEVELOPMENT AND INSTITUTIONALIZATION of 'smart sanctions' provides an array of coercive measures to the international community that have proven somewhat effective in particular cases of massive rights abuses and on–going atrocities. As such they provide a basis for scrutinizing if and how these tools might be mobilized to break the hold of dictators on their populations in all areas of social and political life.

Sanctions mechanisms have evolved from a single donor nation withdrawing economic aid and trade to protest human rights violations, coups, and the rise of dictators, to coordinated action by multilateral organizations imposing targeted sanctions against individuals and entities to punish or constrain their specific activities that violate international law or norms. This use of multilateral economic sanctions has been advocated by transnational human rights NGOs for two decades, and their imposition and enforcement has occupied an increasingly prominent place in the coercive tool kit of national policy makers.[i]

Their operational international form has taken shape most pronouncedly in United Nations Security Council resolutions and has been strengthened, if not also extended in scope and enforcement, by sanctions adopted by the European Union, the British Commonwealth, and ad hoc coalitions of states. These intersecting developments have not been without controversy and, sometimes, outright contradiction. As revealed in the five decades of US unilateral sanctions on Cuba and various 1980s Soviet sanctions against its satellite states, some economic sanctions which claim to be enforcing human rights norms are actually designed as a means to punish directly ideological foes, with significant negative impact on rights and the quality of life of the general population.[ii] These cases of big power economic coercion combined with the negative humanitarian consequences of the earliest cases of UN sanctions in the 1990s: Iraq [devastating humanitarian impact], Haiti, and the Former Republic of Yugoslavia [varied from serious to minimal humanitarian impact] led various analysts to question whether sanctions can ever be an ethical tool, or other than harmful, to human rights and human security.[iii]

THE SMART SANCTIONS TOOLKIT

Sanctions measures are precisely targeted or 'smart' in two ways. First, they take aim at specific sub-national and transnational actors deemed most responsible for the policies or actions considered by the imposer as illegal or abhorrent. Rather than punishing the society generally through trade or aid sanctions, smart sanctions aim to constrain identifiable, culpable perpetrators of wrong-doing. Generally, in human rights sanctions these are the abusive government institutions and leaders who authorize and—when identifiable—the individuals who perpetrate the abuses and the killings.

Second, smart sanctions provide a laser focus of economic coercion to a specific micro-level economic activity that can be identified as contributing to increased human rights violations or dictator activities. Most often such sanctions aim at the 'power tools' of a tyrant: his weapons, repressive technologies, and unfettered pillaging of national resources to acquire wealth to bolster his own power.

The measures below comprise the smart sanctions most readily available to constrain or end the rule of a dictator. They include:

1. freezing foreign-held financial assets of [a] the national government; [b] specific governmental agencies, such as

an armed forces unit; [c] members of the government in their individual capacity; or, [d] those entities or individuals designated as key supporters of the dictator;

2. suspending credits, aid, and loans available to the regime, specifically the political or economic actors [a] through [d] listed above that deal with monies involving international financial institutions in the nation; OR

3. suspending credits, aid, and loans available to [a] the national government; [b] specific governmental agencies, such as an armed forces unit; [c] members of the government in their individual capacity; or, [d] those entities or individuals designated as key supporters of the dictator; political or economic actors in the nation that deal with monies involving international financial institutions;

4. denying access to overseas financial markets, often to the target government's National Bank and other governmental entities, as well as to designated private banks and investors;

5. restricting the trade of specific goods and commodities that provide power resources and revenue to the dictator, especially highly-traded, income-producing mineral resources;

6. banning aid and trade of weapons, munitions, military replacement parts, dual-use goods of a military nature;

7. banning computers, cell phone and satellite technologies, as well as related communications 'jamming' and 'surveillance' technologies;

8. banning flight and travel of individuals and/or specific air and sea carriers;

9. denial of visa, travel, and educational opportunities to those individuals on the designee list;

10. denying import of, or otherwise access to, goods labeled as 'luxury items' for the entities and individuals on the designated list.

One advantage of these smart sanctions lies in how they close the direct accountability gap that often surrounds and protects rights-abusing dictators as they perpetrate atrocities. Asset freezes result in the overseas 'rainy-day' funds of dictators becoming inaccessible to them and relatives. Dictators' children lose travel visas and access to tuition monies to attend elite Western schools and universities. Thus smart sanctions ensure that the coercion aimed at the political power figure for their actions has now become intensely personal.

When time is of the essence in responding to unfolding rights violations and mass atrocities, some targeted sanctions are likely to be more appealing and effective than others. But in all cases the effectiveness of sanctions demands a convergence of factors anchored in the willingness of imposers to unite behind a collection of sanctions and to adapt them to patterns of violation by what should be an expanding list of targets. Essentially, my argument in this chapter is that this pattern of sanctions against rights violations provides some confidence that an extension of these same tools against dictators for abuses of power beyond human rights violations could be effective.

Yet even as I extol these attributes of smart sanctions as an anti-dictator tool, there are downsides and a historical record in the human rights area that needs to be acknowledged. First, while sanctions imposed to stop rights abuses have led to some improvements, they have never toppled the abuser government. Secondly, if a dictator is to be toppled by sanctions, the control of weaponry into the ruler's storehouse must be significantly curtailed. Yet, three decades of sanctions illustrate that arms embargoes have been the most difficult sanctions to implement and enforce effectively.[iv]

THE TRENDS IN THE CASES

Prior to imposing sanctions on Iraq for its invasion of Kuwait in August, 1990 the UN's Permanent Five powers and a sufficient number of rotating Security Council members reached agreement on sanctions only twice in the UN's first forty-five years of its existence. Significantly, each time involved an institutionalized racially-based repressive government case: Southern Rhodesia (1966) and South Africa (1977). These might be considered bureaucratic authoritarians or dictators. In the fifteen years following the initial Iraq resolution, the majority of UN sanctions cases – Yugoslavia, Haiti, Somalia, Libya, Ethiopia and Eritrea (which involved primarily governments) and Liberia, Angola, Rwanda, Sudan, Sierra Leone, Afghanistan, Democratic Republic of Congo, and Cote d'Ivoire (which involved nonstate and often multiple violent actors), had some dimensions of rights concerns reflected in the resolutions.[v]

At the same time, such sanctions have been fraught with inconsistencies regarding their design, implementation, monitoring and 'clout,' thus calling into question their impact on human rights and security. Put in its best light, over time the international community—acting through the UN Security Council—has made progress in some specific cases of rights abuse and mass atrocities and in so doing has formulated at least two on-going guiding themes, which some would call them 'global norms.' The first is the protection of innocent civilians (PoC) in armed conflict, while the second is the responsibility to protect (R2P) civilians faced with mass atrocities.

The cases of Liberia, Cote d'Ivoire and Libya are often cited as somewhat positive recent examples of sanctions enforcing and protecting human rights. Yet these stand in contrast to the more troubling realities and significant historical cases in which UN sanctions effectively failed to halt human rights abuses when civilians were under greatest attack – during genocide and in protracted bloody atrocities. In at least four cases—Yugoslavia, Rwanda, Liberia (until 2001), and Sudan/Darfur—UN sanctions resulted in little or no reduction in the killing, because the Council acted late, and then imposed a limited and weakly-enforced arms embargo that was not integrated with other more powerful financial or other sanctions.[vi] Similarly, the limited measures imposed in Afghanistan prior to 2001 also had no discernible impact on the policies of the Taliban regime regarding treatment of cultural artifacts or of Afghan women's rights.

Despite pleas of "never again," the failure of the international community to use sanctions or other means to prevent ethnic cleansing in Bosnia in 1992 or genocide in Rwanda in 1994 was repeated regarding Darfur a decade later. Without question, the Darfur case serves as a glaring example of too few sanctions imposed too late and without the broad targeting of a substantial number of elites that would maximize their effectiveness. Despite near global condemnation of the Sudanese regime for its—and its Janjaweed agents'—actions against the citizens of the Darfur region from 2003 through 2008, a rather watered-down set of financial asset freezes and travel restrictions were imposed against a small number of Sudanese officials in a series of Security Council Resolutions. A draft Security Council resolution targeting more than thirty persons responsible for killings and brutal actions in the region faced serious opposition. Most of this back-tracking was due to the unwillingness of the Chinese and Russians to support extensive sanctions. Ultimately the final resolution adopted designated only four individuals. The UN debate over sanctions continued for so long prior to their adoption that whoever was to face financial penalties surely avoided them.[vii]

The recent Libyan case provides the most contemporary and controversial example of bringing down a tyrant through multilateral action which featured economic sanctions as its cornerstone. With resolution 1970 (February, 2011) the Security Council targeted the Gaddafi regime institutionally and as 'designated individuals' of the dictator's family and inner circle for their role in the brutal repression of protestors who had taken to the streets of various Libyan cities also with the aim of sending a message to Gaddafi that he should halt future government attacks. In addition to an arms embargo, resolution 1970 imposed an extensive assets freeze, other financial restrictions, and a travel and aviation ban. The sanctions also encompassed cargo inspections anywhere in the world if freight were suspected of being bound for Libya. Significant for human rights advancement, the resolution also called for the International Criminal Court to investigate potential government atrocities and to issue indictments where appropriate.

Despite reservations on the part of some Council members, resolution 1970 passed with remarkable unanimity and speed. The timely adoption of the resolution resulted from the convergence of three realities. The first was that 48 hours prior to the Security Council vote many of the same packages of sanctions and their targets had been invoked by the US and EU. There was a comprehensive and extensive reach by these national sanctions imposed by the United States and the European Union such that the bulk of the assets of the Gaddafi regime and family had already locked down, setting the stage for Security Council action.

The second was the defection of Libyan UN ambassador Mohammed Shalgham, who urged Security Council members to impose sanctions in response to the atrocities committed by Gaddafi against the Libyan people.[viii] Also influencing Council thinking was a third factor, the endorsement by UN member states in the region for sanctions, which were also supported by regional actors like Council of the League of Arab States.

Despite the effectiveness of these strong measures it soon became clear that more stringent actions were needed in order to protect the lives of Libyan civilians, specifically in Benghazi, which Gaddafi had vowed to raze in crushing its dissidents like cockroaches. In March 2011, Resolution 1973 expanded existing sanctions, authorizing a no-fly zone and a ban on all Libyan flights. Arab support, critical to obtaining US consent to a military intervention, was quickly provided when the Council of the League of Arab States called for a no-fly zone and the League of Arab States, Qatar and the UAE pledged to contribute to the NATO and international effort in Libya.[ix] Thus, resolution 1973 made clear that "all necessary measures" other than an occupying force could be used to protect civilians.

NATO implementation of the "necessary measures" led to a full scale bombing campaign to destroy Gaddafi's air defense units and command facilities. The success of these strikes and the resulting military victories for the rebels ended Gaddafi's dictatorship. Certainly the fall of the Libyan regime would not have occurred without an armed rebellion and NATO's military support, but the combination of UN, EU and US targeted sanctions played a considerable role in degrading both the regime's firepower and its support among Libya's elites. By cutting off nearly half of Gaddafi's usable monies—some $36 billion in Libyan funds were locked down in the first week of sanctions—the international community immediately denied the dictator the funds to import heavy weapons, to hire foot soldier mercenaries, or to contract with elite commando units bent on doing the killing Gaddafi would order. Had these sanctions not been successfully imposed and enforced, it is reasonable to assert that the Libyan war would have been longer and considerably more deadly for Libyan citizens. Tripoli, for example, was not destroyed in an all-out battle like that which in 2012-2013 engulfed and leveled major Syrian cities.[1]

But this sanctions success proved short-lived in the Security Council. Faced with an equally brutal regime engaged in killing its own citizenry, in part during the same year, the Council could not reach any consensus on taking action against the Assad regime in Syria. Some of this can be explained by Russia's anger over what it considered an over-extended interpretation of SCR 1973 and illegitimate use of force by NATO to overthrow a government militarily. This pronounced backlash to the Libya case led many member states and analysts to conclude that sanctions were being rendered irrelevant as an international tool.

Contrary to this pessimistic view, I suggest that sanctions strategy and tactical application adapt and advance more deliberately as a result of this impasse and condemnation. Specifically, as I argue below, smart sanctions need to move beyond the narrow leader-focused and 'killer-on-the-ground' targeting approach to casting a broader and deeper net. In this casting policy makers should be guided by both what we know about how mass killings and displacements unfold and, as available, evidence-based findings about products and people linked to atrocities and the support systems that maintain the dictators that order them. The aim here is to change the basic dynamics of the dictator infrastructure which bolsters them and to expand who and what we stifle and thwart via the application of smart sanctions.

---

[1] For a debate on the issues of NATO intervention in Libya see *http://kroc.nd.edu/news-events/peace-policy/military-interventionism-libya-pandora-s-box-questions-1261*.

SHARPENING SMART SANCTIONS BY TARGETING ENABLERS

While locking down the assets of dictators is necessary for atrocity prevention, it is seldom sufficient. By exploring the scope and examples of enabling below I offer a new, earlier, and certainly lower level focus of sanctioning targeting. One potentially effective approach is to focus on the means used to commit dictatorial crimes and on those who provide them. Because dictator actions like resource plundering and mass killings are essentially organized crimes, crippling the means to organize and sustain them—money, communications networks, and other resources—can disrupt their execution. A key element of their organization that is particularly relevant to international responses is the role of third parties. History has taught us that perpetrators are seldom able to carry out these crimes on their own. Rather, they are dependent on direct or indirect support from external actors—governments, commercial entities, and individuals—whose goods and services enable them to wage attacks against civilians.

Certainly dictators and their crime-perpetrating allies are generally both creative and resourceful; it is not difficult to identify a core set of activities that **enable** and sustain their violence and activities. By developing approaches to target the third parties engaged in those activities, it may prove possible to decrease or interrupt the perpetrators' and dictators' access to the necessary means. This may, in turn, alter their calculus for committing atrocities. Targeting the **enablers** is not a panacea, but it should lead to a better understanding of the dynamics of atrocities and present a practical lever with significant untapped potential to halt the world's worst crimes.

There are three essential elements to enabling: (1) a third party provides resources, goods, services, or other practical support—directly or indirectly—to the perpetrator of ongoing atrocities; (2) this support is a critical ingredient that enables or sustains the commission of the atrocities, without which the atrocities would not have taken place to the same extent; and (3) the third party knew or should have known about the atrocities and about the ways in which its goods or support were likely to contribute to the commission of these crimes.

The type of support identified in element (1) might take the forms listed below.

(A) Providing the means that are used to commit the atrocities directly, including:

    1. weapons (small arms and light weapons, heavy weapons, chemical and biological weapons);

    2. ammunition;

    3. military equipment;

    4. personnel (private security forces, paramilitary forces);

    5. other instruments (heavy vehicles, bulldozers);

(B) Offering goods and services that indirectly facilitate or sustain atrocities, including:

    1. transportation by air or sea of products used to commit or coordinate violence;

    2. vehicles (trucks and other land vehicles);

    3. fuel;

    4. technology and communications equipment (satellite phones, cell phones, computer hardware and software);

    5. air support;

    6. facilities (buildings, warehouses, training stations);

    7. technical assistance;

    8. information sharing (tip-offs, target lists);

    9. safe-havens, communications routes, and other geographical support.

(C) Providing general support that materially builds or sustains the capacity of the perpetrator to commit atrocities. This includes the large financial reserves accumulated by violent actors, with special attention to the diverse forms such assets now take, from sovereign wealth funds to shadow holding companies. Often such enterprises are linked to substantial networks of illicit extraction or trafficking of natural resources that generate revenue for the perpetrator.

In this formulation, I have chosen to limit "enabling" to a focus on material resources of dictators. For now I do not extend to the provision of moral support, psychological power and propaganda dynamics, hate speech, or 'political cover,' however real and significant those realities are in enabling dictators to control and brutalize their own citizens. I make this choice because these realities do not constitute practical support as described above and they are more difficult to quantify and interdict. For now they stand outside the parameters of these examples.

What I will focus on as examples and cases are the ways in which other national governments, commercial entities, and individuals may all be enablers. In the case of countries, examples include the situations in Syria, Darfur, and Sudan, where transfers of arms by China, Russia, Chad, and other governments or state-owned entities to government and rebel forces have helped sustain the violence against civilians for years. There are many other examples in the recent past in which third party governments provided weapons to their allies or proxies even when it was clear they were being used to commit crimes against humanity. Countries involved in questionable trading chains or opaque transshipment practices involving weapons, vehicles, or other forms of equipment may also be enabling dictators in less direct ways.

In the case of commercial entities, the range of enabling activities is potentially very broad. In Nigeria, multinational oil companies have faced lawsuits after being accused of hiring abusive security forces in the Niger Delta. In Darfur, the supply of Toyota trucks accessed by rebel groups has been essential to their capacity to commit widespread attacks on civilians. One UN Panel of Experts on Sudan reported that Al-Futtaim Motors Company, the official Toyota dealership in the United Arab Emirates, was, along with second-hand dealers in UAE, the source of "by far the largest number of vehicles that were documented as part of arms embargo violations in Darfur ..."[x] That dealership "declined or replied . . . in a perfunctory manner" to three requests by the Panel for information about buyers of the trucks identified in Darfur.

State and commercial actors may also function as go-betweens, thus playing an important, indirect role as dictator enablers. During the Rwandan genocide, even after a UN arms embargo sought to stop the flow of weapons into that country, arms continued to arrive routed through nearby countries and facilitated by international corporations. A 2009 SIPRI study revealed that more than 90 percent of air cargo carriers used by international organizations and humanitarian agencies to transport crisis response supplies were also named in open source reports on arms trafficking. Individual business people can be instrumental as suppliers or middle-men, with international arms merchant Viktor Bout as the most famous example. But others include the Dutch businessman convicted of providing chemical components that Saddam Hussein used against Kurdish civilians. And who supplied the chemical weapons to the Assad dictatorship that killed hundreds and cost the international community hundreds of thousands of dollars to remove?

Countries and commercial actors also act as enablers when they are engaged in the exploitation of natural resources that generate revenues for their dictator clients. Examples include eastern Congo, where windfalls from the illicit mineral trade fuel the rebels' pursuit of arms and thus contribute to atrocities against civilians by various strongmen. In Burma, during their period of repressive rule that may now be drawing to a close, the country's military rulers derived massive export earnings from their gem mines, which help to finance their brutal repression of that country's citizens.

Various efforts to halt or punish enablers—without calling them by that name or viewing them as a distinct set of actors—already exist. The approaches we choose, therefore, must take these efforts into account and could even build on them. At this point, it seems that dictators will likely be most susceptible to approaches by other governments, international organizations, and regional organizations. Because the relationships between the US and governments that act as enablers are likely to be complicated—and, further, often may not prioritize doing away with dictators—we need to be realistic as well as creative about pressure that the US government could apply. Commercial actors will likely be sensitive to approaches from those governments, and international and regional organizations, too. As other boycott situations evidence, they may be particularly sensitive to actions of consumers and other market-based forces, whether acting on their own, through guideline initiatives, or through nongovernmental organizations.

The softest existing approach to 'sanctioning' the supporters and enablers of dictators emphasizes information dissemination. In situations in which enablers are involved unwittingly or are particularly susceptible to concerns about negative publicity, shining a critical spotlight on their role may be sufficient to get their attention. Some entities—particularly multinational corporations with a strong presence in the US or Europe—may then be open to new commitments to transparency and due diligence standards to protect human rights.

For example, at least one company investigated and discussed in the October 2009 Panel of Experts report on violations of the arms embargo in Darfur was willing to cooperate and fully disclose its relationships in Sudan in order to ensure compliance with UN sanctions. On the other hand, as we have seen through the ongoing role of countries such as China and Russia in the crisis in Darfur even in the face of public protest in the US and internationally, public attention alone is often insufficient. While this approach might be a useful first step, over-reliance on it may risk oversimplifying complex situations, thereby limiting success.

A stronger and more concerted approach, but one that pertains only to commercial actors, involves the range of mechanisms that have emerged over the past decade to engage corporations in more responsible practices that protect human rights. A number of these efforts involve the US and other governments, and civil society actors have played a key role in each case. One example is the Kimberley Process, which brings together governments, corporations, and civil society in an effort to regulate the diamond trade. Others include the Voluntary Principles, the OECD Guidelines, and the UN Global Compact.

The work done in the past decade by the UN Special Representative on Business and Human Rights is also noteworthy in this regard. And efforts by nongovernmental actors to provide guidelines to businesses include the Red Flags project, which identifies potential legal liabilities in high-risk situations. This investigative and regulatory work can be augmented by bridging to the work of other agents who share the need for or desire to expose excessive behavior which sustains dictators. These certainly include the UN Panels of Experts, but also Lloyd's Registry and INTERPOL in their ability to chart linkages across illegal and quasi-legal entities. These and other initiatives may provide a foundation and entry points for addressing commercial enablers of dictators.

An even tougher set of approaches to both state and nonstate actors involve the myriad political, economic, or legal mechanisms that can be used against countries, commercial entities, or individuals to deter or dissuade their actions. In its bilateral relationships, the US can bring pressure to bear on enabling governments through public or private condemnations; by suspending business or cultural exchange programs; by withdrawing diplomatic representation; by reducing aid and other forms of support; or by implementing a wide range of other smart sanctions tools.

The US can also pursue broad or targeted bilateral sanctions, or work through the UN Security Council to impose multilateral sanctions against countries or commercial actors. Enforcement of sanctions is a separate challenge, at least as important as their imposition, as we have seen in the case of the Darfur arms embargo. New regulations specifically targeted at certain commercial entities or activities may be useful. In situations in which there is evidence that the enabler-dictator nexus is engaged in illegal behavior or have violated international law (including human rights law), it may be possible to pursue international criminal sanctions and other legal measures against them.

Whether addressing commercial actors or states in a given situation, information about who the third parties are and what role they are playing is critical. By enhancing its intelligence gathering and analysis related to enablers, the US government and like-minded states should be able to better assess the levers that can be employed to target them. Including information on third party actors in intelligence reports on enabler-dictators situations and in interagency discussions about policy options may be useful approaches. The US could also seek to engage international partners in information sharing to supplement its own intelligence sources on enablers and to help enlist others in the effort to halt enablers of dictators.

CONCLUSION

Even as some consensus is emerging among civil society actors and policymakers that confronting and stifling dictators should be a foreign policy and international community priority, the mobilization of the range of tools for so doing has lagged behind this recognition. The poor record of the international community in addressing atrocities committed by dictators makes clear the complexity to mounting a successful response. Although renewed efforts to stop arms flows or to embargo dictator-pillaged minerals will enhance a government's ability to stifle a dictator, these will probably not suffice to depose him.

I have argued two themes in this article. First, I maintain that smart sanctions have had some success in curtailing the ability of brutal leaders to engage in actual or potential atrocities against their own citizens. As such they provide a strong set of tools with which to bring down the dictators. Second, because dictatorships are systems as well as a strongman, and because dictators always have a set of external political, military and economic 'partners' which enable their crimes, the application of smart sanctions should include the targeting of corporate, nonstate and other enablers.

With a success rate hovering just over 33 percent, smart sanctions must be only one tool in the toolbox. While coordinated action via UN sanctions have the great advantage of requiring all member states in the international order to take this coercive action against dictators, UN sanctions often suffer from taking time to mobilize, legislate and implement. The very rumor of UN action may be enough to spark potential dictator enabler targets to move and hide their assets, or begin to spin off shadow companies, falsified passports and laundered bank records. Smart sanctions work best when they are accompanied by good diplomacy to maximize their leverage. Their aims need to be consistent, and clearly articulated so that they are fully understood by the targets. And creative expansion of the target list to enablers is imperative.

Notes

i.   George A. Lopez, "Matching Means with Intentions: Sanctions and Human Rights" in William F. Schulz, ed., *The Future of Human Rights: US Policy for a New Era* (Philadelphia: University of Pennsylvania Press, 2008).

ii.   See especially Richard Falk, ed., *United States Economic Measures Against Cuba. Proceedings in the United Nations and International Law Issues*, (Northhampton, MA: Aletheia Press, 1993).

iii. George A. Lopez and David Cortright, "Economic Sanctions and Human Rights: Part of the Solution or Part of the Problem?" *The International Journal of Human Rights*, vol. 1, no. 2 (May 1997), p. 1-25; Joy Gordon, "Smart Sanctions Revisited," *Ethics & International Affairs*, volume 25, no.3 , September 2011, p. 315-335.

iv.   See George A. Lopez and David Cortright, eds. *Towards Smart Sanctions: Targeting Economic Statecraft* (Boulder, Co: Rowman & Littlefield, 2002).

v.   Regarding the historic dimensions of human rights in UN sanctions resolution see Andrew Clapham, "Sanctions and Economic, Social and Cultural Rights," in Vera Gowlland-Debbas, ed. *United Nations Sanctions and International Law* (The Hague: Kluwer Law International, 2001).

vi.   Alix J. Boucher and Victoria K. Holt, *Targeting Spoilers: The Role of United Nations Panels of Experts* (Washington, D.C.: Stimson Center, 2009).

vii. For an analysis of such patterns of sanctions preparation see Michael Brzoska and George A. Lopez "Sanctions Design and Security Council Dynamics," in Thomas Biersteker and Sue Eckert, eds., *UN Targeted Sanctions as Instruments of Global Governance* (Forthcoming, 2013).

viii. Natalia Dannenberg and David Levitz, "UN Security Council unanimously passes sanctions against Gaddafi," *Deutsche Welle,* February 26, 2011, accessed November 19, 2014, *http://www.dw.de/un-security-council-unanimously-passes-sanctions-against-gadhafi/a-14876262.*

ix.   "Italy, France sending troops to advise Libyan rebels," *CNN,* April 20 2011, accessed November 19, 2014, *http://www.cnn.com/2011/WORLD/africa/04/20/libya.war/index.html.*

x.   United Nations Panel of Experts established pursuant to resolution 1591 (2005), *Report of the Panel of Experts established pursuant to resolution 1591 (2005) concerning the Sudan (S/2009/562)*, p. 158, (United Nations, 2009), accessed November 19, 2014, *www.geneva-academy.ch/RULAC/pdf_state/S-2009-562.pdf.*

CHAPTER 14

A Diplomat's Handbook for Democracy Development Support

Jeremy Kinsman

O VER THE PAST SEVEN years, co-author Kurt Bassuener and I have worked with the invaluable aid of diplomats and civil society representatives from many countries to record the ways in which they have been able to support democratic aspirations of peoples in every region of the world.

The *Handbook*[i] charts the rise of civil society as the critical force for change and development within countries. The Introduction to the third edition asserts that "How democratic governments and their representatives abroad relate to civil society both at home and abroad, and how civil society relates back to them, is the overarching challenge" set out in the *Handbook*.

The challenge has major implications for the practice of diplomacy which needs to adapt to the reality that civil society's connections and networks, strengthened by ubiquitous information technologies, now accounts for much of the actual content of international relations.

The late Ambassador Mark Palmer, who conceived of the project, intended the *Handbook* to underline the necessity for diplomats to reform a profession that had been typically viewed as conservative and cautious, identified with local elites often on the wrong end of change. We document how diplomatic representation that had traditionally been monopolized by state-to-state contacts conducted behind closed doors has indeed increasingly become public diplomacy aimed at civil society itself as audience and virtual partner.

A more activist and "expeditionary" diplomacy addresses what the *Handbook* appraises as a widespread popular search for agency by people everywhere.

"Across the globe, the relationships of people to their governments are changing. Individuals are asserting their own agency over decisions that affect them. The expansion of economic opportunities in many emerging economies is accompanied by a growing impatience with old authoritarian ways." The ability of people to translate such aspirations into effective governance is the challenge of our age.

It is natural that democracies should make support for such aspirations a foreign policy priority and assign diplomatic assets to assist the strengthening of civil society, not in a sense of influencing political outcomes that must be in the hands of the people in question, but through capacity-building, and solidarity with the quest for human rights that have long been considered to be universal entitlements.

At the same time, we have had to take account of a strenuous defensive tightening by important authoritarian regimes. Nervousness about the perception of outside interference in internal affairs affects public and political opinion even in established democracies, some of which are preoccupied with an uncertain economic landscape and internal governance challenges of their own. Pew polls showed that US public support for democracy promotion and human rights abroad had plunged by 2009 to 10 and 24 percent respectively. For the first time since World War II, no doubt in the throes of fatigue from over-exposure to intractable barriers to change in Iraq and Afghanistan after lengthy and costly wars there, as many as half of Americans polled judged that the United States should "mind its own business." The ragged experience of Arab countries in efforts to adopt inclusive and effective governance because of lack of capacity after initial expressions of euphoria over the "Arab Spring," has been another contributing factor.

The good news is that the percentage of the world's population that is "free" has increased from 25 percent in 1992 to 43 percent today, though with some recent backsliding. The wide radius of the "Arab Spring" shows that no region or religion is immune to democratic aspirations.

Vaclav Havel (who wrote a Preface to the *Handbook*) spoke to the enduring need for engagement represented by the *Handbook* project: "In today's world, more and more people are aware of the indivisibility of human fate on this planet, that the problems of anyone of us, or whatever country we come from – be it the smallest and most forgotten – are the problems of us all; that out freedom is indivisible as well, and that we all believe in the same basic values, while sharing common fears about the threats that are hanging over humanity today."

At its conception seven years ago, the *Handbook's* central functional focus was on the activity and example of diplomats in the field. Our aim was to create a descriptive manual primarily for diplomatic practitioners that set out in a fact- and interview-based way how diplomatic support has been provided over the last decades by a wide variety of democracies, individual representatives, and in multiple and always varying situations, with a view to providing helpful examples.

The Handbook sets out "fifteen ways that diplomats have made a difference" through the description of a virtual "tool box" of skill sets. From the "golden rules" of listening to, respecting, and understanding local conditions and the citizens of host countries, we cover a range of activities from practicing and supporting truth in communications, through essential messaging to governments to defend freedom of speech, and in public outreach, within a general purpose of contributing to building civil society.

We cited experiences that were successfully supportive and those which were less so. In terms of method and voice, we avoided being prescriptive. Our interviews and workshops outside the United States kept us very informed of the extent to which an overly-interventionist US "Freedom Agenda" was divisive among other democracies, especially after being invoked *post hoc* to justify the invasion of Iraq. We always made clear in presentation we were not suggesting any specific form or experience of democratic governance should be a model for others. We tried to channel the full range of democratic points of view and approaches, including especially the experience in democracy development support of countries such as the Czech Republic and Poland which have themselves re-emerged as democracies only relatively recently. Our ecumenical approach enabled the manual's content to be used in the foreign service institutes and diplomatic academies of a wide variety of the member states of the Community of Democracies that endorsed it as a project.

The current third edition goes well beyond the original purpose of presenting examples of supportive diplomatic activity. The considerably expanded project increasingly aims to provide a normative analysis of democratic transitions themselves. We have tried to catalogue what has been learned about why some succeed and why others fail.

The expanded scope of the *Handbook* addresses the interests and activity of practitioners at all levels of engagement including international civil society and national nongovernmental organizations, whether devoted to human rights defense or functional purposes, and the research and interests of scholars and students of international affairs and political development.

We also relate more explicitly and thoroughly to the policy and decision-making processes in democratic capitals, and their bearing on developments. Recent country case studies on Tunisia and Egypt tackle the history of noncriticism of authoritarian Arab regimes due to other over-riding interests and under-estimation of popular resentment. In the extensive case study on Russia's twenty-five year experiment with democracy, considerable analysis is given to the policy approaches, misperceptions, and mis-steps of partner democracies as Russia (and Ukraine) faced the wholesale re-makes of their societies and economies with no template or comparable experience to guide them.

The central conclusion to our analysis of democratic transitions is that the most important key to successful democratic governance is inclusivity. All societies are pluralist, by ethnicity, language, religion and sect, by race, regional tradition and culture, and by economic situation. Inclusiveness of governance is based on the building blocks only civil society can provide through experience with compromise and coalition-building. An essential difference between the transitions from authoritarian and arbitrary government between Tunisia and Libya lies in Tunisia's much greater history of development of a variegated civil society, which had never been permitted by the Quadafi regime to develop in Libya.

Our country-case studies make clear that the skills required for a successful transition are more behavioral than institutional. As democracy theorist Thomas Carothers has put it, the rule of law is more than statutes and courts, but resides in what is in the heads of citizens, in their reflexive habituation to transparency, accountability, meritocracy, tolerance and openness to compromise. A sobering lesson of the last quarter-century is how much time and patience it takes to learn and build these necessary skills, beginning, of course, under authoritarian rule.

Once a transition is underway, to secure popular acceptance, an elected government has to deliver successful outcomes of justice, economic progress, and social fairness. This means that the support of developed democracies must not lapse once free and fair elections have taken place. As Fareed Zakaria has warned, the long, hard, slog of democratic consolidation means that donor and partner democracies must accept "constant engagement, aid, multilateral efforts, and a world not of black and white but of grey."

Repeatedly, our country case studies emphasize that it is what happens after elections that counts the most. Most important is the principle that a majority is not authorized by electoral success to smother electoral losers or ethnic or sectarian minorities.

On the issue of assessing the legitimacy of outside support for civil society, we identify a need for solidarity among democracies. Even some democracies cite historic reasons to be sensitive on the issue of "outside interference," and resist giving NGOs status and standing as a legitimate interlocutor of government.

The *Handbook* notes ways in which democracies have responded to constantly shifting boundaries of how much direct outside support is permissible. The overall position is to acknowledge there are limits in international practice but that there are also permissible rights to support civil society that need to be defended internationally.

Our third edition's case study on Tunisia makes clear "there was no outside 'hidden hand' in what occurred" there. "Tunisian, Egyptian and Libyan citizens were not acting in favor of 'Western values,' but on behalf of their own right to inclusiveness and dignity, and their desire to reconcile religion and civics in their respective societies." This was equally true in the context of Ukraine.

And yet, "the reaction of some authoritarian regimes to developments in North Africa" has led them to impose "greater intransigence at home, curtailing modest political rights and attempting to smother civil society's connections with potential supporters from civil society outside."

We note some of the more egregious examples of authoritarian governments playing the false card of outside "interference" in order to create a pretext for clamping down on dissidents and activists, as has happened in Russia, and as the deposed president Yanukovych attempted in Ukraine. Authoritarian governments are reverting to populist nationalist rhetoric condemning members of civil society who accept support from outside as being unpatriotic or "foreign agents." Legislation is drawn up criminalizing forms of cooperation with democracies that were customary in the early 1990s after the fall of the Berlin Wall.

> "The new case study on Russian democracy identifies misguided claims by Russian authorities that international civil society's solidarity with Russian civil society is a surrogate for Western democracies' alleged ambitions to co-opt the nation's political development in order to weaken the Russian state."

> "The mouthpiece of the ruling Communist Party of China, the *People's Daily*, described perceived Western efforts to export democracy and human rights to China as a 'new form of colonialism.'"

Such reactions are easily identifiable as stemming from the fear the search for agency will be contagious and will extend to political competition at home.

The world remains a community of interests for many trans-border issues requiring cooperation. It is important that democracies show they reject the inevitability of an "us against them" world divided once again, even though there is much talk today about the "return of geopolitics." National assertiveness is commonplace, especially by regional powers vis-à-vis their neighbors.

"Independent Diplomat" Carne Ross notes that in "the hierarchy of priorities, security ranks at the top, followed by economic interests." However, dual-track strategies can enable democracies to sustain partnerships essential to peace, security, and prosperity but also to represent foreign policies that consistently defend human rights as a core value. They won't always work at once, as Vladimir Putin's pushback against a US dual-track strategy described in our Russia case study demonstrates. But longer term, they generally will because the dual track represents a combination of the leverage of real interests and the authenticity of genuine values. As thrusts of policy, they are ultimately interdependent, not competitive.

In diplomacy, consistency is a basic currency. As our case studies on Egypt and Tunisia make clear, democracies belatedly recognize they have needed to replace a long-established preference for the illusion of stability through uncritical relationships with authoritarian partners by a better ability to imagine popular sentiment favoring change within the countries concerned, while also acknowledging that ill-prepared transitions can be counter-productive.

The *Handbook* supports emphatically the argument that the use of violence to effect change is generally a failure, inviting decisive counter-force and alienating the public by overturning security and safety which predominate in the hierarchy of needs. Nonviolent civil resistance has obtained a vastly superior track record of success, as demonstrated by the Maria Stephan-Erica Chenoweth research presented in this volume. It moreover has the very important additional merit of being inclusive and thereby serving as an incubator for the sort of coalition-building and accommodation of diversity that is essential for a successful transition.

Diplomats on the ground will continue to serve as vital deployable assets of democracies, serving as connectors and entrepreneurs between civil societies. Now, of course, embassies routinely blog and show their followers the composite human face of their representation from their own country, as testimony to the emphasis today on values as well as interests.

It may be that diplomats find themselves less directly involved in building government-financed programs for democracy support than when we began the project. We have learned, as the *Handbook* concludes, that "the best vehicles for such outside support are rarely governments and their own programs, however well-intentioned. They are not good at it. Outside support for democratic capacity-building potential comes best from international civil society partnerships, with the lead partner being the one inside the country [...] The lesson that democracy promotion is best done when it's not called 'democracy promotion' has become a truism of policy and research." In any event, the search for agency and the building of democracy flows from earlier experiences of empowerment. Our case study of Cuba, for example, recounts the formative experience of young single mothers who are trusted with running Catholic Church day-care centers. For the first time in their lives, they are able to make decisions about their own situation. Much of the developmental content of democratic governance emerges not from political advocacy but from such functional experience in civil society, more often than not on the local level.

It is vital that individual diplomats continue to feel confidence in their ability to take inspiring and exemplary actions in favor of democracy and human rights defense. The *Handbook* chronicles how EU diplomats accompanied the brave Las Damas de Blanco on their modest marches from mass in Havana to protest the imprisonment of their husbands; how EU, US, and Canadian Ambassadors attended vigils for murdered Syrian dissidents, just as their colleagues had done in South Africa decades earlier; how democracy's diplomats seek to witness political trials of dissidents and human rights defenders in China, Iran, Zimbabwe and elsewhere, as they had witnessed the trials of dissidents in Czechoslovakia and Poland back in the day. Such activities valorize and to some extent protect the brave struggles of activists on the front lines of the assertion of human rights. Australian diplomat Roland Rich, now with the United Nations Secretariat, has described the acknowledgment of their value to activists in East Timor: "Having foreigners alongside was like borrowing a little piece of their democracies."

Of course, developed democracies are highly imperfect. But their norms nonetheless radiate as beacons to citizens of exploitative authoritarian regimes where oligarchy and corruption deny fairness, justice and opportunity. Twenty-first century democratic diplomacy channels our own basic democratic values. The *Handbook* asserts in concluding consequence that

> "outside democracies judge that a key and legitimate role of their diplomatic representatives is to engage directly with civil society in the host country [...] Their primary tasks are to pay attention to change, and in a spirit of solidarity of free peoples, support legitimate aspirations of people everywhere to widen their democratic space."

A Diplomat's Handbook demonstrates how this has been done in the past with a view to facilitating the efforts that lie ahead for the many people who believe they are entitled to human rights. Democracies too often take for granted even though they increasingly recognize they have a duty to support all those who seek them.

Notes

i.   Jeremy Kinsman and Kurt Bassuener, *A Diplomat's Handbook for Democracy Development Support*, 3rd ed. (Waterloo, Candada: The Centre for International Governance Innovation, 2013).

CHAPTER 15

Checklist for External Assistance to Nonviolent Movements

Maria J. Stephan
Senior Policy Fellow, United States Institute of Peace
Nonresident Senior Fellow, Atlantic Council

WITH AUTHORITARIANS LEARNING FROM each other and aggressively restricting civil society activity globally, how should external actors respond? What tools do governments, foundations, NGOs, tech firms, and others have to support nonviolent pro-democracy activism in an era of "closing space"?[i] Given that nonviolent resistance has a positive track record against even ruthless regimes—certainly when compared to armed struggle—and is strongly associated with both democratization and civil peace, it is worth examining and prioritizing the most promising activities.

Donors may be wary of supporting such activities in light of the tumultuous Arab Spring. After all, a mainly nonviolent popular uprising in Syria has been replaced by a disastrous civil war, people-powered Egypt has back-pedaling toward a new secular authoritarianism, and in Bahrain, the nonviolent opposition has been largely silenced. However, an international approach that fails to recognize that repression often prompts resistance, and that when that resistance turns violent the result is often catastrophic, is destined for repeated failure.

The discussion of nonviolent policy options is not new. Scholars and practitioners have been debating the pros and cons of various forms of external intervention to stem violence and advance democracy for years. Much of that conversation has centered on sanctions and military intervention—far less on the tools specifically designed to assist nonviolent campaigns and movements. There is a growing sense of urgency, as evidenced by the Obama administration's Stand with Civil Society initiative, launched at the 2013 UN General Assembly meeting and renewed last year, which calls on governments and nongovernmental organizations to develop new ways to help civic actors facing uneven playing fields.[ii] The Civic Space Initiative is a parallel nongovernmental project that aims to protect and expand civic space by fostering an enabling legal environment for civil society organizations.[iii]

The international legal basis for supporting nonviolent activists and movements, as Elizabeth Wilson described, is rooted in international human rights and international labor law with its guarantees of freedom of nonviolent assembly, movement, organization, and expression. Although such support has never been conceived of as a tool to prevent mass atrocities, the Responsibility to Protect (R2P) community might consider how such nonmilitary options focused on civil society could strengthen the international norm.

PRINCIPLES OF EXTERNAL SUPPORT[IV]

Before considering some of the tools available to support nonviolent activists and movements it is important to begin with a set of principles to guide external actors. The discussion below is meant to jump-start a wider conversation about whom, when, and how to most effectively support nonviolent activists.

LOCAL CONTEXT

The starting point for any discussion of external support to nonviolent campaigns and movements must be the local context and the expressed needs of local activists. Decisions about external support should be based on an examination of the place and people in question, cognizant of the fact that no two countries are alike—and therefore no two strategies can be alike.

Understanding the local context is best achieved through frequent interactions with a broad range of civil society and other actors from that country. Preliminary conflict analyses involving local actors that highlight conflict drivers, societal resiliencies, pillars of support, and an assessment of past nonviolent mobilization would help provide an analytic framework for external support. Peace technologists could consider how crowdsourcing and meta-data collection could be used to facilitate an analytic process to help both activists and external supporters.

CONSENT

Domestic actors and their interests, concerns, and desires must be the drivers of any external support. "Do no harm" thinking should ground the conversation. External actors must be aware of the legal, political, and social constraints faced by activists and the potentially negative repercussions of any type of external support. They must be aware of the domestic restrictions on foreign funding for civil society and make a studied determination about when it is acceptable to ignore such rules because they fundamentally violate international law. External actors must make a strong and inclusive effort to get the consent and input from those inside the country and ensure that their support is in line with their demands and risk comfort.

RISKS AND REWARDS

Local civic actors are in the best position to assess the risks and opportunities associated with any particular type of foreign aid. Support from a particular country may be counter-productive in a particular context given characteristics of the bilateral relationship, historical or other considerations. Diversifying the sources of foreign funding may be helpful in certain cases.

External actors must be mindful of trade-offs associated with any particular course of action and cognizant of how such support could help or hurt domestic activists in the short and long-term. Still, as Erica Chenoweth noted, the "authoritarian playbook" includes denigrating opposition movements for following foreign agendas no matter the level of external involvement.

CORE VALUES

Interventions should be selected in accordance with core values shared by external actors and local activists. A reasonable degree of transparency and accountability should accompany any support, though external actors should prioritize the safety of the local partner(s) when deciding how to engage. To the extent possible, external support activities should be equitable and inclusive, such that the same small numbers of "famous" civic groups are not the exclusive beneficiaries of external support. Donors should have a 'movement mindset'[v] when providing support to civil society.

THE CHECKLIST AND TOOLKIT

Peter Ackerman and Hardy Merriman's "Checklist to End Tyranny" offers a useful analytic starting point for considering how external actors can support the key variables associated with successful nonviolent campaigns. The "Outsider's Guide to Supporting Nonviolent Resistance to Dictatorship," meanwhile, provides a wide menu of options available to different categories of external actors. This next section considers *only a sampling of these tools* in light of the checklist. Further research and data collection will help to reveal the types and timing of effective external support to nonviolent campaigns and movements.

If achieving a **unifying vision** based on shared goals, methods, and leaders is a core attribute of successful civil resistance, there are many ways governmental and nongovernmental actors can help opposition movements achieve greater unity.

SAMPLE OF TOOLS:

1. **Diplomatic Convening:** As Jeremy Kinsman and Kurt Basseuner described in the *Diplomat's Handbook*, diplomats are in an excellent position to support civic movements. They can convene various elements of the opposition to encourage unity and arrange meetings between opposition

members and government officials. This can be particularly
useful when opposition elements are bickering or when
mistrust is deep, as was the case in Serbia with the shaky
Democratic Opposition of Serbia and most recently with
the Syrian opposition. Diplomat-facilitated meetings
between regime loyalists and the opposition can provide
a vehicle for the peaceful transfer of power as occurred
between the ANC and South African authorities.

2. **Peer-to-Peer Learning:** Training and education in
   strategic nonviolent action and coalition building can
   help improve the skills and capacities of local activists. The
   peer-to-peer learning between Serbian youth and Slovak
   civic leaders greatly improved the former's understanding
   of dealing with donors and how to mobilize around
   fraudulent elections in the lead-up to the popular ouster of
   Milosevic in 2000. As Shaazka Beyerle noted, workshops
   involving anti-corruption activists from India, Kenya and
   Afghanistan, facilitated by the Open Society Foundation and
   International Budget Partnership, proved to be particularly
   useful to the colorful counter-corruption campaigns in
   those countries. Optimal trainings are led by activists
   and include strong mentoring components such that the
   learning and sharing of best practices can continue after the
   formal workshop(s) end. On-line courses in civil resistance,
   open to activists and civic leaders around the world, are now
   provided by such organizations as the International Center
   on Nonviolent Conflict and the US Institute of Peace.

3. **Alternative Media:** Independent media are often
   the first targets of authoritarian regimes. Support for
   independent media outlets, both traditional and social
   media, can help highlight shared grievances, expose regime
   propaganda, and present governance alternatives. Radio
   Free Europe and Radio Liberty are widely credited for
   having introduced alternative news to those living under
   communist dictatorships in Eastern Europe. The Polish
   Solidarity movement (supported by the Solidarity Center and

international trade and labor unions) relied extensively on the samizdat underground press, while B-92 radio in Serbia gave the opposition a live voice. Colorful, unifying television ads inviting Chileans to vote "no" in the referendum of 1988 preceded Pinochet's ouster. Graffiti featuring unifying symbols and slogans of the Arab spring were the most ubiquitous alternative media in the recent wave of popular uprisings.

4. **Tools to facilitate communication:** Authoritarian regimes invest significant effort and resources to intercept communication between activists and between activists and the outside world. The "Outsider's Guide" lists a number of ways external actors can support low- and high-tech ways for local activists to communicate around repression, including support for color-coded public spaces, cultural resistance, unconventional message carriers, and HAM radio. External supporters can provide cyber-circumvention tools and organizations like Open Technology Institute have helped develop mesh network, a type of wireless communications network that connects laptops, cell phone, and other wireless devices to form a parallel communications network capable of operating outside of the Internet.

To support an opposition movement's **operational planning** efforts, a critical capacity-building tool, external actors can encourage the movement to set a realistic timeline for achieving progress while providing timely information about regime capabilities and characteristics that could help movement planning. They can help connect activists to veterans of previous nonviolent struggles to share best practices and lessons learned.

SAMPLE OF TOOLS:

1. **Diplomatic Advising:** In their consultations with activists and members of civil society, diplomats can communicate the need to establish a realistic time frame for their

struggles and suggest where there are reformist allies in the government. They can provide safe spaces (at diplomatic or other facilities) to support meetings and planning sessions for members of civil society. Diplomats from countries that have experienced transitions from authoritarianism, like Poland, the Czech Republic, and (more recently) Tunisia, may be useful sounding boards for civic leaders in the midst of a transition process.

2. **Trainings by Activists:** Activists have cited learning from those who have led nonviolent campaigns and movements (notably from same geographic region) and mentoring as being helpful to planning their resistance. Foreign experts financed by NGOs like the National Democratic Institute, the International Republican Institute, Friedrich Ebert Stiftung, Konrad Adenauer Stiftung, the Westminster Foundation for Democracy, or Alfred Mozer Stichting may provide training for domestic activists in nonviolent resistance, political party building, mobilization methods, and electoral monitoring. However, trainings are often criticized for being devoid of follow-on mentoring and being inadequately informed by context. Investment in a small but reliable global cadre of "rapid reaction" trainers with different cultural and linguistic expertise could significantly improve the timely execution of trainings in strategic nonviolent action and transition-related topics.

3. **Capacity building tools:** Low-tech teaching tools that tap into popular culture, like cartoon books, songs, and public art are creative ways for outsiders to invest in the mass dissemination of civil resistance know-how. *People Power: The Game of Civil Resistance*[1] is specifically designed as a computer simulation tool to enhance strategic and operational planning in civic campaigns and movements. Players are exposed to analytic and planning tools as they lay down goals, sequence tactics, build coalitions, deal with repression and assess progress across a range of different scenarios.

---

[1] See http://peoplepowergame.com/.

Maintaining **nonviolent discipline** becomes more difficult the larger the size and diversity of popular participation in civil resistance and the greater the level of regime repression. External actors can support the organizational capacity of opposition movements and train in techniques for maintaining nonviolent discipline in the face of violence. They can engage in acts of solidarity with dissidents and nonviolent activists and provide material support to help movements stay resilient in the face of repression.

SAMPLE OF TOOLS:

1. **Training in Nonviolent Discipline:** Capacity-building trainings for activists and civil society should highlight practical ways to maintain nonviolent discipline and deal with *agent provocateurs* and radical flank elements in repressive environments. Examples of codes of conduct, lessons in dealing with security forces, and diversifying tactics to maintain resiliency—translated into multiple languages—should be catalogued and widely disseminated through appropriate on and off-line channels.

2. **Engaging the Media:** The oft-heard journalistic adage, "if it bleeds, it leads," poses a challenge to nonviolent activists, particularly when they are engaged in tactics that don't involve mass street protests or sit-ins. Not only do journalists need to be sensitized to the dynamics of civil resistance (and why, for example, an organized consumer boycott may be more consequential than an act of vandalism); nonviolent activists also need to be effective spokespeople, to target specific audiences effectively and counter inevitable regime propaganda. "Pressing Your Case" is a helpful new media training module for nonviolent activists that addresses these challenges.[2]

3. **Material support:** Material aid from donors may include the provision of laptops and printers, power generators,

---

[2] See http://www.nonviolent-conflict.org/index.php/learning-and-resources/3732.

portable fax machines, satellite phones, mobile phones, and campaign paraphernalia such as buttons, whistles, and bullhorns—key elements of movement infrastructure. Small, targeted grants that are flexible and able to respond in a timely fashion to the needs of campaigns and movements are generally the most impactful.

4. **Diplomatic Solidarity:** Diplomats can demonstrate solidarity with nonviolent protestors and encourage nonviolent discipline by monitoring trials of dissidents and attending nonviolent rallies. Ambassadors Robert Ford and Eric Chevallier's decision to defy the Assad regime and travel to Hama to show solidarity with the nonviolent protestors there was an example of diplomatic deployment that empowered the Syrian nonviolent movement, which, as Julia Taleb and Maciej Bartkowski wrote, was unfortunately overshadowed by armed struggle.

To help enhance **civilian participation** outside actors can target resources to support the outreach and mobilization activities of nonviolent activists. They can help convene representatives of diverse groups and support media and cultural productions that encourage civic mobilization.

SAMPLE OF TOOLS:

1. **Diplomatic Shuttling:** Diplomats can diversify their own outreach to civil society, notably engaging civic groups outside of capitals, and perform shuttle diplomacy-of-sorts between civic actors when high levels of regime repression discourage mobility. In 2008 in Zimbabwe, the ambassadors from the US, UK, EU and Japan drove in an 11-car convoy to the north of the capital to investigate allegations of government-led crackdowns on opposition supporters following the first round of elections.

2. **Labor solidarity:** Labor and trade unions have been key organizational backbones of many nonviolent revolutions,

including in Poland, South Africa, Egypt, and Tunisia. International labor solidarity, backed by treaty law through the International Labor Organization (ILO) and provided by such organizations as AFL–CIO and the Solidarity Center (under the NED umbrella), has taken the form of technical assistance, advocacy and political support. In an era of shrinking space for traditional civil society groups, external assistance in support of labor and workers rights could become increasingly important.

3. **Flexible grants to nontraditional groups:** The ideal civil society recipients of small grants designed to expand citizen participation in nonviolent movements may not be registered NGOs. They are more likely to be artists' groups, soccer fan networks, doctor's unions, or blogger circles— groups with a volunteer base and mobilization potential. Developing donor infrastructure to provide small grants and maintain regular communication with nontraditional grantees in fluid conflict environments is a challenge that requires greater scrutiny.

4. **Political capacity-building:** Training in traditional political activities like political party development, voter mobilization, and election monitoring, provided by European foundations and US democracy promotion organization in places where such support is allowed, can helpfully complement support for civil resistance activities. The failure of many popular movements against repressive regimes to consolidate democratic gains in the post-transition period, as we have seen in Thailand and Egypt, highlights the need to invest in long-term institutional development, administrative capacity-building and rule of law – involving both government officials and civil society in the process."

To **diminish the impact of repression** external actors can use various diplomatic, political, economic, and military tools to influence security force behavior. Diplomats can coordinate démarches, demonstrate diplomatic solidarity with nonviolent activists, and offer protection to oppositionists. Governments and the private sector can impose targeted sanctions to weaken the regime's repressive apparatus.

SAMPLE OF TOOLS:

1. **Military Engagement:** As Dennis Blair noted in this volume, educational exchanges, joint military trainings, and informal communications are all opportunities to discuss a professional military code of ethics, rules of engagement vis-a-vis nonviolent protestors, and to inculcate the importance of civilian control. Enlightened military officers who refuse to obey illegitimate orders from their superiors, as happened most recently in the Tunisian revolution, are often the unsung heroes in democratic transitions.

2. **Secure communications:** Training and tools to support secure communication can help mitigate efforts by regimes to monitor, intercept, and block opposition communications. In Syria, the Assad regime's Iranian-backed surveillance apparatus allowed it to identify and target for repression some of the most effective nonviolent organizers. Front Line Defenders has produced useful on-line manuals for cyber-activists.[3] Engaging security tools that combine digital and off-line security, translated into multiple languages and disseminated through proper activist channels, could be additionally helpful resources to protect civil resistors.

3. **Targeted sanctions:** George Lopez described how targeted, multilateral sanctions that freeze the bank accounts and other assets of regime officials (and their families) and shrink their international travel options help weaken their repressive apparatus. The current US and EU sanctions regime targeting Russian elites for their role in destabilizing Ukraine is an example. Unilateral sanctions or blanket sanctions that punish entire sections of a society tend to

---

[3] See http://www.frontlinedefenders.org/security-training.

be less effective and allow regimes to project themselves as defenders of the people against outside punishment.

4. **Solidarity and strike funds:** Even small amounts of funding directed at activists, labor, and civic groups can help nonviolent movements maintain resiliency in the face of repression. Human rights defenders' funds and legal defense grants given by organizations like Freedom House and PEN International have provided a boost to imperiled civic leaders. Strike funds from international labor groups allowed workers in places like Poland to weather martial law and a lengthy civil resistance struggle.

To **accelerate defections** external actors can develop and execute a coordinated defections strategy that employs a wide range of tools such as targeted sanctions, golden parachutes, strategic communications, defection funds, technologies that support whistleblowers, and the aggressive dissemination of information about how to defect safely.

SAMPLE OF TOOLS:

1. **Golden parachutes:** Incentivizing defection can take many forms. Although paying regime elites to leave the scene and offering them some kind of amnesty can have serious implications for international justice, this could also accelerate a transition and prevent further bloodshed. But for every Marcos and Ben Ali who is willing to accept a paid vacation, there is the Bashar al Assad who will fight to the bitter end. In certain highly repressive environments, defections-in-place, whereby regime functionaries remain in place while supporting the opposition using quiet, discreet means may be preferable to physically leaving the country.

2. **Financial incentives:** A defections or whistle-blowers' fund(s) could be established to help ease the financial burden for potential defectors and truth-tellers in authoritarian regimes. Such a fund could be modeled on the Mo Ibrahim Foundation monetary awards for former African

heads of state who leave office within their term limit and show excellence in leadership. In addition, in cases where sanctions are in place, potential defectors could be assured that their names would be removed from the sanctions list were they to defect.

3. **Targeted Sanctions:** Asset freezes and restrictions on the ability of authoritarian elites to travel, purchase luxury goods, and send their children to private schools overseas are examples of targeted sanctions, most recently applied by the US and EU against Russian government and business elites for their role in supporting aggression against Ukraine. Travel bans and asset freezes might be usefully expanded to include the spouses, families and supporters of regime elites responsible for mass human rights abuses.

4. **Defection communications toolkit:** Support for the development and dissemination of information about how to defect safely, targeting civil servants and security force members, might be helpful in certain authoritarian contexts. Leaflets, billboards, graffiti, radio and social media spots and campaigns (possibly even mobile applications) that encourage truth-telling as a form of patriotism and warn of the consequences of engaging in rights abuses—as was used to lure soldiers away from the LRA in Uganda—are all defections tools.

This is only a sampling of the tools available to external actors to support nonviolent activism in the lead-up to and during political transitions from authoritarianism. Further quantitative and qualitative research should yield insights into the factors, including timing and sequencing, that make external interventions helpful (or not) in different civil resistance contexts.

In the post-transition period, sustained external support for political and economic development and institution building is crucial, as is technical support for reconciliation processes. Government and nongovernmental actors have a key role to play in helping civil society move from confrontation to engagement with institutions and "normal" political pathways—whether as watchdogs, participants in constitutional and electoral reform processes, or as leaders in local and national reconciliation processes. As in the pre-transition phase, peer-to-peer learning about democratic consolidation processes and participatory governance can help civic actors move from protest to politics.

Notes

i.   Thomas Carothers and Saskia Brechenmacher, "Closing Space: Democracy and Human Rights Support Under Fire," Carnegie Endowment for International Peace, February 20 2014, accessed November 19, 2014, *http://carnegieendowment.org/2014/02/20/closing-space-democracy-and-human-rights-support-under-fire/h1by*.

ii.   See President Obama's discussion of Stand With Civil Society at the Clinton Global Initiative, on the sidelines of the 2014 UN General Assembly meeting: Barack Obama, "Remarks by the President at Clinton Global Initiative" (speech, Clinton Global Initiative, Washington, DC, September 23, 2014, accessed November 19, 2014, *http://www.whitehouse.gov/the-press-office/2014/09/23/remarks-president-clinton-global-initiative*.

iii.   The International Center for Not-for-Profit Law (ICNL), ARTICLE 19, CIVICUS: *World Alliance for Citizen Participation, and the World Movement for Democracy are driving the Civic Space Initiative (CSI)*, accessed November 19, 2014, *http://www.wmd.org/projects/civic-space-initiative*.

iv.   Principles adopted during a two-day workshop in New York City in November 2011 with activists and NGO leaders focused on external support to nonviolent activists and movements. See "An Outsider's Guide to Supporting Nonviolent Resistance to Dictatorship", November 2011, accessed November 19, 2014, *www.outsiders-guide.org*.

v.   Maria J. Stephan, Sadaf Lakhani, and Nadia Naviwala, "Aiding Civil Society: A Movement Mindset," USIP Special Report, February 2015.

Index